The Word Is Out

Other books by Chris Glaser
    published by Westminster John Knox Press

Coming Out as Sacrament

*Uncommon Calling: A Gay Christian's Struggle to Serve
    the Church*

*Coming Out to God: Prayers for Lesbians and Gay Men,
    Their Families and Friends*

Unleashed: The Wit and Wisdom of Calvin the Dog

The Word Is

Daily Reflections on the Bible
for Lesbians and Gay Men

CHRIS GLASER

Westminster John Knox Press
Louisville, Kentucky

Unless otherwise noted, scripture quotations are from the New Revised Standard Version of the Bible, copyright © 1989 by the Division of Christian Education of the National Council of the Churches of Christ in the U.S.A., and are used by permission. All rights reserved.

First published in 1994 by HarperCollins Publishers under the title *The Word Is Out: The Bible Reclaimed for Lesbians and Gay Men*. Reprinted by arrangement with HarperCollins Publishers.

First Westminster John Knox Press edition
Published by Westminster John Knox Press
Louisville, Kentucky

Cover design by Eric Handel/LMNOP
Cover art courtesy of The Pierpont Morgan Library/Art Resouce, NY
Jonathan warns David of his peril by the shooting of arrows.
c. 1250. M.638, f.32.

This book is printed on acid-free paper that meets the American National Standards Institute Z39.48 standard. ∞

PRINTED IN THE UNITED STATES OF AMERICA
99 00 01 02 03 04 05 06 07 08 — 10 9 8 7 6 5 4 3 2 1

Library of Congress Cataloging-in-Publication Data
  Glaser, Chris.
    The Word is out : daily reflections on the Bible for lesbians
  and gay men / Chris Glaser.
      p.   cm.
  Originally published: San Francisco : HarperSanFrancisco, c1994.
  Includes index.
  ISBN 0-664-25820-4 (alk. paper)
  1. Gays—Prayer-books and devotions—English. 2. Bible—Devotional
  literature. 3. Devotional calendars. I. Title.
  [BV4596.G38G59 1999]
  242´6—dc21
                                                          98-41834

Thanks be to God
for my lover,
Mark King

Contents

Preface to the
Westminster John Knox Press Edition
Spiritual Pleasures

Originally I wanted to call this book *Biblical Pleasures.* But for too many people, such a title would be an oxymoron. Many readers find the Bible tedious or intimidating or confusing——and often all three. For lesbians, gay men, bisexuals, and the transgendered, who have been spiritually abused by certain biblical passages, the Bible has also been a source of suffering at the hands of those who want to deny our sexual or gender integrity.

Yet the Bible is what got me through the rough times growing up "queer." The Bible told me that I wasn't alone, that others also had a tough time being who God created and called them to be. Long before I knew there was a gay community, I recognized a spiritual community on the pages of scripture that included people like me. After all, the Bible is about people like us: created and blessed by God, oppressed but then delivered, wandering in the wilderness in search of a promised land, exiled and yet returning "home," outcast and then welcomed into the family of faith.

Picking up the Bible and, in a sense, holding it to one's ear is like picking up a shell at the seashore and listening for the sound of waves. What one hears are voices of people like you and me chattering over the centuries about the nature of life and of love, of faith and of God. Though many think of the Bible as monolithic——that is, of a single point of view, the Bible is rather a compendium of viewpoints on a variety of issues. To enter the Bible is like entering any community: there may be some common beliefs, but there is also disagreement.

The dialogue of the Bible therefore invites rather than inhibits further conversation. "The Bible says it, I believe it, and that settles it" is not a way of thinking that's true to the nature of scripture. For one thing, it presupposes that any reader can be absolutely sure of the meaning of a sacred text. It also excludes the work of the Holy Spirit in interpreting and applying a given scripture. And finally, it forgets that the community of faith has both the right and the responsibility to find its own way in discerning God's will in the present.

For me, to meditate each morning on a sacred text is pleasurable. It allows me to bask in the presence and love of God, and it makes me feel good inside, like doing a charitable act or working for social justice. Indeed, feeling good inside prompts me to act charitably and justly. The Bible is not my only source of sacred texts, of course, but it is my primary and authoritative source. Its words and stories both comfort and challenge me. The course of my life changes ever so imperceptibly each day I reflect on the messages of the Bible.

My hope and prayer is that this book will help you enjoy the spiritual pleasures of meditating on the Bible as the person God has created and is calling you to be.

C.R.G.

Acknowledgments

Thank you, Westminster John Knox Press, and specifically, executive editor Stephanie Egnotovich for making this meditation book available in this new edition.

Thanks also to Kandace Hawkinson, the original editor who challenged me to write this book and helped shape it. I thank Mark King, my lover, for being the first reader and catching me when I became too academic or irrelevant to lesbian and gay readers. And I thank George Lynch, D.Min., who offered his considerable expertise in the Bible, religion, and theology as the second reader, and who gave me the title of the book.

Thanks to all the people involved in the production, publicity, marketing, distribution, and sales of this book. Especially I thank you, the reader, and the God we all seek, for this opportunity to claim the Bible story as also our own.

Introduction

My lover has searched for God in several kinds of churches throughout his life. The condemnation he met with as a gay man discouraged and alienated him. The "in" language of Christians made our faith unintelligible. The complex and ancient setting of the Bible did not render it user-friendly. Mark is HIV-positive and feels a great urgency in his inquiry into life's meaning and purpose, the spiritual quest.

A lesbian woman I met many years ago shared this urgency. Her quest, which I've recounted in two previous books, still motivates me. She had no religious background, but she told me that in her lovemaking with her lover she had touched a spiritual realm never before known to her. She explained that she wanted to know more about God.

This stranger and my lover deserve a devotional book that helps God's Word to them emerge from the closets of the Bible's ancient stories and theological language. The "Word" within the words of scripture is an intimate encounter with God. No writer, not even a biblical writer, has the power to "out" the Word. The Spirit at work within us——writer and reader——introduces us to God.

For Christians, Jesus Christ is the primary Word of God, the primary way we meet God. Through Christ, the Word comes out to embrace us. Just as our love is out, God's love is out.

I traveled much during the time I was selecting the verses for this book. As I sat on planes full of straight strangers and on a cruise ship full of gay and lesbian strangers, I became aware that I was trying to hide the fact I was looking at a Bible! I feared both "friend" and "foe." I feared someone who might look at my scripture reading approvingly, lest they be antigay. I feared someone who might look at my work disapprovingly, lest they be anti-religion. This revealed to me how necessary it is for lesbian and gay Christians to reclaim the Bible from those who would use it either as a weapon or a target!

In the meditations that follow, I approach the Bible more as a student than as a scholar. I seek within its stories spiritual truth rather than historical fact. Each day begins with a scripture, taken from the New Revised Standard Version of the Bible, unless otherwise noted, and modified to avoid exclusively male references to God. The more ambitious readers may choose to look up the context of the verse or verses, but that's not necessary. A reflection on the biblical text is followed by a short prayer or affirmation. Hopefully, what you read will open your own meditation and prayer.

It says good things about the Bible that there were many more verses I wanted to use than could be selected for this book. The scriptures have been arranged by themes, one per month, at times coinciding with the church year, at other times coinciding with events of the lesbian and gay community.

May this book serve as a personal invitation to you and to us all to reclaim the Bible as lesbians and gay men, as bisexuals and transgenders, and as people who love them. Little do we know what spiritual pleasures await us as we work through the Bible together.

Chris Glaser
Atlanta, Georgia

EPIPHANY

The heavens are telling the glory of God; and the firma-
ment proclaims [God's] handiwork.

Psalm 19:1

Epiphanies are manifestations of divine glory. "Natural"
epiphanies may be less evident to us than to the Psalmist.
Landscapes are choked with asphalt and concrete. The
dome of sky is cluttered with buildings, signs, and smog,
and city lights interfere with the billion-year-old light
show that even now proclaims God's handiwork.

Yet we don't have to look far to see that "the world
is charged with the grandeur of God," as Gerard Manley
Hopkins wrote in the poem "God's Grandeur." A wild-
flower growing through a crack of concrete, a cat
jumping from a high wall, the smile of a passing
stranger — all may be epiphanies, manifestations of
God's presence.

And we may look within ourselves as lesbians and
gay men for epiphanies, manifestations of the sacred in
our world. A sparkle in a lover's eye, freedom from a
closet, struggles for justice, tender care in the AIDS crisis — all proclaim that we are also God's handiwork.

From all that obstructs our pleasure of your presence,
deliver us, O Holy One.

*In the beginning . . . God created the heavens and the
earth. . . . And God saw that it was good.*

Genesis 1:1, 25

Our religious upbringing may have emphasized the holiness of heaven over the holiness of earth. Yet God created
both. This earth and our earthly lives have as much sacred
worth as any life that is to come.

Lesbians and gay men struggle to affirm this. We
have often been expected to deny our sexuality "for
the sake of our spirituality," but we resist this. Some of
us believe we have chosen sexuality over spirituality,
since spirituality has been presented to us as an "out of
body" experience. But spirituality, like sexuality, is bodily. We experience the Creator and the creation
through our bodies.

Our spirituality, then, includes physical sensations.
It may provide pleasure, as we enjoy communion with
God and creation. But it may also give us pangs of compassion, as we seek help with our own burdens and as
we lift the burdens of others.

*Help me to recognize my sacred worth, Divine Creator,
and the sacred worth of others.*

Then God . . . formed a human creature of dust from the ground, and breathed into the creature's nostrils the breath of life; and the human creature became a living being.

Genesis 2:7 (Inclusive Language Lectionary)

In Genesis, two separate accounts describe creation. The more ancient one appears second, in chapter two, and describes a "hands-on" Creator who personally sculpts the human body from earth (Hebrew *adamah,* from which we get *Adam*) and breathes into its nostrils the breath of life. In biblical times, the breath was associated with the soul, an indivisible unit of spirit and body that was life. Later, God creates a partner so that the human would not be alone. Both were "naked, and were not ashamed" (2:25).

This story proclaims God's valuing of both our bodies and our need for relationship. If God values our bodies enough to shape each and every part, then we may value our bodies——each and every part. We need not be ashamed of our bodies. And, since God values our need for intimate relationship, then we need not deny ourselves a lover. We need not be ashamed of our sexuality.

Thank you for the glory of our bodies, and the glory of the bodies of our lovers, Sacred Sculptor.

When I look at your heavens, the work of your fingers,
the moon and the stars that you have established;
what are human beings that you are mindful of them,
mortals that you care for them?
Yet you have made them a little lower than God,
and crowned them with glory and honor.

Psalm 8:3–5

The Psalmist is properly awed by the responsibility of such glory and honor and by God's mindfulness and care for human beings. Why are we given this special place in the universe? What is our purpose? What is our calling?

All of us who are sexually unique might ask the same question. What gift does one who is attracted to her or his own gender bring to the world? What insight does one who is attracted to both genders offer? And what is the purpose of one who resists being confined to a gender?

Human ego and humility interweave in this hymn. That God has given us "dominion over the works of [God's] hands" (8:6) means responsible stewardship of creation, but it has come to mean domination, exploitation, and control.

Those of the majority culture may presume to have dominion over the rest of us, wanting to exercise their control. Rather than allowing this, we can teach them to be responsible stewards of our human rights just as they might be of nature, as when protecting an endangered species!

Loving Creator, thank you for shaping my sexuality!
Teach me what gifts it may offer the world.

In the beginning was the Word, and the Word was with God, and the Word was God. . . . And the Word became flesh and lived among us.

John 1:1, 14

We know what it means to give flesh to a word. To many people, the words "gay" and "lesbian" isolate, stereotype, and limit their experience of us. Only when they come to know us do the words take on new meanings, opening their experience beyond sexual acts and social stigma.

Followers of Jesus witnessed God's Word at work in him. Regardless of what one believes to be authentic in the biblical record of his life, there is little doubt that the glory of God must have been present in Jesus to cause such a stir in the conscience of the world. God, in a sense, *came out* in Jesus of Nazareth, overcoming the way people isolated, stereotyped, and limited their experience of God.

To many lesbians and gay men, the words "Christian" or "spiritual" also isolate, stereotype, and limit their experience *of us.* They may have difficulty disassociating us from the antigay positions of much of the church. Yet we may make the words "Christian" and "spiritual" flesh in a new way that unites rather than divides our community.

The gospel writer John affirms that the Word became flesh, "full of grace and truth" (1:14), asserting that we are thereby empowered to become children of God, embodying that grace and truth.

From your fullness, Christ Jesus, let us receive grace upon grace so that we may embody your grace and your truth.

*And when Jesus had been baptized, just as he came up
from the water, suddenly the heavens were opened to him
and he saw the Spirit of God descending like a dove and
alighting on him. And a voice from heaven said, "This is
my Son, the Beloved, with whom I am well pleased."*

Matthew 3:16–17

In workshops I sometimes invite participants to make a
similar affirmation of one another by calling each by
name, followed by, "is my beloved child, with whom I am
well pleased." How we would have loved to hear this
growing up as children, particularly when we doubted
our sense of belonging and identity and calling because
we were "different"!

The gospel writers viewed Jesus' baptism as the
threshold of his ministry. Though he would be
tempted in the wilderness immediately afterward, the
event signified his strong sense of belonging and identity and calling.

Those of us baptized as infants and those of us baptized as youths or adults began a similar journey. We
might have sojourned in a wilderness and been
tempted to give it all up, but we are still God's children, called for a purpose.

If Jesus had not fulfilled his ministry, his baptism
would not have been remembered as significant. As we
fulfill our ministry, our awareness of the significance of
our own baptism increases.

*With Jesus, we are your beloved children, with whom
you are well pleased.*

Just as we have borne the image of the one of dust, we shall also bear the image of the one of heaven.

1 Corinthians 15:49 (Inclusive Language Lectionary)

The "one of dust" is Adam, who sinned, and the "one of heaven" is Jesus, who did not. The apostle Paul writes to the church at Corinth about sanctification, the sanctifying process by which Christians were to become less like Adam and more like Christ. It was not a process of "spiritualizing" the body; it was a process of God *resurrecting* the body, resurrecting how we should have been in a world without sin.

Coming out is a similar process. We are still our bodies, but we are more fully ourselves. Our bodies have in a sense been "glorified"——as Paul writes—— merely because they are no longer denied the fulfillment God intended. We are learning what it means to live in a world without closets.

Coming out may be both a painful and joyful journey in which we never finally arrive. It requires discipline, changing one's patterns of denial and coping and avoidance, and adopting a newfound sense of responsibility and response-ability. Coming out parallels becoming like Christ.

Neither coming out nor becoming like Christ makes us perfect, but both offer us an integrity——an integrity of body and soul, of sex and spirit, of the personal and public self.

Grant us the integrity by which we may harmonize all we are, all we believe, all we say, and all we do.

We are God's work of art.

Ephesians 2:10 (New Jerusalem Bible)

This is a stunning assertion. It takes us by surprise. Scripture was never this positive when I was a child, you might think. And indeed, other translations of this same text do not state it so boldly.

But we *are* God's work of art. We are a work in progress, perhaps. But we are beautiful.

Vincent van Gogh viewed Christ as "an artist whose medium is human flesh" (*The Letters of Vincent Van Gogh*). The scripture continues, "created in Christ Jesus for the good works which God has already designated to make up our way of life." We are God's good work, and we are to create good works. The scripture offers us confidence in our beauty and in our ability to do good.

The gay community shakes our confidence in our own beauty by creating the cult of the body beautiful. The church shakes our self-worth by creating the cult of heterosexuality and the cult of the perfect saint.

But God sees to the heart of the matter and to the heart of *our* matter. Like an artist who believes in her work, God expresses confidence through this scripture that we are good and that we are capable of doing good. Unlike most artists, God can afford to have chutzpah.

Holy Artist, we are your work of art, created in Christ Jesus. Help us to live the good life you intended.

Make a joyful noise to the Lord,
all the earth. . . .
It is [God] that made us,
and we are [God's].

Psalm 100:1, 3

If only Christians could know the multitude of gay and lesbian musicians and vocalists who "make a joyful noise to
the Lord" in their churches every Sunday. Yet the majority
of Christians resist believing that it is God who made us,
and that we are God's. (The very fact that we can praise
God *anyway* says much about our faithfulness.)

Many of *us* also resist believing that it is God who
made us, and that we are God's. We've felt forced to
make a choice by those churches that present an
"either/or" to us rather than a "both/and."

Jon Bailey was disinvited from the leadership of a
church musicians' gathering because he directed the
Gay Men's Chorus of Los Angeles. The keynote
speaker, William Sloane Coffin, refused to come unless
Bailey was reinvited. Bailey was, along with the Gay
Men's Chorus. The opening worship of "joyful noise"
proved healing for the church musicians as well as for
the gay chorus, many of whom had never felt welcomed in worship.

God, forgive us for equating the church's response to
us with your response.

For it was you who formed my inward parts;
you knit me together in my mother's womb.
I praise you, for I am fearfully and wonderfully made.

                        Psalm 139:13–14

God wove together our bodies. God wove together our
gender and our sexuality. The tender intimacy of God's
personal involvement in our embryonic creation is a
cause for praise, awe, and wonder.

God must have conceived us the way we are: not
the way we express ourselves——that is up to us——
but who we are. If we are gay, God made us that way. If
we are lesbian, God made us that way. If we are bisexual, God made us that way. If we are transgender, God
made us that way.

Our sexual differences have made us a cause for
blame, fear, and horror to those who don't understand.
Rather, they should be a cause for praise, awe, and
wonder that we exist. God is very creative and not
committed to one formula of existence. God is not as
dull or unimaginative as people seem to think!

Thank you for intricately weaving me "in the depths of
the earth," my mother's womb, Creator God.

Can a woman forget her nursing child,
or show no compassion for the child of her womb?

Isaiah 49:15

Before it became "P.C."——politically correct——I had already come to believe that the image of Father God on which I'd been raised did not adequately account for my experience of God. I began to open the Lord's Prayer with, "O God, Mother and Father of us all." This opened me to a broader sense of God.

Biblical writers knew this. A multitude of names and metaphors were used to refer to Yahweh, the Hebrew name for God, which was never spoken aloud out of reverence. Today's scripture is just one instance: Yahweh is characterized as a mother whose intimate love of carrying a baby in her womb and feeding it at her breasts reminds us of God's visceral love and loyalty. I believe this is more than metaphor; a loving mother *incarnates* divine love.

There are mothers and fathers who forget and mistreat their children. Some parents' negative visceral reaction to homosexuality overrides their otherwise positive response to gay and lesbian children. For those children, praying to a father or mother God may either alienate them from God or serve as a substitute for an absent, distant, or cruel parent. The Bible assures us that we will always have a Father God who welcomes us home and a Mother God who holds us on her lap.

Mother and Father God, hold me in my fear. Keep me safe and warm. Kiss me and make me better.

I do not cease to give thanks for you as I remember you in my prayers.

Ephesians 1:16

A lesbian friend who joined an evangelical Christian group when in college told me that the worst threat its members could make was, *"I will pray for you . . . "* It meant that they believed your thinking or behavior was seriously awry.

What a contrast is Paul's letter to the members of the Ephesus church: "I do not cease to give thanks for you as I remember you in my prayers." This is preceded by commendations on their faith and love and followed by a prayer for their wisdom and hope.

One of the central lessons of the *One Minute Manager,* a quick guide to better business management, is the concept that it is better to catch someone doing something right than to catch someone doing something wrong.

This is also true spiritually. It is better to give thanks to someone, building self-worth, than to blame and shame. Shaming makes it all the more difficult for persons to believe themselves *capable* of doing something right. Sadly, most religious training is shame-based. We have been shamed about our bodies, our sexuality, even our spirituality.

Instead of using our prayers as a means of control, how much better it would be to use them as a way of thanksgiving!

Thank you, God, for lesbians and gay men all over the earth struggling to keep faith!

Does not wisdom call,
and does not understanding raise her voice? . . .
"The Lord created me at the beginning of [God's] work. . . .
Happy is the one who listens to me."

Proverbs 8:1, 22, 34

Many religious people fear wisdom. Wisdom questions. Any of us may want answers rather than inquiry because we want a handle on life that is certain.

And yet Wisdom was God's first creation, according to the wisdom literature of the Bible. And she was viewed in some ancient cultures as the feminine principle of the divine. Referred to as feminine in the Bible, she is associated with the Word that became flesh, the Christ. She is acclaimed as the guiding principle in the diversity of creation by the Psalmist: "O [God], how manifold are your works! In wisdom you have made them all; the earth is full of your creatures" (Ps. 104:24).

She is integral to life and to faith. Wisdom is more insight than information, as much intuition and emotion as she is reason. She requires an open heart as well as an open mind. Wisdom visits in moments of reflection. She offers perspective and understanding and hope.

Lady Wisdom, visit me. Offer me insight into myself and into the self of each person I meet this day.

For everything created by God is good, and nothing is to be rejected, provided it is received with thanksgiving; for it is sanctified by God's word and by prayer.

1 Timothy 4:4-5

It is said that atheists are very quiet in their lovemaking because they have no one to address. The spontaneous and unrehearsed "oh God" that we emit in the throes of sensual delight may be more genuine thanksgiving than the expected and memorized grace we offer before meals.

A gay member of my church used to give thanks to God for putting nerve endings in all the right places! Yet how many of us wince at the notion that God might be pleased in our sexual pleasuring, while we look with approval on those who thank God for another sensual delight: eating a meal. The wince reveals how separated or segregated our sexuality is from our spirituality.

Young Timothy is being advised to watch out for religious fanatics who "forbid marriage" and "demand abstinence from foods." Spiritual discipline is not abstinence from sensual pleasure but remembrance to thank God for earthly delight. Recognizing rather than denying its sacred worth prompts responsibility.

Sacred Lover, thanks for the many intimate ways by which you caress me with your love.

I am black and beautiful.
                          Song of Solomon 1:5

The Song of Solomon revels in the sensual delight of two lovers. The woman begins her self-description this way, and though it is a self-affirmation, it is part of an explanation of why her skin is dark.

My high school principal was an African-American of deep spiritual conviction. Every time I heard him speak, his words seemed golden, carefully orchestrated into insight. He became my primary role model for speaking and writing. Though he was dearly loved at our school, no real estate agent would sell his family a home in our neighborhood because of his color. And this was in "liberal" California!

When you think about it, most prejudice and related injustices grow from a response to bodies: bodies different from our own (gender, race, disability), bodies who love their own sex or both sexes, bodies believed unattractive, bodies who are poor or powerless. All injustices are linked because they are what the body suffers for being different.

If we link our bodies against injustice, then, as Martin Luther King, Jr., prophesied, "The chain of hatred must be cut. When it is broken, brotherhood can begin" (Coretta Scott King, *My Life With Martin Luther King, Jr.*).

Bless our bodies, Lord, for it is through them we love you and one another. Amen.

The Lord spoke to Moses: . . . I have filled [the artisan] with divine spirit, with ability, intelligence, and knowledge in every kind of craft, to devise artistic designs.

Exodus 31:1, 3–4

"Your people are so creative" may be a somewhat patronizing stereotype of the gay community, but I'm pleased to say that I believe it's true. It is also true that gays and lesbians can be as tacky and tasteless in clothing and furnishings as anyone else.

My mother always told me that visual and verbal artists had to suffer, and if this is so, it may account for our disproportionately extensive creativity. Aesthetic sensibility may arise from the ascetic sensitivity of the closet——if life is confining, oppressive, and now short, then make it as beautiful, gay, and elegant as possible.

What we may not notice is that our creative spirit is *divine.* It is a godly response to the chaos of our anti-gay world. As suffering may evoke a godlike response in our compassion, so it may prompt a godlike rejoinder in our creativity.

It is not that suffering is good. It is rather that our response to suffering is often of greater spiritual significance than we realize.

Divine Spirit, inspire my work and my play and my love and my meditation with fresh approaches and designs.

Ah, you who rise early in the morning
in pursuit of strong drink . . .
whose feasts consist of lyre and harp,
tambourine and flute and wine,
but who do not regard the deeds of the Lord,
or see the work of [God's] hands!

Isaiah 5:11–12

Our community believes living well is the best revenge, and "Party *down!*" is a frequent cry. The problem is that those who "rise early in the morning in pursuit of strong drink" end up dead or in Twelve-Step meetings.

Isaiah is not an antiparty kind of guy. What bothers the prophet is that people are not noticing God's work. They're not picking up the newspaper to see what the Spirit is doing: the fall of the Berlin Wall, the end of apartheid in South Africa, the democratization of Eastern Europe, the stirrings of peace in the Middle East, the work of homeless shelters, the efforts of AIDS caregivers, the advances of minorities. They are also failing to pick up scripture to see what God has done in the past.

And they may not notice God's presence in ordinary events: a spider weaving a web on the deck, a phone call from a faithful friend, the innocence of a sleeping lover.

Filling one's life with artificial and temporary highs can make one miss the cosmic and eternal party.

Divine Mover and Shaker, open my eyes to your influence in our world, inspiring mercy, justice, and peace.

"Be still, and know that I am God!"
                    Psalm 46:10

You might expect an idyllic setting for this admonition from Yahweh, but the command comes in the midst of tumult: an earth that changes, mountains that shake, waters that roar, nations in an uproar, tottering kingdoms. God "makes wars cease . . . breaks the bow, and shatters the spear" (46:9). Then to the nations God charges, "Be still, and know that I am God!"

We, too, face tumult. Religious groups attack our rights, society rejects us from the military to the ministry, surveys question our numbers, scientists quiz our genes, the media exploits the sensational, AIDS kills friends and leaders, issues divide us. We wish God would make these wars cease.

The beginning of the end of wars is a cease-fire. Though those who line up against us may not stop their attacks, we need to be still and remember who is God. God is not them.

As a young Jewish woman facing the Holocaust in Europe, Etty Hillesum wrote to God, "all we can manage these days and also all that really matters [is]: that we safeguard that little piece of You, God, in ourselves. And perhaps in others as well" (*An Interrupted Life* [New York: Simon & Schuster, 1985], p. 187).

In this moment, I quiet myself and remember that you are in my heart, O God, "our refuge and our strength, a very present help in trouble" (46:1).

All scripture is inspired by God and is useful for teaching.
											2 Timothy 3:16

I am grateful to have been reared in a Baptist church and a fundamentalist Christian school that were intensely passionate about my learning scripture. The Bible helped me get through the rough parts of my youth and helped lead to my self-acceptance. It also helps me refute those who misuse it as a weapon against us, while it helps me connect with those who love scripture and resist using it as a club.

All this suggests to me that there is a lot more good in scripture than bad. Yes, I'm Pollyanna all over again, who discovered more blessings than curses in the Bible.

Of course, the scripture that Timothy is advised on is what we call the Old Testament. The New Testament was not yet collected. The experienced missionary advising Timothy tells him that Jewish scriptures have had life breathed into them ("inspired"), much like the first human being. That means they are alive and well and worthy guides.

But because they are *living,* I believe, they are open to dialogue and interpretation. Jesus freely dialogued with his tradition and interpreted scripture differently from his peers. So did the early church and the church through the centuries. So why should the dialogue and interpretation stop now?

Instruct and guide me through your words in scripture, Holy Wisdom, but especially through your Word Jesus Christ.

*You have been born anew, not of perishable but of imper-
ishable seed, through the living and enduring word of
God. . . . That word is the good news that was announced to you.*

1 Peter 1:23, 25

The author here did not know he was writing a book of
the Bible. So "the word" in this case is not scripture, it is
the mystical *kerygma,* Greek for *proclamation,* which is
communicated (that is, given and received) more through
the Spirit than through reason or words. It is an *experience*
of the *gospel,* the *good news* of God's love in Jesus Christ.

It is often difficult to *experience* good news, especially coming from God or the Bible. So much of what
we have heard from religion has been bad news. Evan-
gelists and evangelicals, whose names come from the
Greek verb for bringing good news, connote "bad
news" to many of us.

In my book *Come Home!* I wrote of a gay member
of my church who pleaded to speak with me privately.
I braced myself for a serious problem. "Yesterday
morning," he said, "I woke up . . . and felt surrounded
by God's love." He was "born anew" by this experience
of the gospel.

Meditation prepares us for our own rebirths within
God's love. It also helps us to remember other times
when we felt welcomed by the universe. A friend had
such an experience when coming out, and sent birth
announcements to family and friends!

*May I be born anew by the imperishable seed of your
word, your good news, in my life.*

*Now there was a great wind, . . . but [God] was not in the
wind; and after the wind an earthquake, but [God] was
not in the earthquake; and after the earthquake a fire,
but [God] was not in the fire; and after the fire a sound of
sheer silence.*

1 Kings 19:12

God is not always a drama queen. Epiphanies, or manifestations of divine glory, do not always come in dramatic
events. The prophet Elijah learned this on a holy mountain. God was not in the storm, earthquake, or holocaust,
but rather, in the "sheer silence" after, also translated as
"the sound of a gentle stillness," or "a still, small voice."

A friend with HIV described the death of his closest
friend to AIDS. "Nothing spiritual happened," he told
me. "No rustling of the curtains at the window as he
died. Just a group of his friends looking on horrified as
their friend breathed his last." I replied, "Spirituality
isn't *'Hollywood'!*" What was "spiritual" was the love
of the friends who gathered around him. Even my
friend's terrified recognition that this could have been
him was compassionate identification, a sign of spiritual connection.

Beyond or within the dramas of our lives we may
discover God's presence in sheer silence.

*Wind, earthquake, fire. In the silence that follows, may I
feel your presence and listen for your voice, O God.*

But Moses said to God, "If I come to the Israelites . . . and they ask me, 'What is [God's] name?' what shall I say to them?" God said to Moses, "I am who I am."

Exodus 3:13–14

God's voice boomed from a bush that was burning but not consumed. Moses stopped to listen and heard the call to lead his people out of Egyptian bondage. But——oh——what was that name again?

Before some of us came out, someone asking our name in a gay context could feel threatening. Some of us made up names because we were afraid. In biblical times, it was believed that the name revealed the self, a form of intimacy. That's why God proved evasive. God was not ready. Nor was humanity.

The content of God's identity cannot be "fixed" in time or place. "I am who I am," suggests a God of mystery, asking——like the protagonist in the musical *La Cage aux Folles* who sings similar words——to be accepted *as is*. Another translation, "I will be what I will be," implies a God in process.

Similarly, though we want to be accepted "as is," we do not want others to think that they "know" us by our sexual orientation. We don't want our whole self viewed by one identity, though vital and good. We retain our mystery. And we are in process.

You who will be what you will be, sojourn with me, I who will be what I will be.

Moses came down from Mount Sinai. As he came down from the mountain with the two tablets of the covenant in his hand, Moses did not know that the skin of his face shone because he had been talking with God.

Exodus 34:29

Moses had one of the first mountaintop experiences in the recorded spiritual history that we know as the Bible. Any of us who have been on an enriching retreat know the glow with which we come away. *Retreats* are in reality *advances.* We retreat to reflect on who we are and where we are headed. We retreat to restore our resources for what's next. We retreat to know what life would be like without the burden of everyday agendas, which may cause us to modify those agendas.

When I began to take personal retreats, I modified my schedule to provide time for everyday "retreats": my morning prayer time. I need that time to maintain a healthy glow.

Moses' experience, of course, was no ordinary retreat. It transformed a scraggly assortment of recently freed slaves into a people. It gave them the resource they would need to survive and thrive: the Law of Moses, the tablets of the covenant. It called them to a land that God would show them, a land full of promise. And forever it changed human history.

May our collective meditations with God do the same.

May others see your divine reflection in our faces, O God of the mountaintop, the valley, and the plain.

Jesus took with him Peter and James and John, and led them up a high mountain apart, by themselves. And he was transfigured before them, and his clothes became dazzling white. . . . And there appeared to them Elijah with Moses, who were talking with Jesus.

Mark 9:2–4

Jesus communed with Moses and Elijah, signifying his relationship with liberation and prophecy. Like the mountaintop experiences of Moses and Elijah, the disciples heard God's voice: "This my Son, my Beloved; listen to him!" And as Moses' face shone talking with God, Jesus glowed from the experience.

We might wonder why Peter would later deny Jesus, while better understanding why James and John squabbled over the places of honor on his left and right hand in the coming kingdom. Peter's self-protecting panic during Jesus' trial made him forget an epiphany that may have inflated the egos of James and John.

Without trivializing this mystical experience, there are parallels to our own "epiphany," our own coming out as lesbian and gay Christians within the church. It causes a panic of denial among the patriarchs like Peter, who fear for their very lives and the life of the church. But it may also inflate our egos, so that we think of ourselves more highly than we ought and fail to build mutual relations with other disciples, especially those who have also been denied full access to leadership and service.

Transfigure us, Christ Jesus, that we might stand with other liberators and prophets in a collegial communion.

And all of us, with unveiled faces, seeing the glory of [God] as though reflected in a mirror, are being transformed into the same image from one degree of glory to another; for this comes from [God], the Spirit.

2 Corinthians 3:18

When the largely gay congregation that I served was small, we worshiped around the communion table, looking into one another's faces. This embodied our belief that God's Spirit was not "up front," closeted behind an altar, but "out" in our midst.

Upon Jesus' death on a cross, scripture holds that the curtain that divided the Holy of Holies from the rest of the temple was torn in two from top (the heavens) to bottom (the earth), signifying God's coming out from sacred shadows to fully dwell with humankind (Matt. 27:51).

Paul wrote of this free Spirit to the church at Corinth. The old covenant of Law was externally binding, but the new covenant of Grace was internally guiding. The glow that Moses experienced with his encounters with God was temporary, but the glow that is possible with God within us is eternal. The people made Moses veil his face because God's reflection was overpowering, but we are to unveil our faces so that we can be transformed by God's glory reflecting out of one another.

Open my vision to your glory revealed within persons I meet today. Unveil your glory within me.

Wisdom makes one's face shine,
and the hardness of one's countenance is changed.

Ecclesiastes 8:1

Our countenances changed when finally accepting our sexual orientation. Many of us improved our appearance, smiled and sparkled more, and relaxed. Many of our countenances changed again as we "got wise" about relationships. The constant cruise disappeared. We relaxed about our appearance, sought conversation rather than conquest, surrounded ourselves with friends rather than strangers, enjoyed solitude.

And we know people whose countenance changed when they became wise about lesbians, gay men, bisexuals, and transgenders. They smiled welcomingly when they saw us, glowed because they better accepted their own sexuality, grieved with us about AIDS, cheered us at pride events.

This biblical pearl about wisdom changing the countenance is ironically found under an ignorant, misogynistic passage, which reminds us that, even in scripture, God's glory is veiled by human limitations. If *we* are wise, we won't discard that glory because it's wrapped in words revealing the ignorance and evil of human attempts to capture that glory.

Transform our countenances with the wisdom of your glory embedded in scripture and embodied in us.

. . . and the angels came and ministered to him.
                     Matthew 4:11 (Revised Standard Version)

In his first major battle with human suffering and temptation, Jesus was blessed with the ministry of angels.

A friend who had just had his first major battle with AIDS told me that, near death, he had seen angels. His profession was in medicine, so he knew it was possible that what he witnessed may have been a hallucination induced by the drugs he'd been given. But he chose to believe they were angels.

Angels are emanations of God's glory. They may come to us in dreams, or they may come to us in reality.

The lover of a friend was in a final, deep sleep in a long struggle with AIDS. He feared God would not receive him in death because he had never resolved his faith and his sexuality. I had been holding his hand for quite some time, when I decided to pray aloud with him. It could have been my own wishful thinking, but his hand seemed to grasp mine tighter as we prayed.

In his semiconscious state, I could have appeared as an angel to him. In reality, I was a friend reaching out to him as best I knew how. But I hope he chose to believe I was an angel.

After all, we are all emanations from God.

In our suffering, send angels and visions of your love.

But filled with the Holy Spirit, [Stephen] gazed into heaven and saw the glory of God and Jesus standing at the right hand of God.

Acts 7:55

Stephen enjoyed this mystical vision as he became the first martyr of Christian faith, accused as Jesus had been of wanting to destroy the temple and to change customs.

Today's lesbian and gay Christians are similarly accused of wanting to destroy the church and to change customs. And though few of us have died for our witness (*martyr* comes from the Greek word for "witness"), many of us have given our lives and our livelihoods to proclaim our vision of God's inclusive glory and of a living Christ that calls all of us to service.

A religious fundamentalist named Saul "approved of their killing" Stephen. Thus began Saul's persecution of the early Christians, and he did not simply cast them out of synagogues. He took away their rights and "committed them to prison." Sound familiar?

On the road to Damascus Saul himself saw the glory of God in Christ. Temporarily deprived of sight just as he had temporarily resisted the vision, the champion of Law and orthodoxy became Paul, the evangelist of Grace and the Christian revolution.

We pray for those who persecute us, that your transforming glory may shine on them on their own roads to Damascus.

*"Every valley shall be lifted up,
and every mountain and hill be made low;
the uneven ground shall become level,
and the rough places a plain.
Then the glory of the Lord shall be revealed,
and all people shall see it together."*

Isaiah 40:4–5

Departing from his prepared text on the steps of the Lincoln Memorial during the 1963 March on Washington, Martin Luther King, Jr., awed the quarter of a million souls gathered that day on the Mall with his "I Have a Dream" speech, stirringly quoting this scripture from Isaiah.

"Where there is no vision, the people perish" (Prov. 29:18, KJV). Where there is no vision, there is no spirituality. Where there is no spirituality, there is no vision.

Spirituality is about the whole picture. Spirituality is our view of reality. But it is not simply *today's* reality. It is yesterday's and tomorrow's. It is memory and it is hope. It is history and it is vision.

Thank God for visionaries. They are the ones who "prepare the way of the Lord" (40:3). If it weren't for them, I wouldn't be writing this and you wouldn't be reading it.

Prepare us for your way, O Lord, that we may be on the Way and not in the way.

I will sing to the [Sovereign] as long as I live;
I will sing praise to my God while I have being.
May my meditation be pleasing to [God],
for I rejoice in the [Sovereign].

Psalm 104:33–34

Recently I realized that my lover's scriptures were popular songs. Scriptures are texts that speak of and to our experience, offering us a sense of wholeness and meaning. Not all texts need be from the Bible. When he decided to take a position with an AIDS agency in Atlanta, Annie Lennox's "Little Bird" became his text for our move. His desire to fly away to a new city and a new life was given voice and mythic meaning by her music.

There's nothing new in this. The Jews collected their favorite "hits" in the Psalms. These were songs sung at various occasions: religious, cultural, civic, political, personal. They gave voice and meaning to life. They also offered lilt, a lifting of the spirit only melody and rhythm and beat can give.

Anyone who has sung, played, clapped, or danced to music, whether in their hearts or with their bodies, knows how it inspires the embodiment of praise. Worshiping once with a gay, charismatic congregation in Texas, I learned that praise in music may also be an aerobic activity!

Teach me to sing and dance your praise, O God, not just with lips but with feet and with soul.

God bless you and keep you;
God make God's face to shine upon you, and be gracious to you;
God lift up God's countenance upon you, and give you peace.

Numbers 6:24–26 (Inclusive Language Lectionary)

How rarely we bless each other! And yet how often we curse one another!

When I was a teenager, I would pray a blessing on those I considered enemies. I figured a blessing would have the effect of a curse on those who didn't deserve it, a somewhat innocent but immature interpretation of scripture. Jesus told his disciples that if they blessed a home that didn't deserve it, the blessing would return to them (Luke 10:5-6). He also said to "bless those who curse you" (Luke 6:28). Paul quoted Proverbs, saying we should give food and drink to our enemies, "for by doing this you will heap burning coals on their heads" (Rom. 12:20). But the gist of these sayings comes in Paul's next comment, "Do not be overcome by evil, but overcome evil with good" (Rom. 12:21).

We are so overcome by evil that we don't even bless those who are good. Sometimes we're jealous of them and secretly wish they'd trip up! We would do well to practice this blessing that Moses gave Aaron with which to bless the Israelites——first on ourselves, then on one another.

Bless me and keep me; make your face to shine upon me, and be gracious to me; lift up your countenance upon me, and give me peace.

LAMENTATION

"Do not human beings have a hard service on earth . . . ?
Like a slave who longs for the shadow . . .
Remember that my life is a breath . . .
What are human beings, that you make so much of them?"

Job 7:1, 2, 7, 17

Why do the good suffer? This is the question raised in the book of
Job, in which a good man loses family, wealth, and health in a
bizarre bet between Satan (not yet the fallen angel) and God to
test his faith. Job laments the hardship and brevity of human existence, mocking the Psalmist's affirmation, "what are human beings that you are mindful of them?" (Ps. 8:4). Job would prefer a
little less attention, thank you very much!

The intimacy with which God created us makes God either an intimate friend or an intimate foe in the face of suffering and death, depending on our faith. If God is worthy
of praise for good, many of us think that God must be responsible for evil. For example, if God blesses us with sexual variation, then some might hold God accountable for
heterosexism, discrimination, gay-bashing——possibly even
AIDS.

God can take our anger. I've shaken my fist at God and
lightning has not struck, nor have I felt abandoned. God is
not some positive-thinking congregation that abandons a
member dying with AIDS because of "negative thoughts."
Nor is God some spiritual health guru who refuses to attend
a funeral because of its "negative energy."

Hear our anger as well as our love, Dear God. Hold us in our
suffering and in the many deaths we experience.

As a deer longs for flowing streams,
so my soul longs for you, O God.

Psalm 42:1

We have a deep longing for God. A thirst. A desire to "behold
the face of God" (42:2). This can't be all there is. Life has some
greater significance yet to be revealed to us. We are here for a
purpose. As people. As gay people.

The author of Psalms 42 and 43 (which should be read as
one) is prevented from worshiping Yahweh at the temple.
The Psalmist remembers leading others "in procession to
the house of God, with glad shouts and songs of thanksgiving, a multitude keeping festival" (42:4). Now adversaries
taunt, "Where is your God?" (42:3).

Many of us have felt prevented from the worship of God
because of our sexuality, either because of internal doubts of
our worthiness or because of external prohibitions of our
presence or leadership. This is *our* Psalm. "I say to God, my
rock, 'Why have you forgotten me? Why must I walk about
mournfully because the enemy oppresses me?' " (42:9).

Deep down, we also know the answer of the Psalmist:
"Hope in God; for I shall again praise [God], my help and
my God" (42:11).

"O send out your light and your truth; let them lead me; let
them bring me to your holy hill and to your dwelling" (43:3).

"Blessed are the poor in spirit, for theirs is the kingdom of heaven."

Matthew 5:3

"Blessed are you who are poor, for yours is the kingdom of heaven."

Luke 6:20

The Sermon on the Mount in Matthew becomes the Sermon on the Plain in Luke. Matthew alludes to Moses giving the Law on a mountain to demonstrate Jesus' authority. Luke suggests Jesus' egalitarian approach by placing the sermon "on a level place" (6:17).

There's another big difference. In Luke's version, physical needs are emphasized; in Matthew's, spiritual needs. The "poor" in Luke become the "poor in spirit" in Matthew; those "who are hungry" in the first are "those who hunger and thirst for righteousness" in the latter.

Jesus' ministry reveals he cared about both physical and spiritual needs. He teaches as well as feeds the multitudes. His healings reveal the integral relationship of body and spirit. While rejecting the notion that sin causes illness or disability (John 9), he recognizes the power of a woman's faith to heal herself (Luke 8:43–48).

Aware of our needs, spiritual or physical, we are blessed, for we will be satisfied.

May our hunger for your Spirit remind us of those who hunger for our bread.

How could we sing the Lord's song in a foreign land?

Psalm 137:4

The majority of us probably were not aware of another person whom we knew to be gay or lesbian when we were growing up. Or, if we were, the person was frequently portrayed by adults or our peers as strange or "queer." How could we sing a gay song in a straight land?

As we finally met others like ourselves, many of us discovered difficulties talking of spirituality with people who had been abused by religion. And the places where we met may not have been conducive to such conversation. How could we sing God's song in the midst of spiritual alienation?

When the Babylonian empire conquered the children of Israel, they were exiled from their homeland to prevent an uprising. The Psalmist laments as the exiles are required by their captors to sing "one of the songs of Zion," of Jerusalem, their Holy City devastated by Babylon.

The Psalmist's cry for vengeance against the enemies' children ("Happy shall they be who take your little ones and dash them against the rock!" [137:9]) may offend us. But then consider all those who oppose us whose children *we* might wish were gay as both retribution for and transformation of their bigotry!

How can we sing your song in the church and in the gay and lesbian community, lands alienated from one another?

Those who wait for the Lord shall renew their strength,
they shall mount up with wings like eagles,
they shall run and not be weary,
they shall walk and not faint.

Isaiah 40:31

Anticipating the return of those exiled from Palestine by the
Babylonian conquerors, Isaiah glories in the newfound power
God provides the reuniting community of Israel.

Lesbians and gay men, who grew up essentially in exile
from one another, now unite as a community. Those with
shared interests find one another in a variety of local and national groups. Those who share faith exult that now they
have a chorus with which to sing God's song. Organizations
in most denominations and traditions provide support, networks, and worship for them. Congregations in many denominations welcome them home, as well as a whole
denomination inspired within the heart of a gay Pentecostal
pastor.

In the midst of our lamentations we reassure one another that God will renew our strength, help us fly and run
and walk and wheel our way home to one another.

We wait, O God, exultant in our expectation of the return of
souls we have yet to meet.

"But you are doing away with the fear of God,
and hindering meditation before God."

*"As long as my breath is in me
and the spirit of God is in my nostrils . . .
I hold fast my righteousness, and will not let it go."*

Job 15:4; 27:3, 6

Good for Job! He rebukes his associate Eliphaz, who claims
that Job and his lamenting are somehow interfering with the
people's respect for God and traditional values and becoming a
stumbling block to worship. Job affirms both his creation by
God and his righteousness.

And good for us! We, too, are rebuking those who claim
we are antireligious or antifamily. We, too, are taking to task
those who claim our presence in church will inhibit worship.
We, too, affirm our creation by God and our righteousness.

If other Christians truly feared God they'd be less quick
to judge. If other Christians truly held God in awe, they
would not limit the divine capacity for sexual diversity. If
other Christians truly knew God, they would not question
that God's grace covers every condition of people. If other
Christians truly worshiped God, they'd leave their gifts at
the altar and first be reconciled to their lesbian sister and
gay brother.

*Help us hold fast to our righteousness, and bear witness to
your Spirit within us.*

*More in number than the hairs of my head
are those who hate me without cause. . . .
I have become a stranger to my kindred,
an alien to my mother's children.*

Psalm 69:4, 8

We live the Psalmist's lament. We are among the most openly and widely hated people in the world. Think how that affects our psyches and our spirituality, individually and corporately!

Voters and legislators and judges deny us our rights. Religious bodies, governments, and corporations refuse our full participation. Our families and friends may reject us or draw away. We are bashed by strangers. We even "eat our own" because of our own homophobia.

It's a miracle that we survive and thrive!

The Psalmist is bombarded by gossip, drunken bashers, insults, shame, and dishonor. Alluding to this Psalm, the gospel writers claim Jesus also lived this lament in the crucifixion: "for my thirst they gave me vinegar to drink" (69:21).

"More in number than the hairs of my head are those who hate me without cause," cried the Psalmist, and yet Jesus reminds us of God's care in adversity, "But even the hairs of your head are all counted. Do not be afraid" (Luke 12:7).

You care enough to count the hairs of our head; deliver us from those who hate us without cause.

The servant was despised and rejected by every one,
was full of sorrows, and acquainted with grief,
and as one from whom people hide their faces,
was despised and not esteemed by us. . . .
But this servant was wounded for our transgressions,
was bruised for our iniquities.

Isaiah 53:3, 5 (Inclusive Language Lectionary)

When you were a child, did your peers decide that someone among you had "cooties," and that, if you touched them, you could get "cooties," too? It was a cruel children's game intended to ostracize someone who was different.

I felt sorry for the object of the game, and I nearly always befriended her or him, probably because no one knew that *I* had cooties, too. At a school reunion, I happily discovered that one person with cooties now owned her own computer software firm!

Adults are no less cruel than children, just more subtle. Many have decided that those who are sexually different have cooties. Just as in childhood, the judgment says more about those who judge than the judged. It reveals their own insecurities about sexuality.

The "suffering servant" whom Isaiah describes bears a similar fate. Small wonder that early Christians identified Jesus with this servant. Jesus had cooties in a big way.

Forgive us, God, when we wound others for our own inade-
quacies. Heal us when we are bruised by another's insecurity.

Then [God] answered Job out of the whirlwind: . . .
"Where were you when I laid the foundation of the earth?"

Job 38:1, 4

For my thoughts are not your thoughts,
nor are your ways my ways, says [God].
For as the heavens are higher than the earth,
so are my ways higher than your ways
and my thoughts than your thoughts.

Isaiah 55:8–9

God finally responds to Job's laments with a little gracious chiding. It doesn't answer Job's central question of why the good suffer. But it places human life in perspective. Creation is a mighty achievement even if there is suffering.

God's comments in Isaiah occur as part of an assurance of God's faithfulness. God is way out of our league; best to trust God's benevolence. God's word has been planted like a seed that, God says, "shall not return to me empty, but it shall accomplish that which I purpose" (55:11).

New Yorker magazine once quoted a heading from a hymn of the Presbyterian hymnal: The title of the hymn, "God Is Working His Purpose Out," was followed by a reference to the tune, "PURPOSE Irregular." The *New Yorker* wryly commented, "How true."

God help us with our need to always be in control. Help us discern the times to let go, and let God.

"Come, let us build ourselves a city, and a tower with its top in the heavens, and let us make a name for ourselves."

Genesis 11:4

Human——and male——arrogance at its pinnacle! Whether it's the Tower of Babel, or a church tower, or New York's World Trade Center, it's all about whose erection is bigger.

The citizens of Babel wanted to make a name for themselves by building a city whose tower could reach God's heaven. Babel means "Gate of God" and refers to a pyramid-shaped temple tower believed by the Mesopotamians to reach into heaven. The country's capital of Babylon became the urban symbol for excess.

According to this Bible story, God didn't appreciate uppity human neighbors dropping by uninvited. So God confused their speech, which explained to ancient Hebrews why there were so many languages. The English word "babble" is probably derived from this.

The message is: we can't take heaven or God on our own terms. God alone is God, and we can't trespass on divine territory or sovereignty. The Bible tells of a self-revealing God, though the revelation may come through human experience, reason, science, nature, history, and scripture.

A little humility is called for, from Babel to the World Trade Center, and all the steeples between.

Sacred Mystery, forgive our human arrogance. Reveal yourself as we build prayers rather than towers, and as we study your language, scripture.

*[God] said to Cain, "Why are you angry, and why has your
countenance fallen? If you do well, will you not be accepted?
And if you do not do well, sin is lurking at the door; its desire
is for you, but you must master it."*

Genesis 4:6–7

The story of Cain and Abel served a dramatic purpose: to affirm the shepherding of the ancient Hebrews and their practice
of animal sacrifice over against their agrarian neighbors and
their practice of fertility rites. That's why God is depicted as accepting Abel's offering of firstlings from his flock and rejecting
Cain's offering of produce from his fields.

Biblical stories were often written to support and later
used to reinforce the lifestyle of the "in crowd," the majority
culture. That explains why our opponents point out that
God created Adam and Eve in the Garden of Eden, not
Adam and Steve or Addie and Eve.

The heterosexual majority today asserts heterosexual
marriage as the only acceptable offering to God. This appropriately frustrates and angers us. As God advised Cain, we
must be careful that our frustration and anger do not give
rise to the violent and murderous impulses of our human
nature. We must keep faith that, if we do well, we will be
accepted, and our offerings welcomed.

*God, grant the acceptance of our offerings by others just as
you graciously receive them from us.*

No one, when tempted, should say, "I am being tempted by God"; for God cannot be tempted by evil and . . . tempts no one.

James 1:13

I once wrote a skit based on a story of God testing a biblical figure that ended with the mocking conclusion of the civil defense alerts on radio and television: "This has been a test. Had this been an actual alert . . . "

It is hard for the biblical writers and for people of faith today not to see God at work in adversity or challenges, testing people of faith. But God does not need to test us. Life is test enough. And some of us are given harder exams, by circumstance rather than by providence.

In the Lord's Prayer, we pray for God to "lead us from temptation," but we also pray for God to "deliver us from evil," because a temptation-free life is not possible. In today's verse from James, the writer asserts that we are tempted by our own desire, which leads to sin. Our most tempting desire may be to live without suffering.

For example, there is nothing good or godly about AIDS. But AIDS does challenge us, calling forth God-like compassion. Compassion means "to suffer with." We fail the test of life if we give in to our desire to avoid suffering and withhold love and care from those living with HIV.

Lead us not into temptation to avoid suffering at the risk of losing our souls.

"God, be merciful to me, a sinner!"
Luke 18:13

We are called "unrepentant" if we are well-adjusted and self-affirming. But we *are* repentant: of closets, of duplicity, of complicity with the oppression of other lesbians and gay men, and of a heretical belief that we could be beyond God's creativity and grace.

And we are still sinners. It's just that our sexuality needs no repentance. There may be instances of how we reach out to another sexually (or fail to reach out) that we confess as sin. And there may be instances of how we affirm (or fail to affirm) our sexuality that are inappropriate.

In this quote from a parable of Jesus, the tax collector——considered an enemy of the Jewish people because he was a collaborator with Rome and typically a thief——beat his breast and asked for God's mercy. The self-righteous religious leader thanked God that he was not like others, such as this tax collector. Jesus said the tax collector went home justified, not the Pharisee, "for all who exalt themselves will be humbled, but all who humble themselves will be exalted" (18:14).

God, be merciful to me, a sinner!

Yet even now, says the Lord,
return to me with all your heart; . . .
rend your hearts and not your clothing.
Return to the Lord, your God,
for [God] is gracious and merciful,
slow to anger, and abounding in steadfast love,
and relents from punishing.

                                        Joel 2:12–13

God is our first, best, and current lover.

Our ideal lover is what God offers to be. One who wants *us,* wants our love, forgives our turning away, and loves us steadfastly. Romantic love, eat your heart out: you can't ever quite match this. God loves us as no human lover could.

And yet God is also human. In the person of Jesus, we feel God's touch. Jesus touched the strangers he healed or allowed them to touch him. Unprovidentially, scripture hides his sexuality. But, in Luke 7:38, we see he is unafraid of what people will think when a woman described as a sinner washes his feet with her tears, dries them with her hair, kisses them with her lips, and anoints them with ointment! And the Gospel of John depicts the disciple "whom Jesus loved" reclining next to Jesus at the Last Supper (John 13:23) just after Jesus washed the disciples' feet.

Touch us, Holy Lover, through Jesus, and inspire us to touch others with the same healing and delight.

The saying is sure and worthy of full acceptance, that Christ Jesus came into the world to save sinners—of whom I am the foremost.

1 Timothy 1:15

Those of us who attend church have probably heard the first part of this verse in an assurance of pardon after the prayer of confession. But we've probably never heard the minister or priest conclude "of whom I am the foremost"! Spiritual leaders are often reluctant to admit to sinning because of the high but false expectations we have of clergy. Those the church calls saints were as keenly aware of their own sinfulness as the apostle Paul was writing to young Timothy. Many of them had also been blasphemers, persecutors, and people of violence, as Paul described himself. Many openly continued to struggle, despite their devotion to God.

Martin Luther was a perfectionist who drove his spiritual confessor crazy——until he broke down and broke through to the heart of the gospel: we are saved by grace through faith, not by following all the rules. Christ Jesus came to save sinners, not saints.

Those we call saints may simply be those who most realize that they have benefited from this.

The saying is sure and worthy of full acceptance, that Christ Jesus came into the world to save me.

"O Lord! Is not this what I said while I was still in my own country? . . . I knew that you are a gracious God and merciful, slow to anger, and abounding in steadfast love, and ready to relent from punishing."

Jonah 4:2

What sounds like praise is actually Jonah raging angrily against God! God has forgiven the Ninevites because they repented upon hearing Jonah's prophetic word. The reader might think Jonah would be pleased with success, but Jonah had resisted going to Nineveh because it was an oppressor of his people. He wants to see it destroyed, not forgiven.

Lesbians and gay men may be reluctant to preach to our oppressors, and we may run from the responsibility as Jonah ran to Tarshish, the farthest possible point to which he could have traveled. But like the storm that forced Jonah's return (via the belly of a big fish!), the storm caused by our own unresolved feelings about the church, the confusion about spirituality in the gay community, and the crisis of AIDS may drive us to preach repentance to a homophobic church.

Yet, when repentance comes, I wonder how eager we will be to see God forgive those who have battered and bruised us. I remember how angry and unforgiving *I* became when someone who attacked her brother for being gay announced months later that she herself was a lesbian.

Gracious and merciful God, grant us the success of Jonah as well as the grace to cope with it.

"For if you forgive others their trespasses, your heavenly [Creator] will also forgive you; but if you do not forgive others, neither will your [God] forgive your trespasses."

Matthew 6:14

"Do not judge, so that you may not be judged."

Matthew 7:1

Forgiveness is not something you hoard.

The more I feel forgiven, the easier it is for me to forgive others. The more I am trusted and the less I am judged, the more I trust and the less I judge.

The gay community is filled with the misjudged and the unforgiven. And so we judge and begrudge our leaders, lovers, strangers, organizations, and our own "deviates": cross-dressers, bisexuals, transexuals, and those with specialized erotic interests. Our community even distrusts its religious "deviates" who say God loves lesbians and gay men.

The judgment we give will be the judgment we get, but like other cycles of abuse, it's hard to stop. The best way is to let someone love us who offers unconditional love—God: to meditate on God's mercy and to trust in God's trust. Then pass the Word along.

Let us bask in your forgiveness and grow in your trust.

My God, my God, why have you forsaken me? . . .
Yet it was you who took me from the womb;
you kept me safe on my mother's breast.

Psalm 22:1, 9

How could a God who gave us life forsake us? Yet many of us
felt the anguish of that question the day we began to realize we
were different from others. We suspected it must somehow be
our fault, because God was good and we were not. We didn't
dare talk to anyone about it. So we grew up, fearing our difference and fearing others might find out.

Jesus was queer. Not in our sense, perhaps. But queer
enough to be mocked, scorned, despised, shamed, and forsaken just as the Psalmist he quoted from the cross. Jesus
knows what it was like for us growing up, what it is like for
us now. From the cross he saw his mother, possibly remembering when he felt safe at her breast.

While Psalm 22 expresses bitter despair, it also speaks of
hope and praise. Could this be why Jesus says its first line
while on the cross (Matt. 27:46)? Surely he knew
the Psalm's conclusion: "future generations will be told
about the Lord, and proclaim [God's] deliverance to a people yet unborn" (22:30–31).

Save future lesbians and gay men from feeling forsaken by
you. May they proclaim the deliverance you effect in us.

As my life was ebbing away,
I remembered the Lord;
and my prayer came to you,
into your holy temple.

                    Jonah 2:7

Ever feel like you were swallowed by a whale, and there was no hope left? That's how Jonah felt. Escaping from God, he knew he was the cause of the storm that threatened the ship he booked passage on. So he told the crew to throw him overboard, which would have made him feel hopeless enough, but then God "provided" a large fish to swallow him up.

There he stayed three days and three nights, and there he prayed these words, according to this fantastic story. What a metaphor for many of our experiences: testing positive to an HIV antibodies test; attacked by gay-bashers; the abrupt departure of a long-term lover; complete rejection by our family; losing one's best friend to AIDS; outed as gay and losing one's job; losing a gay rights vote. Swallowed by a whale, with no hope left.

Jonah's assurance, however, can be our own. Though our prayers are not allowed in many churches, our prayers will be welcomed in God's holy temple. Especially when we feel overwhelmed as Jonah in the belly of a whale.

Holy One, thank you for welcoming my prayers, even of despair!

"Keep awake and pray that you may not come into the time of trial; the spirit indeed is willing, but the flesh is weak."

Mark 14:38

Likewise the Spirit helps us in our weakness; for we do not know how to pray as we ought, but that very Spirit intercedes with sighs too deep for words.

Romans 8:26

Meditation and prayer may relax us so well that we fall asleep. That shouldn't concern us. Maybe we need the sleep. Or maybe we're working things out in our sleep.

Other times, in prayer, our words fail us. We may not be sure what to pray for, or how to say it. That shouldn't concern us either. Placing ourselves in God's presence is enough; God knows what we need even before we ask. God interprets our sighs "too deep for words" and comforts us.

On many occasions, the Bible warns us to "Keep awake!" so that we may be prepared for what is to come. In the verse from Mark, Jesus speaks to his disciples, who have fallen asleep in the Garden of Gethsemane where he is soon to be arrested. In the other verse, Paul writes to the Romans about the power of the Spirit in the midst of human limitations.

When we're too tired, or ill, or speechless, our willing spirit works with the Spirit to make our intent known to God.

Thank you, Spirit, for receiving my sighs too deep for words. My spirit is willing even when my body is weak.

*We are afflicted in every way, but not crushed; perplexed, but
not driven to despair; persecuted, but not forsaken; struck
down, but not destroyed.*

                                                    2 Corinthians 4:8

Witnessing how the church has frequently become the perse-
cutor today, it's hard to believe that it once itself was persecuted for the lifestyle it promoted, the "heresy" it proclaimed,
and the kind of people it included.

A campus priest once objected to a leather group using
his building because "they dress funny." This said by a man
who wore a robe, stole, and cross to say the Eucharist!

Some Christians are horrified when I tell the story of a
lesbian who began a search for God because of a profound
lovemaking experience in which her sexuality became a
conduit for spirituality.

Many of my own denomination who oppose ordination
of gay people will say to me privately, "But we would ordain *you!*" as if my apparent "normalcy" gave me access denied others.

The church has forgotten its early persecution. Or
maybe the church acts it out, just as abused children frequently abuse their own children. The fierce anger toward
the church within our community cannot be adequately explained unless we understand it as the result of the church,
in turn, abusing its own children.

*Father and Mother God, heal the child within us, afflicted,
but not crushed; persecuted, but not forsaken by you.*

We also boast in our sufferings, knowing that suffering produces endurance, and endurance produces character, and character produces hope, and hope does not disappoint us, because God's love has been poured into our hearts through the Holy Spirit that has been given to us.

Romans 5:3

We may be loath to admit it, but suffering has shaped the characters of many of us in positive ways. At the same time, we recognize that suffering has destroyed others of us through suicide, abuse, addiction, mental illness, or denial.

It would take chutzpah to take credit for our survival. And to say, "There but for the grace of God go I" is to imply God was not gracious to others. Better simply to give thanks to God that we survived.

And better to consider what suffering has done for us, or rather, how suffering has been transformed into our stamina, character, and hope. Standing alone, we developed inner resources to cope with the world. When everyone else seemed to hate us, many of us opened up to God's love all the more. Abandoned by the church, we "freelanced" our spirituality, and the Spirit transformed our suffering into the hope that we would move beyond our pain and prevent suffering for others.

Justified by our faith, "we boast in our hope of sharing [your] glory" (5:2), O God!

I consider that the sufferings of this present time are not worth comparing with the glory about to be revealed to us.

Romans 8:18

This truth is obvious to those who remember the pain of coming out as lesbian or gay. When I counsel those beginning the process, I am reminded of my own birth pangs. In later verses, the suffering is compared to a woman in childbirth.

Standing inside the threshold of my closet, I remember paralyzing fear, overwhelming grief, profound sadness, undirected anger, physical pain, and spiritual terror. My soul was at stake. My self-image. Others' opinions. My friends. My family. My career plans. My future. My God.

All were at stake. Yet the moment I stepped beyond that threshold, I began to breathe easier. Freedom. No longer pretending. Honesty. Open to the future. Open to people and to God, I discovered afresh my family and friends and God. I met a lover, and the delightful agony and ecstasy of that relationship made all the suffering worth it.

This experience of risking our lives to save them offers us a power that is unique. Coming out was not dramatic for all, but for the rest, the experience keeps us mindful that "the sufferings of this present time are not worth comparing with the glory about to be revealed to us."

God of all times and destinations, in the suffering of our present, keep us mindful of the glories of your future.

*Many, even of the authorities, believed in [Jesus]. But because
of the Pharisees they did not confess it, for fear that they would
be put out of the synagogue; for they loved human glory more
than the glory that comes from God.*

John 12:42–43

A delegate to a national church assembly once told me that she
supported the ordination of gays and lesbians but felt compelled to vote against it because how she voted would get back
to her congregation. A minister once said that he supported
us, but would vote against us because he thought our issue
would split the church. A newly elected moderator of a church
body once said he would have appointed me as vice moderator, but he was looking for a new pastoral position and feared
it would queer his chances.

According to John, on the eve of Jesus' arrest, trial, and
crucifixion, many believed in him but did not say so, fearful
of religious conservatives who might kick them out of the
synagogue. Perhaps they could have averted his death.

The resistance to lesbians and gay men in both church
and culture is not simply because religious conservatives
oppose us. It is because many of those who support us are
not willing to risk their reputations in speaking out.

*Give power and courage to those who believe in us to come
out of their closets.*

*Many, even of the authorities, believed in [Jesus]. But because
of the Pharisees they did not confess it, for fear that they would
be put out of the synagogue; for they loved human glory more
than the glory that comes from God.*

John 12:42–43

No, this is not a mistake. It's easier to hear a scripture directed
at others than to hear it directed at ourselves. So yesterday's
scripture for others becomes today's scripture for us.

While preparing this book of meditations, I took a gay
cruise. How strange I felt sunning myself on the deck of the
ship with rows and rows of gay sun worshipers as I pe-
rused the Bible for verses to use for daily meditations! Even
stranger on the clothing-optional beach at Mykonos! I was
afraid someone might see the Bible, and I'd possibly have to
deal with their scorn or hostility. Here I was willing to expose my body but not my spirituality!

Many within our community and many of our leaders believe in God and in Jesus. Because it may not be thought politically correct or socially acceptable, many keep silent,
fearing rejection. We love human acceptance more than
God's.

*Give power and courage to those who believe in you, God, to
stand with you as you stand with us in Christ Jesus.*

*"Truly I tell you, whoever does not receive the kingdom of God
as a little child will never enter it."*

Mark 10:15

Recently, I had my first church summer camp experience. I felt
nostalgic for this childhood experience I had missed, even as I
sadly remembered my lover's childhood search for God at such
camps. There he had his first sexual experience with another
boy, but he feared it would cut him off from God. I had never
had a sexual experience with another as a youth, and I grew
up feeling alone in my desires.

There is much talk these days about how the *bad* we do
to others in later life grows out of negative childhood experiences. But much of the *good* we do for others may also
grow out of the poverty of our own childhood. I do what *I*
do so that another gay child will have an easier time.

Eileen Lindner of the National Council of Churches
spoke at my church summer camp of a group of children
living under a bridge in urban Brazil. The eldest, a child
himself, had said, "Today we've got to get our baby some
shoes." Lindner wondered how someone without home or
parents could learn to care for the youngest child of the
pack in this way. Perhaps the answer was the poverty of his
own childhood.

Jesus said that a little child shall lead us. That child may
be the one within us who knows what's missing and tries
to fill the need.

*Awaken the child within us, Jesus, to notice what's missing
in the world and "get our babies some shoes."*

"Whoever wishes to become great among you must be your servant."

Mark 10:43

How could a church whose founding figure said this turn out to be so hierarchical?!? A church of popes, bishops, elders, priests——where are the servants? Deacons come the closest. Their name comes from the Greek word for service, which literally means "waiting on tables." Gay waiters and lesbian delivery persons may be more of what Jesus had in mind.

The carefully guarded secret is that Jesus did not actually found the church. His followers did, and rather loosely on his teachings. Jesus was more interested in the movement of the Spirit than in institutionalizing it.

Yet, to be fair, when Jesus left, something needed to be done to keep his followers together, preach the gospel, and heal the sick. Though warned by Jesus not to imitate current political structures, that's generally what the church has done through the ages. Popes were like kings. While the church was often a step ahead of the culture in democracy, major democratic reform didn't occur until the Protestant Reformation.

Christian lesbian feminists point out that another revolution is needed: one that turns the church on its side, so that communal circles characterize our relationships rather than the alienating ladders of hierarchy.

Encircle us with the movement of your Spirit, that we may commune through a Christ without walls.

"I believe, help my unbelief!"
                    Mark 9:24

When it was evident to my father that his cancer would be fatal, we talked about death. My father was completely accepting of me, but he was also a fundamentalist Baptist, very sure of his faith, active in the church, honest and generous in his dealings. What moved me was that this man, so deeply convicted by his faith, could openly share his doubts. That made his faith all the more real to me. It wasn't a mindless conformity; it was heartfelt and human.

My biggest lament in life is my doubt. I could better accept suffering and death and love and happiness were it not for my doubt. So this cry is my most common confession: "I believe, help my unbelief."

This is not a foreign experience to any of us. In the Bible, a father is seeking healing for his epileptic child. Jesus' disciples cannot cast out the spirit causing the boy's distress. (Epilepsy and mental illness were understood by the ancients as demonic spirits.) Jesus says, "All things can be done for the one who believes." The father doubts if he has enough belief. Later, the disciples ask why they couldn't heal the boy, and Jesus explains that this healing could only happen through prayer.

Healing our doubts can only happen through prayer. Prayer together, prayer apart, prayer for each other.

Sacred Spirit, we believe. Help our unbelief!

"Blessed are those who have not seen and yet have come to believe."

John 20:29

When people say they love us, we are all suddenly from Missouri and have a "show me" attitude. But even when they show us by their actions, we do not have proof positive that their motivation is love. Yet we begin to develop a faith that what they say is true.

When people say about us that they "hate the sin, but love the sinner," we properly have doubts about their love. We know that loving us cannot mean hating our desire to love and be loved. We doubt that what they say is true.

We can neither absolutely prove that a lover loves us nor that a religious conservative hates us. Yet our spiritual well-being depends on our determining what true love looks like. It may require a leap of faith in our own discernment.

Our spiritual well-being also depends on discerning what's life and what's not. Does our faith offer us life? Does the Bible still speak to us? Is Christ still present in our world? Again, it's a matter of faith, not of facts, because the Resurrection was only revealed to the faithful.

Thomas doubted and then believed because he saw. We are the ones of whom Jesus then said, "Blessed are those who have not seen and yet have come to believe."

May we grow in the faith of your presence in our world, Christ Jesus.

PASSION

•
•
•
•

Love is strong as death,
passion fierce as the grave.
Its flashes are flashes of fire,
a raging flame.
Many waters cannot quench love,
neither can floods drown it.

Song of Solomon 8:6–7

Theologian Carter Heyward has said that women and gays and lesbians are not welcomed by mainstream churches partly because we represent *passion* to Christians who have become dispassionate about faith. The "Gentleman God" (as she puts it) that they worship is ambivalent about our presence in the church: too polite to throw us out, but embarrassed by our strong feelings about justice and love.

This was apparent when my own denomination rejected a report on human sexuality that recommended an ethic of "justice-love" to govern all sexual expression. How shocking it was that people reacted to the term with hostility, claiming it was unbiblical! But justice and love are correlated in scripture. Justice without love is heartless, and love without justice is cruel.

Love and justice are passions that can't be squelched. They flash like fire and cannot be quenched by floods. Death has two adversaries that can match it.

Thank you for love that cannot die. Bless us with a passion for justice that makes us live.

"For God so loved the world that [God] gave [God's] only Son, so that everyone who believes in him may not perish but may have eternal life."

John 3:16

Passion begins with God. "God *so loved* the world" makes God sound like a lovesick kid, an unabashed romantic. And "God so loved *the world*" suggests God is very this-worldly, not as other-worldly as some might have us believe.

Is this some form of global narcissism, to believe that God loves our world this passionately? Yet God created our world, and an artist is likely to be biased, especially for those made in the creator's likeness.

God so loved *you* that God gave you God's own Child, so that believing in the Christ, you may not perish but have eternal life.

You, too, are the work of God's hands. You also have been made in the divine likeness. God passionately loves *you*. That's awesome, because we usually don't feel worthy of *human* love, let alone *divine* love. But that's why God sent that message in human flesh——Jesus——so we wouldn't be overwhelmed.

And, unlike many other passions, this love is forever.

God, help me love the world as you do: the whole of it, not just my small corner.

[O God,] Where can I go from your spirit?
Or where can I flee from your presence?
If I ascend to heaven, you are there;
if I make my bed in Sheol, you are there.

Psalm 139:7-8

If I reach the heights of sexual ecstasy, you are there. If I make my bed in a closet, you are there. If I make my bed in compulsive behavior, you are there.

If I go to the bars or a club, you are there. If I go to church or Twelve-Step meetings, you are there. If I stay home alone or go to a party, you are there.

God will meet us anywhere. God is indifferent to the place, but passionate for us. If a human lover behaved this way, we would have a court issue a restraining order. But there is no restraining God.

God is our most intimate *compañero,* Spanish for "companion," literally one we break bread with (*pan* is "bread" in Spanish). God is so intimate, there is even a Hebrew thanksgiving to be offered after visiting the toilet.

This is not the time to get shy or embarrassed about the wrong things. God has seen us naked (indeed, created us naked!), and God has seen us sexually aroused and pleasured and pleasuring (indeed, created within us the capacity!).

Thank you for being there, God. Help me understand that there is no place where you do not love me.

If God is for us, who is against us? . . . For I am convinced that neither death, nor life, nor angels, nor rulers, nor things present, nor things to come, nor powers, nor height, nor depth, nor anything else in all creation, will be able to separate us from the love of God in Christ Jesus our Lord.

Romans 8:31, 38–39

So many people are against us. And so many things! Homophobia. Heterosexism. Sexism. AIDS. Cancer. Closets. Rulers. Prejudice. Backlash. Power. Hierarchy. Hatred.

Yet the apostle Paul assures us in the very book of the Bible quoted against us by our opponents that *nothing* and *no one* can separate us from the love of God in Christ Jesus our Sovereign: neither sexuality, nor homophobia. Neither gender, nor sexism. Neither HIV, nor AIDS-phobia. Neither breast cancer, nor silence about lesbian health issues. Neither self-affirmation, nor rejection. Neither human rights, nor human wrongs.

Nothing shall separate us from the love of God. If God is for us, who dares to stand against us?

In all these things we are more than conquerors through you who love us (8:37), O God.

There is no fear in love, but perfect love casts out fear; for fear has to do with punishment, and whoever fears has not reached perfection in love.

1 John 4:18

A victim of an intimate, abusive relationship is always afraid. Whether parent-child or lover-lover, if verbal or physical abuse is present, as Tina Turner sings from experience, "What's love got to do with it?"

Victims of a public, abusive relationship are also afraid. Whether pastor-parishioners, employer-employees, or police-citizens, if abuse is present, one might similarly inquire, "What's justice got to do with it?"

Neither love nor its civic expression of justice can be inspired by an overwhelming fear of being treated as less than human, or a fear of being wounded or killed.

Many of us are in an abusive relationship with God. We didn't get there by ourselves. Sunday school teachers, nuns, priests, pastors, parents, and peers all played a role, often innocently passing on what they'd been taught: the fear of a wrathful, angry, punishing God.

It's appropriate that God's awesome love and justice give us pause if we ponder doing an unloving and unjust deed and require repentance if we've done such a deed. But, as we trust that God is love, that love governs us rather than fear.

We confess our fear of you, O God. We trust your love of us.

Those who say, "I love God," and hate their brothers or sisters, are liars; for those who do not love a brother or sister whom they have seen, cannot love God whom they have not seen.

1 John 4:20

It seems easier to love someone you can't see than a brother or sister whose foibles and faults you may live with daily. We sometimes make of God an imaginary friend over whose character and behavior we have perfect control: our pet God. But brothers and sisters, whether in the family or the church or the world, cannot be as easily regulated.

In reality, God is out of our control and any human regulation. God is absolute love. If we want to love God, we must love, period. And what do we have to love but brothers and sisters? If we don't love them, creatures of God that they are, how do we express any love to God?

"We love because God first loved us," 1 John prefaces the verse for today. If we do not feel loving toward sisters and brothers, maybe we are not adequately enjoying God's love. If we do not choose to be loving toward others, maybe we are not adequately comprehending God's will.

Sometimes, God, I don't see what you see in other people to love, but then, sometimes, I don't see what you see in me.

*The quiet words of the wise are more to be heeded
than the shouting of a ruler among fools.*

Ecclesiastes 9:17

A leading figure of the religious right appeared on a *Phil Donahue* show, opposing a new gay soap opera filmed for cable
television. The man came across as a nasty, arrogant dema-
gogue, shouting down his more soft-spoken opposition.

If I'd been on the program, I would have asked the audience, "If you had a personal problem for which you were
seeking spiritual guidance, would you go to this man?
Would you identify him as someone you could trust as a
spiritual authority?"

Zealous passion does not make someone right. This man
had none of the gentle qualities of the Spirit described in
the Bible, but he had all the marks of the self-righteous religious leaders who tried to shout down Jesus.

Often it is the soft-spoken woman or man who has spiritual wisdom to offer us. Those who turn up their volume to
drown out another's views are probably more interested in
control than guidance.

*Jesus, protect us from your followers. Help Christians listen to
"the quiet words of the wise" rather than "the shouting of a
ruler among fools."*

Behold my servant, whom I uphold,
my chosen, in whom my soul delights:
I have put my Spirit upon my servant,
who will bring forth justice to the nations.

                    Isaiah 42:1 (Inclusive Language Lectionary)

Israel viewed itself as God's servant, proclaiming Yahweh's justice to all nations. The Church saw Jesus as this servant, preaching a kingdom of God that knew no boundaries. These insights were both the cause and result of their suffering. We also suffer as gay and lesbian people, and as gay and lesbian Christians. Our suffering, too, leads to spiritual insight. God is not just the God of straight people.

But God is not simply our God, either, but the God of all who suffer. Prejudice against us may help us recognize our own prejudices. Our humiliation at antigay jokes may prompt us to question sexist and racist jokes. Bias against us calls us to work against all discrimination.

Yet God is not just the God of those who suffer. God is the God of those who oppress, prejudge, ridicule, and discriminate. God not only delivers us from the role of victim, God delivers us from the role of oppressor as well.

May our own suffering redeem us from imposing suffering upon others, so that your soul may delight in us, and your spirit of justice rest upon us.

They have treated the wound of my people carelessly,
saying, "Peace, peace," when there is no peace.

Jeremiah 6:14

"There now, that's a good girl." How infuriating this "comfort"
is within its context of control, as hollow as the proclamation
of "Peace, peace" when there is no peace!

The remark is from *Masterpiece Theater's* production of
"Beyond Yellow Wallpaper," based on a semiautobiographi-
cal story by the early feminist Charlotte Perkins Gilman. It
depicts the frustrated passion of a woman who yearns to be
a writer. Believing that this is unsuitable for a woman's "del-
icate" nature, her husband and her doctor sequester her in
an isolated country house, removing her pens and paper
"for her own good."

She hates the yellow wallpaper of her room, and it
comes to symbolize her oppression. In an emotional break-
down, she rips the paper from the wall, and her trapped
self emerges and escapes. As lesbian comedienne Robin
Tyler quips, women don't have breakdowns, they have
breakthroughs!

We may identify with the woman in the story because, as
Jeremiah described, our wounds have also been treated carelessly, glossed over and ignored. Just as women have been
placated when questioning their traditional roles, we have
been advised "not to make a big deal" of the way we have
been treated. But, as every emerging cause reminds us,
peace without justice is still violence.

Dear God, "from prophet to priest, everyone deals falsely"
(6:13). Give us the passion to speak the truth!

But let justice roll down like waters,
and righteousness like an ever-flowing stream.

Amos 5:24

The prophet Amos declared that God preferred justice and righteousness to songs and sacrifice, reminding his people of their sojourn in the wilderness when offerings were not necessary to have access to Yahweh.

In our own sojourn with God, we do not need the church nor its worship to arouse God's favor. We have access to God because we are seeking justice.

But sometimes we come to an oasis in the wilderness on our way to the Promised Land, and we are hesitant to go on. The oasis may be a home with a lover, or an accepting congregation, or a comfortable job. We settle for less than the Promised Land because we, at least, have what *we* want.

Yet none of us are free until all of us are free. We cannot confuse a sojourn with our destination; we cannot confuse an oasis with the Promised Land. We journey with the lover, the congregation, and the job, but our journey toward justice for all continues. We may occasionally enjoy the mirage of "having arrived," but we do not quit till "justice rolls down like waters, and righteousness like an ever-flowing stream."

As we travel with you in the wilderness, Holy One, thank you for the occasional oasis and the eventual Land of Promise.

*If I give away all my possessions, and if I hand over my body
so that I may boast, but do not have love, I gain nothing.*

1 Corinthians 13:3

No matter how much we sacrifice, no matter for what good
cause——even justice——if we do so without love we "gain
nothing."

Consider the spiritual discipline of fasting, going without. Its purpose is not simple sacrifice, but to make room
for something. We may be identifying with Christ's or the
world's deprivation. Or, we might be giving up a lunch
hour to pray. The maxim of physical workouts, "No pain,
no gain," is reversed in spiritual "workouts": "No gain, no
pain." In other words, disciplines such as fasting are intended to offer some spiritual benefit. This saves us from
spiritual masochism.

Love is its own reward. We do not love to gain materially.
We actually may lose things for love. We do not love to gain
God's love——that's ours already. We do not love as life in-
surance, for love may require risking our lives.

We love by allowing another to touch us, to move us, to
shake us. Whether one more justice movement or one
more soul, we act in love only if we allow ourselves to be
touched, to be moved, to be shaken. That will offer us the
passion by which we gain our lives.

*Transform my sacrifice, God of Love, into an offering pleas-
ing to all.*

"Which of these three, do you think, was a neighbor to the man who fell into the hands of the robbers?" [The lawyer] said, "The one who showed him mercy." Jesus said to him, "Go and do likewise."

Luke 10:36–37

Jesus broadened the Hebrew concept of loving thy neighbor. In this conclusion to the story of the Good Samaritan, who helped a beaten man along the road, the one who proved to be a neighbor was the one who got close enough to be moved to action by the robbed man's plight. The religious figures in the story——the priest and Levite——avoided doing so, possibly because they feared being rendered ritually unclean. It was a Samaritan, a member of a mixed race and an unorthodox religious sect, who showed compassion.

In a shopping mall, I caught my last live glimpse of a friend with AIDS. I had been to see him in the hospital, but this time, I chose to avoid him. He was with a mutual friend, so he was not alone. From afar he looked considerably emaciated, and I just couldn't bear to deal with him that day. Though God and my friend would forgive me, I will always regret my decision.

With the priest and the Levite, I passed by on the other side, not wanting to get involved.

Jesus, lead us to risk our comfort to comfort others.

*If one offered for love
all the wealth of his house,
it would be utterly scorned.*

   Song of Solomon 8:7

Some of us have tried to buy love, either for the night or for a lifetime. But love is a work of the Spirit, a serendipitous gift of grace that we can neither demand nor expect.

But, just as placing ourselves close to a neighbor or a cause may move us to compassion, so allowing someone close to us may prompt love. The wealth we have to share is within us. Our big fear is that we are not inwardly wealthy. We cover our imagined emptiness inside with bravado, with show, with attitude. Yet poverty, rather than wealth, is spiritually valuable. Vulnerably sharing our poverty with another person, we discover how much we have to offer.

Henri Nouwen told of a woman sent to visit him by Jean Vanier, founder of the l'Arche religious community. While Henri was away, the woman took it upon herself to fix them both dinner. Upon his return, Henri was mystified to find the dinner table elaborately set by a woman who had brought nothing with her. "Where did you get all this?" he asked. "From your own cupboards," she replied.

Our own cupboards may not be as bare as we think.

In love, rather than for love, we offer the wealth of our bodies and souls.

So Sarah laughed to herself, saying, "After I have grown old, and my husband is old, shall I have pleasure?"

Genesis 18:12

Sarah laughed because she had just overheard a prophecy that, though old, she and Abraham would conceive and bear a son. The couple had offered hospitality toward three strangers, unaware that they entertained God and two angels. In answer to her laughter, God said, "Is anything too wonderful for the Lord?"

Sexual passion is pleasurable. We all know that, but most of us think of it as "a little wicked" pleasure. In reality, the pleasure of sexual passion is divine. The physical sensations that it provides are both a gift of God and a clue to the cosmic reality of the gravitational pull and the coming together of celestial bodies, whether our own or those of the macroscopic heavens or the microscopic atomic universe. As the cosmos is expanding, so are we. Age does not necessarily limit our capacity for pleasure and passion; it may expand it.

Pleasurable sensation is God's way of rewarding passion toward a person or a cause. That's why to love someone or to do a good deed makes us feel good inside.

Sensational Creator, thank you that we may feel pleasure and pleasure others.

Then [Delilah] said to [Samson], "How can you say, 'I love you,' when your heart is not with me? You have mocked me three times now and have not told me what makes your strength so great."

Judges 16:15

A passion that pleasures us may lead to a downfall, something ultimately unpleasurable. Addictions, unhealthy relationships, and compulsive behaviors may initially deceive us, but finally reveal their idolatrous nature. Since the revelation first comes to those who care about us, we must listen for any warning signals from them. It is also vital that we sound the alarm when we see it in others.

Delilah was just another bad relationship Samson got into. Enemies wanted the secret of his strength, and Delilah had already attempted to deliver Samson into their hands. But Samson suffered under the delusion that he had his addiction to danger and to Delilah under control. When he finally revealed that his strength came from his unshorn locks, he hit rock bottom.

We wonder, how could he have been so stupid? It's harder to look at ourselves and see how stupid we are to let alcohol control our emotions, or work control our relationships, or relationships control our identity, or order control our lives.

God grant me the serenity to accept the things I cannot change, the courage to change the things I can, and the wisdom to know the difference.

So Jacob served seven years for Rachel, and they seemed to him but a few days because of the love he had for her.

Genesis 29:20

A gay friend told me that he once went to bars searching for F.E.R.N.'s: fast, easy, and right now. While most of us would not be so frank, many of us would confess to a few Mr. or Ms. Right Now's while we were looking for Mr. or Ms. Right.

In a consumerist, instant gratification society, it is not surprising that relationships would be viewed as one more commodity to be instantly served up with the question, "Do you want fries with that?"

Jacob's willingness to work for Laban seven years to marry his daughter Rachel seems incredible to those who have yet to have a *relationship* last seven years! But it does remind us that worthy relationships require time. As it turned out, Laban tricked Jacob to work another seven years!

Christian ethicist Margaret Farley writes of our desire to make commitments over time in her book *Personal Commitments:* "Commitment is our way of trying to give a future to a present love" (p. 40). It may limit choices, but it opens us to new possibilities. Love over time is qualitatively as well as quantitatively different.

God, give us passions for persons and causes that empower us to offer our lives to their fulfillment.

"But I say to you, Love your enemies and pray for those who persecute you, so that you may be children of your [Creator] in heaven; for [God] makes the sun rise on the evil and on the good, and sends rain on the righteous and on the unrighteous."

Matthew 5:44

Saint Patrick was an English youth captured for slavery by the Irish. When he regained his freedom, he returned to Ireland to proclaim the gospel, rapidly converting the nation.

This is the love Jesus counsels for enemies. We may not *feel* love for our opposition, but we *behave* with love, much as God sends rain and sunshine on both sinner and saint. We pray the best for those who persecute us, hoping that includes a conversion of attitudes about lesbians and gay men.

Mahatma Gandhi, the great spiritual leader of India, called his opponents "the opposition" rather than "enemies," to avoid their dehumanization. We know how *we* resist those who dehumanize *us*.

When I get a hostile question or statement, I know my response will have little effect on the one who has presented it. But, on a good day, I respond as well and as gently as possible for the sake of others within earshot who might be receptive. How we behave in the face of our opposition's misdirected passion reveals our passion for Jesus' words.

Jesus, teach me the gentle answer and a benevolent love for all who oppose us.

Then Saul's anger was kindled against Jonathan. He said to him, "You son of a perverse, rebellious woman! Do I not know that you have chosen the son of Jesse to your own shame, and to the shame of your mother's nakedness?"

1 Samuel 20:30

Delilah used Samson's secret about his strength to destroy him. King Saul used his son Jonathan's passionate love for David (the "son of Jesse") to insult him, and did so by insulting his mother.

We've all had those closest to us use our secrets to attack us. We've all had those we considered family insult our passionate love, whether for our own gender or for God.

In breaking off our relationship, my seminary lover told me that I ran "like a fag." When I described this "insult" to another gay friend, he simply said, "So?" *Oh,* I thought, *I am gay, so however I run is how a gay man runs!*

The people who know how to punch our buttons are those closest to us. They punch our buttons by tapping into our shame. Shaming silences; it never transforms. Shaming humiliates us rather than calls us to responsibility. Much of our religious upbringing is based on shame.

We are shamed by our family or our lover or a friend if we do not conform to their expectations or bend to their control. There may be just cause for changing our behavior, but shaming is more about conforming than converting.

Teach me how to love without shame and to love without shaming.

They kissed one another, and wept with one another, until David [exceeded] himself.

1 Samuel 20:41 (Revised Standard Version)

"Your love to me was wonderful, passing the love of women" (2 Sam. 1:26), David eloquently spoke after learning of Jonathan's death. David and Jonathan were not ashamed of their passion for one another, whether as friends or lovers. They physically demonstrated their love in kissing and weeping, two things "real men" are shamed from doing today.

In brackets I've used the alternate translation of the old Revised Standard Version, because it better renders the ambiguous sense of the underlying Hebrew term. Translators have blinders that affect their work, and we must consider views of other scholars, such as Tom Horner, who argues in *Jonathan Loved David* that the phrase has sexual implications.

Regardless of genital sexuality, Jonathan and David serve as models for male love. Jonathan willingly gave up his right to fight for his father's throne out of his love for David, who had been anointed king by the prophet Samuel. Jonathan's giving up power to another man was his most unnatural act, and a compromise worth imitating as we work to make our own love relationships mutual.

Bless us with unashamed love and mutuality of passion in our relationships, God of In-Your-Face Love.

The women said to Naomi, "Blessed be the Lord, who has not left you this day without next-of-kin. . . . He shall be to you a restorer of life and a nourisher of your old age; for your daughter-in-law who loves you, who is more to you than seven sons, has borne him."

Ruth 4:14–15

Without the violence, the story of Ruth and Naomi is the Bible's *Thelma and Louise.* As lesbian theologian Mary Hunt documents in *Fierce Tenderness,* women have had to bond together to survive the machinations of patriarchy. Such a passionate friendship could offer all of us survival techniques.

Naomi's husband and sons died. She returned to her native land of Judah, and daughter-in-law Ruth insisted on going with her, leaving her own homeland of Moab. The book of Ruth describes how they work together to establish an economic and then familial foothold in Bethlehem. They scheme for Ruth to marry Boaz, which she does, bearing a son, giving occasion for the other women's praise of Ruth.

Ruth has secured the future care of the older Naomi by offering her social security, progeny to care for her in her old age. Both women used what resources were available to them——including their passionate friendship——to succeed.

Help us create and value friendships of strength, stamina, and endurance, God of Ruth and Naomi.

The peasantry prospered in Israel,
they grew fat on plunder,
because you arose, Deborah,
arose as a mother in Israel.

Judges 5:7

The Song of Deborah, from which this text is taken, is probably the most ancient part of the Bible. Before kings, judges governed Israel. The fact that Deborah was a judge suggests
Israel's religion may not have always been as male-dominated
as it became.

It must have felt threatening for the leader of the
Israelite army to be forewarned by Deborah that people
would say that God had given the enemy "into the hand of
a woman" (4:9)——as it turned out, a woman named Jael.
In contrast, it must have felt empowering for the marginalized that under Deborah's respected leadership "the peasantry prospered."

Similarly, feminist critiques of scripture may seem threatening to men whose basis for control is found in the Bible's
words, but such critiques are encouraging to women and
minorities whose basis for liberation is found in scripture's
Spirit.

Male interpretations of scripture alone are inadequate,
as are heterosexual interpretations. Our reflections as lesbian and gay Christians are all the more vital for a fuller understanding of God's Word to us.

Holy Spirit, guide me in my own interpretation of scripture.
Thank you that I am not alone in this endeavor.

David danced before the Lord with all his might; David was girded with a linen ephod.

                                                          2 Samuel 6:14

We can probably think of a sensual experience that made us want to dance. And we can probably remember a political victory that called for happy feet. But perhaps only the charismatics and Pentecostals among us can probably recall a *religious* event that prompted dance.

David danced because of all three. He was dancing almost naked, which may have been why his wife, Michal, looked at him with contempt. He had consolidated the northern and southern kingdoms of Israel and made Jerusalem its capital. And now he escorted the Ark of the Covenant, Israel's primary religious symbol, into the new capital with all the fanfare of a Pride March. The Ark contained the tablets of the Law of Moses.

Everything was coming together, and David, the darling of Jewish scripture, was a hero. His personal ambition coincided with God's calling and his nation's pride, a biblical version of Camelot.

Camelot, or heaven, is when all things come together and work together for good. The harmony created when all parts of ourselves become integral——sexual, spiritual, and political——serves as music for our dance.

Dear Dancing God: teach us to dance!

Steadfast love and faithfulness will meet;
righteousness and peace will kiss each other.

Psalm 85:10

Passions are fueled by dreams. Those who have forgotten to dream run out of fuel. Scripture may stimulate our dreams once more, thus restoring our passion.

The Psalmist's dream of God's steadfast love meeting our faithfulness fulfills the hope of God's love and our faith. The Psalmist's dream of God's righteousness kissing world peace, so that it is not bereft of justice, fulfills divine and human hope.

God's steadfast love is not disembodied. It is found in the ground that anchors our feet, in the food that nourishes us through the day, in the arms that embrace us at night. Nor is our faithfulness disembodied, but it is expressed in how we direct our feet, in how we transform the food to action, in how we embrace another.

When justice "inspirits" peace, righteousness kisses peace in our beds as well as at the polls, in our homes as well as on our streets, in the church as well as out in the world. When peace is the product of coercion and control, it spits on God's righteousness.

Grant us your peace, the passion of your justice, and the kiss of their integrity.

As an apple tree among the trees of the wood,
so is my beloved among young men.
With great delight I sat in his shadow,
and his fruit was sweet to my taste.

Song of Solomon 2:3

Oh, may your breasts be like clusters of the vine,
and the scent of your breath like apples,
and your kisses like the best wine
that goes down smoothly,
gliding over lips and teeth.

Song of Solomon 7:8–9

Just as religion disembodied spirituality and love, so some religious interpreters have spiritualized this sensual rapport between lovers. Maybe they've never known a lover whose "fruit was sweet," or kisses "like the best wine that goes down smoothly."

But we have, even if only in fantasy. "With great delight" we have sat in a loved one's shadow, and yearned for breasts or chests "like clusters of the vine" on which we might lay our faces.

The opposite mistake of spiritualizing this text is to simply sensualize it. Within the sensual is the spiritual; these bodies are souls who communicate their sacred love by a reverent touch.

Bless this body; bless this body's capacity to bless another body with my flesh and my soul.

"But you have kept the good wine until now."
                                              John 2:10

That Jesus would contribute wine to a wedding party at Cana contradicts the somber image most of us carry of him. That it would be better than the wine the host ran out of is less amazing; after all, this wine was divinely inspired. Yet his use of divine powers for something seemingly so frivolous may surprise us.

One of the themes of his teaching is how frivolous religious legalism is. Could it have been an ironic slap at legalism that he chose to make wine of the water in six stone jars intended for religious rites of purification?

Water purportedly changed to wine in the temples of Dionysus on his festival day, which "just happened" to be the day the early church chose to celebrate Jesus' miracle. Dionysus was the Greek god of fertility, ecstasy, and sensual pleasure. Maybe Jesus was offering a nod to these qualities of spirituality——after all, he was at a *wedding*.

Lest I border on heresy, remember that the wine Jesus contributed was not the cheap stuff intended for drunken revelry. The wine steward commended the bridegroom for keeping the best for last. Jesus' gift added to the *quality* of the party experience.

Jesus, come to the parties of our lives, transforming the ordinary into the extraordinary.

One of his disciples, whom Jesus loved, was lying close to the breast of Jesus.

John 13:23 (Revised Standard Version)

Mary took a pound of costly perfume made of pure nard, anointed Jesus' feet, and wiped them with her hair. The house was filled with the fragrance of the perfume.

John 12:3

Every time a new translation of the Bible comes out, it seems, the beloved disciple moves farther away from Jesus! In the King James Version he "was leaning on Jesus' bosom." In this version he is close to Jesus' breast. In the New Revised Standard Version, he is "reclining next" to Jesus.

Could translators be a little nervous about gay men seeing a hint of homosexuality in the physical intimacy between an especially loved disciple and the Messiah?

Bisexuals and heterosexuals can take heart, however, because it also appears that Jesus was not afraid to be close to Mary, who preferred sitting at his feet to helping sister Martha in the kitchen, and who subsequently anointed his feet with perfume, wiping them dry with her hair. I can still smell the lingering scent.

Perhaps Jesus' sexuality is a mystery because his sexual passion is irrelevant to his message of God's passion for us.

Hold us close to your breast, Jesus. Let us massage your feet with oil, the feet of one who brings glad tidings.

"Judas, is it with a kiss that you are betraying the Son of Man?"

Luke 22:48

The story of Judas may be a story of passion misguided. Tradition holds that he wanted Jesus to be a political Messiah. Though Jesus was surely aware of the political ramifications of his spiritual revolution, he resisted becoming a revolutionary, military hero.

As the builders of the Tower of Babel attempted reaching into heaven on their own terms, could it be that Judas wanted to force God's kingdom rather than let it come of its own accord? Jesus warned of "the violent who take [the kingdom of heaven] by force" (Matt. 11:12).

There are those within the lesbian and gay community who believe a political resolution is the only answer. But legislation, though a necessary interim goal, is not radical enough. We want a transformation of the heart——a voluntary, spiritual conversion.

Whatever Judas' motivation, Jesus apparently intended that the political and spiritual dimensions of the gospel enjoy a kiss of mutuality, not of betrayal.

Deliver us from our own misguided passions, Sovereign God, that we might welcome rather than command your commonwealth.

Then [Elisha] got up on the bed and lay upon the [dead] child,
putting his mouth upon his mouth, his eyes upon his eyes, and
his hands upon his hands; and while he lay bent over him, the
flesh of the child became warm.

2 Kings 4:34

Our heightened awareness of clergy sexual misconduct might
make us question this behavior today. But touch was and is important to all healing, to all restoration of life. Most of us could
testify to occasions when being held in a mother's lap, cuddled
in a lover's arms, or hugged by a stranger rejuvenated our ail-
ing or weary flesh.

So many of us and so many caregivers of the sick or
dying are afraid to touch. In a culture that exiled lepers,
from a religion that considered contact with a corpse defiling, Elijah lay down on the boy, mouth to mouth, eye to
eye, hands to hands. His bodily warmth warmed the boy to
life. This is touch in a full-bodied way.

The resurrection saved the life not only of the child but
also of his mother, who would depend on his care in old
age. So, too, our healing touch reverberates as the rings of a
pebble touching the surface of a pond.

God of the Body, give us the passion to reach out with heal-
ing compassion to all who need our touch.

Jesus began to weep. So the Jews said, "See how he loved him!"
But some of them said, "Could not he who opened the eyes of
the blind man have kept this man from dying?"

John 11:35–37

We, too, have wished that the passion of our love could raise a dead lover or friend, as the passion of Jesus' love raised Lazarus. We, too, know Jesus' love of those who are sick with life-threatening illnesses. And we, too, wonder why Jesus cannot prevent the deaths of those we love dearly.

Jesus must have winced when Mary said, "Lord, if you had been here, my brother would not have died." But he must have been encouraged by her faith in adding, "But even now I know that God will give you whatever you ask" (11:21, 22).

"I am the resurrection and the life," Jesus told her. "Those who believe in me, even though they die, will live, and everyone who lives and believes in me will never die" (11:25–26). Jesus' passion for us transcends death; he will never let us go.

Jesus was "greatly disturbed in spirit and deeply moved" by death's power. Though rabbis avoided the dead to keep ritually clean, the Teacher asked to be taken to him. He prayed, then cried, "Lazarus, come out!" (11:33, 43).

Jesus will not let us rest in peace, in closets or tombs, now and forever.

Thank you, Jesus, for the passion for life you embody which
reminds us that in life and in death we are God's.

"For those who want to save their life will lose it, and those who lose their life for my sake, will find it."

Matthew 16:25

"Very truly, I tell you, unless a grain of wheat falls into the earth and dies, it remains just a single grain; but if it dies, it bears much fruit."

John 12:24

"Your life is hidden with Christ in God," Colossians 3:3 tells us. God has "brought us to life with Christ," Ephesians 2:5 (NJB) declares.

All this talk of life and death, of being buried and bearing fruit! But passion makes us all speak and think in extremes. Passion is itself extreme. It is not lukewarm; it does not measure out life. The passion that comes from nature is willing to kill to live, but the passion that comes from God is willing to die to live and so others may live.

Our old selves die so that we may find new life with our Divine Lover.

We've died before. We died when we let go of a sexual persona that was not us. We died when we let go of self-knowledge that was not true. We died when we let go of societal expectations that were not just. But we died *to live!*

May our passionate love affair with you, Spirit, transform our seed to good fruit.

Jesus answered them, "Have faith in God. Truly I tell you, if you say to this mountain, 'Be taken up and thrown into the sea,' and if you do not doubt in your heart, but believe that what you say will come to pass, it will be done for you. So I tell you, whatever you ask for in prayer, believe that you have received it, and it will be yours."

Mark 11:22-24

Our faith is not magical. We do not, nor can we, manipulate God. Some of us believed when young that if we said the right words in prayer, God would change us, make us like everyone else. It didn't happen, and some of us lost faith in God, angry that God would create us and allow us to be outcast. Others of us changed the tune of our prayer, and prayed to integrate our faith and sexuality.

I don't believe that Jesus is talking about magical power in this quote. Rather, he speaks of the *passion* with which we must pray. My mother passionately prayed for my father's recovery from cancer, and felt her prayers were not answered when he died. But I believe she became the answer to her own prayer, as her passion empowered her compassionate caregiving.

Hear our prayers, O Lord. Incline thine ear to us, and grant us thy peace.

COVENANT

"When the bow is in the clouds, I will see it and remember the everlasting covenant between God and every living creature of all flesh that is on the earth."

Genesis 9:16

After the destruction of the flood, God offered the multi-colored rainbow as a peacemaking gesture. A bow and arrow was an ancient weapon, and the symbolic nature of a bow laid on its side in the heavens implied God's disarmament. Never again would God cause the destruction of all flesh on the earth.

Those who view AIDS or other devastating calamities as a form of God's punishment have not understood God's intent in scripture to save rather than to destroy. Ancient peoples explained illness, disability, and catastrophe by blaming sin and God's judgment. Today, we know that diseases and disabilities are caused by viruses, bacteria, or genes, and that floods and other natural disasters are products of weather patterns.

According to the Bible, God's first covenant with all life on earth was one of peace. Gay people have chosen the rainbow flag as our symbol, and we are people of the rainbow, claiming its promise, celebrating the diversity of God's creation in a world grown suspicious of difference.

Rainbow God, may we also lay down our weapons of prejudice and indifference, and embrace your creative diversity.

And [God] put a mark on Cain, so that no one who came upon him would kill him.

Genesis 4:15

God abhorred human violence both as a way of settling differences and as a way of settling scores. For this reason, God offered protection to Cain after he murdered his brother Abel, threatening a "sevenfold vengeance" on anyone who would kill Cain. This should give pause to any society that engages in executions.

A friend defending the death penalty asked me if I had ever been the victim of crime, as if that would change my view. I said yes, having been burgled and threatened, and having had three friends murdered.

I should have countered with, "Have you ever become the friend of someone who faced the death penalty?" It was such a person who had prompted our church to start a ministry to gay jail inmates. That very week I received word that this person died in prison of AIDS. I suspected that poor prison care had transformed his incarceration to the death sentence he had narrowly avoided.

When Jesus admonished his disciples to turn the other cheek, he was not encouraging them to cooperate with evil. He was enjoining them——and us——to restrain our tendencies toward revenge.

Merciful God, forgive both the murderer within me and my desires for revenge.

"As for me, this is my covenant with you: You shall be the ancestor of a multitude of nations. No longer shall your name be Abram, but your name shall be Abraham."

Genesis 17:4-5

In the Bible, a new covenant often meant a changed name. As a movement, we know that experience. When we affirmed our love, the clinical-sounding "homosexual" became "homophile." When we affirmed our self-accepting lifestyle and community, the paternalistic "homophile" gave way to "gay." As we affirm the different experiences of women and men, the exclusive-sounding "gay" becomes "lesbians and gay men."

Now our radicalized, in-your-face activism prompts some of us to adopt terms that made and makes earlier generations cringe: queer, dyke, faggot. And, in an effort to reunite us, some academics have chosen "lesgay" or "lesbigay."

Now that many "blacks" in this country are choosing the name "African-American," maybe we also have a new name coming. Whatever it is, we, like Abraham and Sarah, have been blessed with a multitude of people with a multitude of opinions from which to choose how we name ourselves, which is better than having no choice at all.

Thank you for our choices, Holy One. Bless us in our decisions.

"I will not let you go, unless you bless me."
                                    Genesis 32:26

In the night, Jacob wrestled with God.

Wrestling with my dad when I was a kid was fun, partly because the playful struggle brought me closer to him. Wrestling with a friend in junior high, I was embarrassed by getting an erection. Though I wanted to take weightlifting in high school, I didn't, because the course required wrestling, and I feared the possibility of sexual arousal.

For women and men, our own wrestling with God brings us closer to God. But as we get closer, we may find ourselves embarrassed by our sexuality.

Jacob was on his way to reconcile with his brother, Esau, whom he had wronged and from whom he had been estranged. God's blessing could certainly help. He received the blessing and a new name——Israel. But most translators delicately dance around an important detail of the story: God ultimately placed a hand in Jacob's groin!

God wrestles even with our sexuality. No part of us can be left out when we wrestle with God. And God will bless all of us.

Wrestle with me God, and please don't let me go until you bless me.

"Where you go, I will go;
where you lodge, I will lodge;
your people shall be my people,
and your God my God.
Where you die, I will die—
there will I be buried.
May the Lord do thus and so to me,
and more as well,
if even death parts me from you!"

Ruth 1:16–17

No more eloquent words of covenant between two human beings is found in scripture. Ruth said them to Naomi, as she followed her kinswoman back to her native land. Ruth's willingness to give up her own country, culture, and theology to adopt Naomi's country, culture, and theology as her own exemplifies the very heart of love.

This covenantal relationship between two women warranted its own book in the Bible, apparently receiving God's blessing and the approval of others. The words of the covenant, said in private between Ruth and Naomi, imply that even a nonpublic and nonritualized commitment contains power that is honored by God and must be honored by us.

Bless our covenants, Covenant Maker, bless the love of women with women and men with men! May I also bless them!

When David had finished speaking to Saul, the soul of Jonathan was bound to the soul of David, and Jonathan loved him as his own soul. . . . Then Jonathan made a covenant with David, because he loved him as his own soul.

1 Samuel 18:1, 3

Many of us will recognize this experience of a love that binds souls. The covenant Jonathan and David make with each other simply *solemnizes an already existing reality.*

One verse later (18:4), "Jonathan stripped himself of the robe that he was wearing, and gave it to David, and his armor, and even his sword and his bow and his belt." In a public way, they *demonstrate the reality* of their covenant by this gesture. And notice the symbolism of the act: Jonathan strips himself of his defenses and offers them to David.

We may see in this passionate covenant something of our own reality: the bonding of souls, the making of covenants, stripping ourselves of our defenses to welcome intimacy. The Spirit somehow makes it past heterosexist, ancient biblical editors and modern translators and delivers good news, a model of same-gender love!

Thank you, Spirit, for David and Jonathan, for Ruth and Naomi, for giving us our reflections in the biblical mirror.

These I will bring to my holy mountain,
and make them joyful in my house of prayer;
their burnt offerings and their sacrifices
will be accepted on my altar;
for my house shall be called a house of prayer
for all peoples.
Thus says the [Sovereign] God,
who gathers the outcasts of Israel,
I will gather others to them
besides those already gathered.

Isaiah 56:7–8

"These" is a reference to foreigners and eunuchs. We are the foreigners, the eunuchs, the outcasts. We are those alien to the mainstream culture. We are those who may not bear children. We are those cast out from society and religious institutions.

Through Isaiah, God assures us that we who worship, do what is right, love God, and hold fast to God's covenant with us will always have a place and be given an everlasting name. God will give us joy, our offerings will be welcomed, and our prayers will find a home. Jesus quoted this scripture when he passionately cleared the section of the temple set aside for you and me.

We have a place of joy, a home of prayer, thanks to you and your covenant, Sovereign God, our creator and redeemer.

But Naaman became angry and went away, saying, "I thought that for me he would surely come out, and stand and call on the name of the Lord his God, and would wave his hand over the spot, and cure the leprosy!"

2 Kings 5:11

Naaman is peeved that the prophet Elisha simply sent a messenger to advise him to wash in the Jordan River seven times to be healed of his skin disease. Why didn't he wave a magic wand? he wonders. His servants point out that if Naaman had been required to do something extraordinary, he would have done it, and so persuade him to follow the simple instructions. "His flesh was restored like the flesh of a young boy" (5:14), the scripture says.

Whether for our spiritual, mental, or physical health, we often expect that the more complicated and the more expensive the process, the better chance we have of being healed. Either we embrace an elaborate regimen or we are intimidated and do nothing.

Simple things like prayer, rest, and reducing stress are overlooked as we search for a guru, a psychiatrist, and a specialist to give us the complex rather than the simple answers. In quest of a magician, we do not notice those around us who offer practical support and guidance. In quest of a magic pill to solve our ills, we do not take the trouble to create our own solutions.

May we be receptive to those who offer us healing, no matter how ordinary or simple their balm.

"If God will be with me . . . of all that you give me I will surely give one tenth to you."

Genesis 28:20, 22

Uh-oh, here it comes.

There are different types of covenants in the Bible. The one between God and humankind is not mutual, like those between human beings. After all, we cannot be God. God offers us blessings. In response, we offer what we have. This is the most ancient nature of sacrifice, the giving up of first fruits to the God who benevolently offers everything. This type of sacrifice occurs in many cultures and religions.

In this story Jacob offers God one-tenth——a tithe——of all that God gives him. Those reared in the church are probably familiar with this concept. My parents, who were not paid much, quietly gave to their church one-tenth of their income *before taxes!*

If gay men and lesbians practiced this concept of giving back to our community centers and organizations one-tenth of what they have achieved for us, they wouldn't have to sweat their budgets each year. If gay and lesbian Christians returned one-tenth of what their denominational support networks have achieved for them, these groups would have the resources to challenge the church in a big way.

If you will be with us, God, we will stand with those agencies and associations that have been given to us.

You shall circumcise the flesh of your foreskins, and it shall be a sign of the covenant between me and you.

Genesis 17:11

As a sign of the covenant unique to the descendants of Abraham and Sarah, the Hebrews believed that the men were to be circumcised. The women were not circumcised, though some other cultures and religions required it.

Circumcision decreases sensitivity. Modern claims of its medical advantages have been refuted. It was the one mutilation allowed by a people who otherwise even forbade tattoos. It was antipleasure, antisensual, and antisexual. I do not believe God wanted a sign of the covenant that contravened divinely intended pleasure. Christianity did not require it.

Nonetheless, the church has circumcised our sexual pleasure with the Bible as we were growing up. Though there is no operation to separate our sexuality from our spirituality, many of us were taught that God was antipleasure, antisensual, and antisexual. The covenant with God took on heterosexual and procreational requirements.

Our experience teaches us that these requirements unfairly limit God's gift of sexual and sensual pleasure.

God of Mercy, help us to forgive those who tried to take away the sexual pleasure you gave us, in body and in spirit.

Real circumcision is a matter of the heart—it is spiritual and not literal.

Romans 2:29

The apostle Paul argues here about who is the truly faithful person. For him, external conditions are not as relevant as internal attitude. In the first chapter of this letter to the church at Rome, he describes the external condition of pagans (Gentiles, the uncircumcised) arising from their internal attitude. Their idolatry leads to immoral behaviors, among which he includes same-gender lust, an inclusion we would question today. Then in chapter two he condemns those people of faith (Jewish Christians, the circumcised) who would judge externals, when they, the judges, are doing the very same things.

Ultimately, he concludes, God looks for a person's internal attitude as a sign of the new covenant in Jesus Christ, rather than at the person's external condition. The circumcision of the heart is even more important to God than behavior, since, after all, we are all sinners whether we live within the law or as outlaws.

Jesus Christ introduces a new covenant that leaves its mark on the heart, not on the body.

Circumcise my heart, Jesus. Heal my attitude toward God.

But this is the covenant that I will make with the house of Israel after those days, says the Lord: I will put my law within them, and I will write it on their hearts; and I will be their God, and they shall be my people.

Jeremiah 31:33

What amazes me about our community is how a bunch of supposed "*out*laws" have "*in*laws"——laws within ourselves that govern our behavior. Yes, there are exceptions, but for people who are "criminals" in half the United States and considered "heretics" in much of Christendom, we behave pretty well.

There are the politically self-righteous who may "out" a public figure, but most of us are caringly discreet about disclosures of another's sexuality. There is less violence among us than the general population. We become the *best* of friends, and befriend the friendless. Our breakups with lovers often end in lifelong friendships. We readily offer hospitality by opening an ear or our homes to those in need. And, in terms of compassion, we were the best-equipped segment of the population to deal with a crisis like AIDS, caring for our community and warning mainstream society.

God's laws got written inside our hearts, I believe, because, like the Hebrews, we suffered and escaped oppression and had to find organizing principles for our journey; and, like Jesus, we elevated love over love-inhibiting laws.

We have been your people, God. Help us know you are our God.

"God . . . will provide the lamb for the burnt offering, my son."
                                                    Genesis 22:8

God asked Abraham to sacrifice his only——and long-awaited——heir on an altar. Abraham remorsefully agrees to comply. But it is a test of his willingness to follow God's will, and both he and Isaac are saved by an alternative sacrifice of a hidden ram in the bushes provided by God.

What may seem like a horrible story about child abuse and an overly demanding God was told by the Hebrews to explain that their God did not require the sacrifice of children, as did the gods of surrounding cultures.

Mistaking God's will, many parents willingly cut off their children upon discovery of their sexual orientation, sacrificing them to a god of conformity. Other parents have the hearts to search for God's hidden sacrifice: their own giving up of control and of prejudice to continue enjoying their posterity.

Too many parents believe faithfulness means sacrificing their children, God. Forgive them, for they know not what they do.

All have sinned and fall short of the glory of God; they are now justified by [divine] grace as a gift, through the redemption that is in Christ Jesus, whom God put forward as a sacrifice of atonement by his blood, effective through faith.

Romans 3:22–25

In the film *Dominick and Eugene*, the mentally disabled Dominick witnesses, in absolute horror, a boy beaten by a violent father. In his church, a tearful Dominick points to Jesus on the cross and cries to a priest, "I would never let that happen to *my* son!"

The concept of an angry God demanding the death of God's own son troubles many of us. Jesus' followers sought a divine plan behind the human tragedy of the crucifixion. The legal atmosphere of the Roman Empire influenced the notion that Jesus had to be punished for our sins. Since the Jews offered animal sacrifices for sins, Christians came to believe that Jesus served as the *final* sacrifice, dispensing with further shedding of blood. To them, this was an *advance* in theology.

The Christian teacher Abelard of the twelfth century taught another view. The atonement or at-one-ment of God and humankind came through Christ's suffering awakening human compassion, what differentiates us from other creatures and makes us one with God. A crucified God offers a new covenant with us by redeeming, or calling forth, our better nature.

As your suffering is redemptive for us, O Christ, may our suffering awaken the better natures of others.

For we do not have a high priest who is unable to sympathize with our weaknesses, but we have one who in every respect has been tested as we are, yet without sin. Let us therefore approach the throne of grace with boldness, so that we may receive mercy and find grace to help in time of need.

Hebrews 4:15–16

If our attitude toward clergy is any clue, then Jesus had better be both perfect and the perfect listener. But the "perfect listener" is usually what Henri Nouwen calls "the wounded healer." If you mess up in a relationship, aren't you likely to go to someone who's had similar problems? If addictive behavior gets the better of you, aren't you likely to go to a Twelve-Step meeting of others who cope with the same behavior?

The perfect sacrifice and the perfect priest were to be without blemish; so, since Jesus was both, he was viewed as being without sin. Yet "one who in every respect has been tested as we are" surely knew the remorse of human error.

Scripture says, "love covers a multitude of sins" (1 Pet. 4:8, quoting Prov. 10:12). Jesus' compassion would have more than adequately compensated were he less than perfect. As many of the saints that followed him, Jesus probably was more sensitive to his own missteps than his followers would have been.

The bottom line is, Jesus knows what it's like for us. We can "approach the throne of grace with boldness."

Jesus, you know us inside and out. Forgive us our sins, and help us forgive ourselves.

Surely God is my salvation;
I will trust, and will not be afraid.
                                    Isaiah 12:2

A gay church member told me that she was disturbed to realize that most of what she did in life was motivated by fear. The approval of others, financial and physical insecurity, health, being alone or having a relationship, sexual adequacy, employment——all give rise to fear, and we may find ourselves scurrying about to keep life all together.

   Writing this book gives rise to my own fear. Will I make the deadline? Will it be meaningful to readers? Are the entries too long or too academic or too simplistic or . . . you understand what I mean. After all, they say a writer is only as good as the next book.

   A spiritually profound writer passed along an observation a woman once made of him. "When you make a speech or take some action," the friend said, "it's as if your whole life depended on it." The writer gave me similar advice in preparing a talk: "You should rely on the Spirit more."

   Isaiah reminds each of us that "surely God is my salvation; I will trust, and will not be afraid."

Surely you are my salvation, God; I will trust and not be afraid. With joy I draw water from the wells of salvation!

Your love is like a morning cloud,
like the dew that goes away early. . . .
For I desire steadfast love and not sacrifice,
the knowledge of God rather than burnt offerings.

Hosea 6:4, 6

A psychologist once suggested that our sexual drive may be, in reality, an affectional drive. That may explain why some choose affectionate relationships over sexual ones. That may also explain why others, not realizing they are hungry for affection more than sex, are confused when sexual encounters do not satisfy.

Whatever feelings of affection accompany a sexual encounter may swiftly dissipate as the morning fog or dew. A gay ethicist has theorized that, for some, the "guilt" experienced afterward may instead be the combination of a naturally occurring chemical letdown combined with a profound sadness that the event did not contain more meaning.

Hosea compared God's relationship with people to the prophet's relationship with an unfaithful lover. God is profoundly sad that the meaning of divine-human encounters dissipates for us as quickly as the morning cloud and dew. Just as we, with Hosea, prefer a steadfast lover rather than one who is unfaithful and constantly apologizing, so God prefers steadfast love to repeated acts of contrition.

To Hosea, God is a lover wronged. We often forget the covenant, while God eternally remembers it.

Keep us constant as the sunrise in the morning, O God,
steadfast as the earth's orbit around the sun.

For by grace you have been saved through faith, and this is not your own doing; it is the gift of God—not the result of works, so that no one may boast.

Ephesians 2:8

Imagine yourself trying to earn someone's love. That's how many Christians felt trying to earn God's love before the Protestant Reformation. Now imagine yourself responding to someone who already loves you. That's how the theologians of the Reformation described our relationship with God.

The Protestant scriptural basis was the phrase, "By grace you have been saved through faith." Grace is God's unmerited favor and unearned mercy. This phrase was to be as revolutionary for religion as the concept that all were created equal would be for politics.

Before the Reformation, the church had gotten stuck in a righteousness-by-works mentality. Christians gained their salvation the "old-fashioned" way, they *earned* it. But Protestants challenged this, feeling that Christianity had returned to the same legalistic requirements Jesus resisted.

Those who require heterosexual conformity also are stuck in a righteousness-by-works frame of mind. As modern day Reformers, we remind the church of the covenant of grace.

Fill me with the knowledge and the experience of your grace, Holy One, so that I may be more gracious toward others.

For if the inheritance comes from the law, it no longer comes from the promise; but God granted it to Abraham [and Sarah] through the promise.

Galatians 3:19

A friend called late one night and asked to come over. When he did, I found him bruised and bleeding. His perfectionist lover had beaten him again for his seeming imperfections. What had seemed at first to be a promising relationship had turned into a nightmare.

Many of us experienced God that way. God's promise of love became a nightmare of bashing. But the bashing was not God's. It was people mistakenly acting for God. God's promise of love is still there behind the church's unyielding expectations.

That's what Paul points out to the Galatians. God gave Abraham and Sarah the Promise 430 years before God gave the Law to Moses. Abraham and Sarah's faith alone "was reckoned . . . as righteousness" (Rom. 4:9). The promise of faith both precedes and supersedes the law.

Our own skirmish with church leaders as lesbians and gay men is part of the church's ongoing struggle to understand that faith in God's promise, or covenant, is more important than playing by their rules.

Thank you for the promise of our salvation, Great Deliverer. Help us live as children of the promise: free and faithful.

[God] brought you to life with Christ.

Ephesians 2:4 (Jerusalem Bible)

The sense of this verse is probably better described as God making us alive *along with* Christ. But one day, reading this scripture during my morning prayer time, it struck me that God had truly brought me to life *with Christ:* that without Christ, much of the meaning of my life and most of the saints in my life would not be there.

Some ancient versions of this text would support this understanding, reading that God "brought us to life *in* Christ." Whatever the case, consider what your life would be if Jesus Christ had never lived. Even our so-called secular life would be different, not to mention how we experience God and one another.

"Get a life," we admonish people who preoccupy themselves with minor concerns or major addictions. I am so grateful to God for the life given to me in Jesus Christ. Were it not for Christ, my world would have been smaller. And I would be smaller, too.

Thank you, God, for expanding our horizons with Christ. Thank you for life's expansive quality in faith.

Therefore, since we are justified by faith, we have peace with God through our [Sovereign] Jesus Christ, through whom we have obtained access to this grace in which we stand.

Romans 5:1–2

"This grace in which we stand."

"Here I stand," was Martin Luther's proclamation of God's grace in the face of an onslaught of criticism, condemnation, excommunication, and death threats coming from peasants to pope.

To enter one of my first gay and lesbian pride festivals in Hollywood in the late seventies, I had to walk through a gauntlet of chanting "Jesus people" carrying antigay banners. One read, "Turn or Burn." In response, the DJ for the dance area just inside the festival played the disco number, "Burn, Baby, Burn."

I smiled. To me it was an appropriately irreverent and mocking version of Luther's "Here I stand." At his famous trial before the Diet of Worms, Martin Luther, relying on "Scripture and plain reason," repudiated church councils and hierarchy. He concluded, "I cannot and I will not recant anything, for to go against conscience is neither right nor safe. . . . Here I stand, I cannot do otherwise."

In such grace, lesbians and gay men at that pride festival not only stood, we danced.

We stand, we dance in the grace of your covenant, O God, "and we boast in our hope of sharing [your] glory" (5:2)!

So if anyone is in Christ, there is a new creation: everything old has passed away; see, everything has become new!

2 Corinthians 5:17

When you have a new love, the world changes. For a friend who fell in love, the world seemed more loving. A friend who found an apartment enjoyed a greater sense of belonging in her city. A friend who discovered photography recognized the hidden beauty of his neighborhood.

A friend who started a roof garden found peace in the midst of a chaotic urban sprawl. A homeless shelter for battered women at which a friend volunteered revealed purpose.

Our new love with God——the new covenant——not only creates us afresh, but transforms the world for us as well. We observe more love. We know that we belong. We gain new perspectives. We find peace. Purpose is revealed.

How are we "*in*" Christ"? Just as we might get into any new love: we spend time with Christ through scripture, we find a church home that is welcoming of us, we look at our world as God might, we enjoy and offer spiritual peace, and we find ways to help others. Most of all, just as with any new love, we *believe*.

Help us trust you, Christ Jesus, so that everything old may pass away and the whole creation become new to us.

All this is from God, who reconciled us to [God's self] through Christ, and has given us the ministry of reconciliation.

                                        2 Corinthians 5:18

Our ministry of reconciliation has a unique twist. As God helps us reconcile our sexuality with our spirituality through Jesus Christ, we help other Christians do the same. Then, in turn, we help reconcile those of different sexualities.

God "came out" in Jesus to overcome the world's misunderstandings of God and to show mercy on the world in its sin and suffering. We come out as gay and lesbian to overcome people's misunderstandings of us. In doing so, we have an opportunity to show mercy toward people who are homophobic, and to alleviate the suffering of those who are erotophobic, that is, those paralyzed by their fear of sexuality.

As Jesus demonstrated the covenant of the human and the divine, so we may demonstrate the covenant of sexuality and spirituality.

Reconcile the sexuality and spirituality of our souls, O God, and bless us in our ministry of reconciliation.

*In this is love, not that we loved God but that [God] loved us
and sent [God's Child] to be the atoning sacrifice for our sins.*

1 John 4:10

We know that love is not dependent on a response. Many of us
have experienced the bliss and bust of unrequited love. Many
of us have made sacrifices out of a love that we did not expect
to be returned, at least not with the same intensity.

We may have become someone's very best friend. We
may have been a surrogate mother or father or daughter or
son. We may have been a benefactor to someone struggling
to get it together. We may have been a teacher's very best
student, or a student's very best teacher. We may have been
an especially caring therapist or minister.

In this is love, not that they loved us but that we loved
them. This is how God loves.

The fulfillment of love comes when it is returned with a
similar intensity and commitment. Jesus loved God that
way. In Christ, it is possible for us to love God as deeply as
is humanly and divinely possible. Mystically, Christ provides
the at-one-ing bond —— the Holy Spirit, the Advocate —— by
which our love may be at-one with God's love.

*You are our very best friend, Sacred Advocate. Inspire us to
return that love through Jesus Christ.*

As shepherds seek out their flocks when they are among their scattered sheep, so I will seek out my sheep.

Ezekiel 34:12

Like the lost sheep in Jesus' later parable (Matt. 18:12), and Jesus' seeking "other sheep not of this fold" (John 10:16), Ezekiel describes God seeking after the beloved as shepherds search for their own.

It's difficult to think of God——the awesome, cosmic Creator——going to the trouble.

One day, coming home from school, I found my sister sitting on the kitchen floor, frustrated, surrounded by pots and pans and drawers taken from the cupboards under the counter. She explained that that afternoon she had brought home a tiny kitten which had managed to disappear behind the kitchen cabinets. She could hear its plaintive meows, but only after more effort did she finally locate where it had wedged itself behind the framework.

God is at least as good as my sister! Why then resist believing that God would listen to our plaintive cries and search for us?

Search for me when I am lost, Yahweh, and restore me to your fold.

As a mother comforts her child,
so I will comfort you.
                              Isaiah 66:13

Today, I wish my mother were not several thousand miles away. I'd like to sit with her on the front porch steps and talk about my recent troubles. I know she doesn't have the solutions, but somehow, being able to tell her would help.

As a child I used to enjoy sitting on her lap, an echo of when I nursed at her breast. When she held me I felt safe. I suppose sitting on her porch steps is the adult equivalent.

That God could comfort me like that suggests the intimacy of God's covenant with me. That I could imagine it at all reflects the comforting intimacy of the bond between my mother and me.

A gay priest once told me that for him, God was his grandmother. It was on his grandmother's knee that he first learned about God. Though he had gone on to learn harsher images of God at the hands of the church, he had chosen to return to the gentlekindness of his grandmother God.

Some of us may unnecessarily bear the burden of an exclusively male deity. To discover the *imago dei*——image of God——within us, we may review the images of God that burden or buoy us.

Mother God, nurse me with your consoling breast, that I may drink deeply with delight, dandled on your knees.

*"Though I have no fear of God and no respect for anyone, yet
because this widow keeps bothering me, I will grant her justice,
so that she may not wear me out by continually coming."*

Luke 18:4-5

Jesus told this parable so that we "pray always and not . . . lose
heart" (18:1). It is not a warm and fuzzy story. An aggrieved
widow seeks justice from a heartless judge. Her bothersome-
ness alone makes the judge relent and give her the justice she
repeatedly demands. God is not the judge in the story, but if
this dispassionate bureaucrat may be persuaded, then surely
God may be.

Hebrew prophets evaluated faithfulness to God's
covenant by how society treated the most vulnerable and
powerless: widows and orphans. Faithfulness to the new
covenant in Christ may be evaluated by how the church
and the society it influences treat today's vulnerable and
powerless, which include lesbians and gay men and people
with AIDS.

In our powerlessness, we are "to pray always and not to
lose heart" as equal beneficiaries of God's covenant. This
parable's legal and political context may encourage us to
seek justice by praying repeatedly with our vote as well as
by praying devotedly.

We cry to you, God: Grant us justice! Do not delay! Help us!

Behold, I send my messenger to prepare the way before me, and God whom you seek will suddenly come to the temple; the messenger of the covenant in whom you delight, behold that one is coming, says the God of hosts.

Malachi 3:1 (Inclusive Language Lectionary)

When we enter into a covenant, we expect something will come of it. There is a future that will be improved by making mutual promises now. Just so, there is an expectation of delight implied by God's covenant. Malachi's concern is that we, especially our spiritual leaders, prepare for it.

In a sermon, Atlanta preacher Ted Wardlaw told the story of an eccentric woman whose presence at a church conference center surprised him. She explained that when she was there decades before, a preacher was handed a message as he stood to preach and announced that World War II was over. She said, "This world today is such a frightening place and there are so many terrible things; and so I thought that, if I could just get back down here, maybe it would happen again. Maybe someone would hand the preacher a note that had good news."

The gospel is such good news. Yet many of us listeners and——sadly, for Malachi——many of our spiritual leaders have not adequately prepared the way for God's delightful message, including the end of the "war" between sex and spirit.

Prepare your way in my heart, Holy One, that I may delight in your messenger of the covenant. Come, Lord Jesus!

As for you, . . . because of the blood of my covenant with you,
I will set your prisoners free from the waterless pit.
Return to your stronghold,
O prisoners of hope.

                                                    Zechariah 9:12

During a debate of a national church assembly, a delegate pointed out a contradiction in the denomination's supposed "welcome" of lesbians and gays as members while rejecting our ordination as leaders. Since all members had the right to hold ordained office, the delegate questioned if there were now two categories of membership.

The denomination's chief interpreter of church law responded. Revealingly, he said we were like people in prison who could be church members but would "obviously" be unable to hold office. Unwittingly he placed us in a grand tradition of prophets imprisoned for their convictions, including Jesus himself, crucified between two criminals.

Some in the gay community also consider lesbian and gay Christians as hopeless prisoners of religious institutions that will never truly embrace us.

I prefer to think of us as "prisoners of hope," held by the covenant by which we will be set free from "the waterless pit," or dungeon, that is the church's closet.

The covenant of God's hope will never let us go.

If we are to be imprisoned, God of Justice, imprison us by our hope of deliverance rather than a closet of despair.

Rejoice always, pray without ceasing, give thanks in all circumstances; for this is the will of God in Christ Jesus for you. Do not quench the Spirit. . . . May the God of peace . . . sanctify you entirely; and may your spirit and soul and body be kept sound and blameless at the coming of our Lord Jesus Christ.

1 Thessalonians 5:16–19, 23

A lesbian and gay charismatic church that takes its name from the Aramaic prayer "our Lord, come!" ("Maranatha") invited me to spend a weekend. I felt deep peace during an evening prayer meeting, caressed by the rhythmic undercurrent of whispered affirmations——"yes, Jesus," "thank you, Jesus"—— as each one prayed. One later got what they called "the holy giggles."

Morning worship began with songs of praise accompanied by hands clapping, bodies swaying. When I preached, I said I had never before thought of worship as an aerobic activity!

A church catechism claims that the chief end of humanity is "to enjoy God and glorify God forever." But, as the old joke goes about mainstream Christians, "many are cold, but a few are frozen." We have choked back the Spirit. What we could learn by lifting our hands during worship!

Being "sound" or "complete" in spirit, soul, and body did not imply a division of these three for the apostle Paul, but rather a covenant among them by which we bring our whole selves to pray, rejoice, and welcome the Spirit of Christ.

Come, Christ Jesus! Baptize us in your Spirit. Hallelujah!

COMMUNITY

For in the one Spirit we were all baptized into one body—Jews or Greeks, slaves or free—and we were all made to drink of one Spirit. . . . If one member suffers, all suffer together with it; if one member is honored, all rejoice together.

1 Corinthians 12:12-13, 26

Suffering and rejoicing together is the heart of community, whether Christian or lesbian and gay. What united early Christians was not only the joy of their faith, but suffering persecution from religious and political authorities. What unites lesbians and gay men is not only the joy of our sexuality, but suffering persecution—also from religious and political authorities.

The Christian community could do better "suffering with" its lesbian and gay members. And the gay community could do better suffering with its members that are people of color, people with disabilities, or those of our various subcultures. And lesbians and gay men could improve our understanding of one another, as well as of bisexual and transgender persons.

Both the church and the lesbian and gay community seem awkward rejoicing with an honored member. As Jesus said, "Prophets are not without honor except in their own country and in their own house" (Matt. 13:57).

Yet both communities have their egalitarian dimensions, rejoicing in their diversity. Whether over a Christian communion table or a gay dining table, I may expect to break bread with people of various economic, educational, and social backgrounds as equals.

As differently-abled bodies of one body, one community, let us suffer with one another and rejoice together.

*[God] said to Joshua, "Israel has sinned; they have trans-
gressed my covenant that I imposed on them."*

Joshua 6:10–11

"Joshua fit the battle of Jericho, and the walls came a- tumblin'
down," we used to sing in Sunday school. This African-American spiritual celebrates the walls that faith can bring down.

But after the battle, God was displeased. The instructions
for disposing of Jericho's wealth had not been followed.
Achan had taken some of the booty "devoted" to Yahweh.
Because of his sin, all suffered a military loss, and "the hearts
of the people melted and turned to water" (6:5).

We know how an individual's sin can affect a whole
community. Lee Harvey Oswald. Watergate. Dan White.
Gary Hart. Patient Zero. Exxon Valdez. All remind us of the
corporate power of individual choices.

That's why confession of sin in Jewish and Christian traditions is corporate as well as personal. We may not understand how our sins affect our community, but they do. And
we may not understand why we have to be responsible for
someone else's mess, but we are. We're all in this together.

*Forgive us for the sins by which we taint the whole commu-
nity and make it less than whole and far from holy.*

[Yahweh], forgiving iniquity and transgression and sin,
yet by no means clearing the guilty,
but visiting the iniquity of the parents
upon the children
and the children's children.

Exodus 34:6–7

When I told my parents that I was gay, my mother's initial reaction was to "blame" herself. She wrote, "But the Bible says the sins of the fathers fall upon the child, so I feel that what has happened to you must be for my sins——I haven't been the best mother, I know."

The organization Parents and Friends of Lesbians and Gays has delivered thousands of parents from assuming responsibility for their children "turning out" gay or lesbian. The more we know that sexual orientation is predisposed at birth, the more we know that God has created us as we are.

The Hebrew concept of corporate guilt extended beyond the present to the future community. We know there is some truth in this as we try to clean up the environment or as we cope with generations-old animosities.

But the prophet Ezekiel rejected the notion of generational culpability for sin, voicing God's word: "Know that all lives are mine; the life of the parent as well as the life of the child is mine: it is only the person who sins that shall [be held responsible]" (Ezek. 18:4).

Keep me from faulting the past and failing the future by resisting responsibility for the present, O God of the ages.

"Whoever does the will of God is my brother and sister and mother."

Mark 3:35

Many of us create extended families for ourselves from within our community, sometimes in the absence of supportive biological families. But, in the presence of his supportive family who had come to see him, Jesus created his own extended family of faith in this scripture.

Doing the will of God would become the organizing principle of the new family. It might set family members against one another (Matt. 10:35–36), but faith must be of more value than family (Matt. 10:37). Jesus called his disciples away from their families, and to the would-be disciple who wanted to wait until his father died, he said, "Follow me, and let the dead bury their own dead" (Matt. 8:21–22). Jesus gave priority to his spiritual family over his biological family.

Just as we are, Jesus could have been accused of attacking "traditional family values"!

Thank you, God, for the family who created me, the family of faith Christ created, and for the family I help create.

"I am the good shepherd. . . . And I lay down my life for the sheep. I have other sheep that do not belong to this fold. I must bring them also."

John 10:14-16

In a friend's church there was a stained-glass window depicting Jesus as the good shepherd, carrying a lost lamb. She told me that she had dismissed the image as religious sentimentality.

But a gay member of her church living with AIDS told her how much the memorial window had come to mean to him. He would often imagine himself as the lamb carried in Jesus' arms, and he would feel better when he was afraid or ill.

My friend began to value the picture in a different way, as a kind of icon of a healing and divine presence. When the young man with AIDS died, the church had the window cleaned and refurbished, rededicating it in his memory. Now his name appears with that of the one for whom the window was originally donated.

We are the other sheep not of this fold. We may see things differently, but we hear the shepherd's voice, and come home.

Thank you, Good Shepherd, for laying down your life for us. Bring us home, so there will be one flock, one shepherd.

"It would be better for you if a millstone were hung around your neck and you were thrown into the sea than for you to cause one of these little ones to stumble."

Luke 17:2

In an exchange of letters between a lesbian pastor of a gay congregation and the straight male pastor of a straight congregation, the latter warned her of the danger of leading her flock astray. One of her flock responded, reminding him of the danger of leading his flock astray.

Antigay pastors seem to think themselves incapable of leading their members astray. Believing themselves immune to God's judgment, such pastors think nothing of reinforcing antigay bias and hatred among straights, confusion within bisexuals, and self-hatred and spiritual anxiety among homosexuals who have not accepted themselves.

It's better to err on the side of grace than the side of condemnation. After all, that's what God did. "To err is human, to forgive divine," we say. On judgment day, wouldn't it be better to be accounted *too* gracious than too judgmental?

We pray for lesbians and gay men coming of age in antigay congregations, lest they stumble and fall.

"It would be better for you if a millstone were hung around your neck and you were thrown into the sea than for you to cause one of these little ones to stumble."

Luke 17:2

It's not just homophobes who can cause "little ones," that is, disciples, to stumble. A gay minister received a letter from a friend who explained how hurtful it was for him when they had had a sexual encounter many years before. The friend had viewed their relationship as pastoral. The pastor had understood the evening as a dinner date.

What the pastor did not know till receiving the letter was that the friend had been seduced repeatedly as a teenager by an older, closeted minister. Now the friend experienced the sexual encounter with an openly gay minister as a betrayal of yet another pastoral relationship.

Mutuality is difficult to gauge in a sexual encounter. The closeted pastor apparently cared nothing for mutuality. The openly gay pastor had no idea what implications a sexual encounter would have for his friend. Rather than cause him to stumble, it would have been better to learn and to love more.

This could guide us all. "To whom much has been entrusted, even more will be demanded" (Luke 12:48).

Keep us from causing others to stumble by our failure to know them adequately and to love them appropriately.

"And who is my neighbor?"

"The one who showed . . . mercy."

Luke 10:29, 37

For the subtitle to my first book, *Uncommon Calling,* I chose, "A Gay Christian Struggles to Serve the Church." But my publisher changed it to, "A Gay Man Struggles to Serve the Church." I told my editor that I did not want to emphasize being male, but rather, being Christian. She explained that to still too many people, "Gay Christian" was an oxymoron.

"Good Samaritan" would have been considered an oxymoron to Jesus' hearers of this story of the Good Samaritan who helped a victim of a roadside robbery. The animosity between Samaritans and Jews for religious and racial differences made this parable fantastic in the literal sense of the term.

An expert in the Law of Moses was trying to limit his liability by asking Jesus who was the neighbor that the law commanded him to love. In the course of his tale, Jesus switched the question to who proved to be a neighbor, and the lawyer was forced to reply, "The one who showed him mercy." Jesus told him, "Go and do likewise."

Mercy begets mercy. As we show mercy——toward one another, toward those who misjudge us, toward all the communities affected by AIDS——we transform hearts.

Help me to show my neighbors mercy, even those who do not prove merciful to me.

"Was none of them found to return and give praise to God except this foreigner?"

Luke 17:18

Ten lepers ask Jesus for healing. He tells them to go and show themselves to the priests, a ritual requirement of those who were outcast for health reasons. On the way, their skin heals, but only one, a Samaritan, turns to praise God "with a loud voice" and give Jesus thanks. Jesus tells him, "Your faith has made you well."

Just as Jesus' listeners would have been unsettled by his story of the "good" Samaritan because Samaritans were despised, so Jesus made use of this Samaritan's expression of thanks to demonstrate the lack of gratitude among his own people.

As lesbian and gay Christians offer thanks for God's grace and for God's gift of sexuality, we model for all people of faith the heartfelt gratitude Jesus praises in this story. With the Samaritan leper we may return to our communities of faith, show ourselves to religious leaders, and proclaim God's healing of sexuality and spirituality.

Praise be to you, Sovereign God. You have restored me to your Body by grace, and you have reclaimed my body by faith.

That evening, at sundown, they brought to [Jesus] all who were sick or possessed with demons. And the whole city was gathered around the door.

                                                    Mark 1:32–33

A disproportionate number of lesbians and gay men are caregivers. Part of the reason may be that we seek approval. Partly it may be that caregiving professions require more years of schooling, and we have an excuse to delay marriage. But mostly, I believe, it is because our own hurt and need makes us want to care for others who are hurting and in need.

Jesus had already had a busy day in Capernaum. He had taught in the synagogue, cast out an unclean spirit, and healed Simon's mother-in-law. But word spread of his capacity for healing, and "the whole city was gathered around the door." There are days in our lives when it feels like everyone needs us, and we have no time for ourselves.

Jesus did not forget that he was human. The next morning, he went alone "to a deserted place, and there he prayed" (1:35). Everyone was looking for him, but he found time for himself and for God.

If Jesus needed such time, think how much more we need to take time for prayer!

Help us receive your care, Sweet God, as we give our care to others.

For thus says the [Sovereign]: . . .
With weeping they shall come,
and with consolations I will lead them back. . . .
Their life shall become like a watered garden,
and they shall never languish again.
Then shall the young women rejoice in the dance,
and the young men and the old shall be merry.
I will turn their mourning into joy
I will comfort them, and give them gladness for sorrow.

Jeremiah 31:7, 9, 12–13

What a vision for those exiled from one another and from their home! Just as it worked for Israel, it works for us. Our community is coming together, with more to come.

We are transforming neighborhoods and congregations, creating oases of joy from places of mourning. Young lesbians are out dancing, mixing in gay male clubs that once were hostile to their presence. Lesbians and gays, old and young, are making merry together. As with Jeremiah, this is part vision, part reality. But it will come.

When I lived in West Hollywood and ran along the median strip dividing that city's "Main Street" ——Santa Monica Boulevard——I saw, felt, and smelled the metamorphosis. The dirt strip of rocks and train rails became a soft grassy lawn adorned by flowers, lined with colorful flags and our own rainbow flag. Our gay ghetto became "a watered garden."

Thank you, Sacred Gardener, for bringing us together, watering our lives, and making us blossom.

Each one heard them speaking in the native language of each.
                                                    Acts 2:6

Devout Jews gathered from all over the known world to observe the day of Pentecost, the day, fifty days after Passover, when the Law of Moses had been given. A wily Holy Spirit, whom Jesus had prophesied "blows where it chooses" (John 3:8, RSV), chose to descend on his followers on that day, filling them with the power to speak in other languages.

If you've traveled abroad, you know how good it can be to hear your own language. Entranced and curious, the foreign visitors gathered to hear in their own tongues of "God's deeds of power" in Jesus Christ.

Today, Christians speak with "in" language that may keep others out. We could use the Spirit's gift of speaking in others' languages to become inclusive. Lesbian and gay Christians could explain even common words like "grace" and "redemption" to bring the Word out to the gay community.

In the church, lesbian and gay Christians already have the gift of tongues. We speak a range of theological and liturgical languages in which to proclaim the worth, hopes, and needs of our community to our denominations.

Bless the words of our lips with a way to speak the meditations of our hearts to others, Holy Spirit.

*"Look, here is water! What is to prevent me from being bap-
tized?"*

Acts 8:36

Once, one might ask someone who formed an unusually
strong attachment, "You're queer for her/him/it, aren't
you?"

The Spirit led Philip to an Ethiopian eunuch, a Jewish
convert who had been to worship at Jerusalem and happened to be reading Isaiah. "Do you understand what you
are reading?" Philip inquired. "How can I, unless someone
guides me?" he replied. Philip helped him understand that
the text about Yahweh's chosen servant spoke of Jesus.

The eunuch, convinced, asked to be baptized. Philip
didn't hesitate——after all, the Spirit had led him there and afterward "snatched Philip away," leaving the eunuch to rejoice.

In the Judaism of that day, the eunuch would have been
at a disadvantage spiritually as much as sexually because
bodily mutilation was forbidden and procreation was expected. His black skin also may have put him at a disadvantage among fellow Jews.

Let's face it, the Spirit was queer for this guy. The eunuch did not fit the standard profile of "acceptability." Yet
the Spirit went out of her way to baptize him into the Christian community.

Thanks to the Spirit, she's queer for us, too.

*Thank you, Spirit! May we be just as passionate for you, lov-
ing God with all our hearts.*

Then Peter began to speak to them: "I truly understand that God shows no partiality, but in every nation anyone who fears [God] and does what is right is acceptable to [God]."

Acts 10:34–35

The Spirit gave Peter a vision and then an experience that made him question the early church's exclusion of Gentiles. To be baptized as Christian, Gentiles converted to Judaism first. Now, as Peter witnessed the Spirit baptize them before this conversion, he cried, "Can anyone withhold the water for baptizing these people who have received the Holy Spirit just as we have?" (10:47).

I believe that spiritual growth makes one's faith more expansive. Mahatma Gandhi, though Hindu, saw himself as Muslim and Christian, too. The Catholic mystic Thomas Merton prayed with Eastern monks. The Christian author Simone Weil resisted joining the church, fearing it would confine her spirituality. Etty Hillesum, whose diaries during the Holocaust reveal a deepening spirituality, is claimed in her native Holland by both Christians and Jews.

If spirituality is about what unites us, why do we let it divide us? If God shows no partiality with regard to our condition, perhaps God shows no partiality to the spiritual way that is chosen, as long as God is reverenced ("feared") and justice is done.

God of every faith and God of my faith in Jesus Christ: help me embrace those of other faiths without neglecting my own.

At the same time, we must recognize that the interpretation of scriptural prophecy is never a matter for the individual. For no prophecy ever came from human initiative. When people spoke for God it was the Holy Spirit that moved them.

2 Peter 1:20 (New Jerusalem Bible)

I believe in the Christian community's responsibility to interpret scripture. But *we who are lesbian and gay Christians also* are the church, and to neglect that responsibility is to give up our rights.

In Latin America, the *campesinos* and *campesinas* ("peasants") took their responsibility to heart and formed Christian base communities to reflect on the Bible. Out of this grew a vigorous resistance to injustice.

This collective expertise is what I pursue when leading workshops or retreats. The collective truth is greater than an individual, partial truth. These meditations themselves grow out of a gathering of experience.

The Bible is also a collective response to the Spirit's leading. Most passages grew out of a community of faith. The texts taken together represent a collective dialogue, which is why Reformed theology affirms that one scripture may be used to interpret or correct another.

With the broader biblical theme of justice, the Spirit has led us beyond biblical affirmations of slavery and the subjugation of women. Now she is leading the church beyond biblical negations of homosexuality.

As you moved women and men of ages past to proclaim your leading, move us, Holy Spirit.

Do not let anyone disqualify you, insisting on self-abasement.
                                                    Colossians 2:18

A friend in seminary had a copy of John McNeill's then newly published book, *The Church and the Homosexual*. She brought it to the dining hall and set it on a table while she selected her food. Out of fear, she placed it face-down. Then she thought, "Oh, what the heck," and placed it face-up.

When she returned to the table, someone asked her if McNeill was gay. She asked him why he wanted to know. "Because if he's gay, he's biased," came the response. What infuriated my friend was not simply the unfairness of the observation, but that it was offered so guilelessly. He had no idea that *heterosexuals* might be biased!

"Do not let anyone disqualify you, insisting on self-abasement," the church of Colossae is advised. Some of its members had gotten carried away, becoming painstakingly punctilious when it came to ritual and austerely ascetic when it came to spirituality. But what mattered was their faith in Christ.

Others may raise a fuss over the gender of our attraction, and question our "bias" when we say that doesn't negate our faith in Christ. But we are more qualified to speak of our experience, not them. We are the experts.

God, give me confidence to speak from my expertise and to challenge the bias of others.

Once you were not a people,
but now you are God's people;
once you had not received mercy,
but now you have received mercy.

1 Peter 2:10

1 Peter is addressed to "aliens and exiles." Christianity first appealed to the poor who had everything to gain by embracing a faith that promised a commonwealth to which they were heirs. The writer of 1 Peter subverts the implicit political message of such a belief by advising slaves of abusive masters and wives of unbelieving husbands to suffer as Christ in the hope of converting them.

Lesbian and gay Christians are more likely to respond to the concept that once we were not a people, but now we are God's people and enjoy God's mercy. Most of us are tired of suffering, no matter how redemptive. We want to celebrate.

Seeing the AIDS Quilt in Washington, D.C., I realized our community was not satisfied with hard, gray tombstones to commemorate our dead; we want soft, colorful quilt panels to celebrate our life. When we returned for the 1993 March on Washington, laments and anger did not typify our show of political strength; rather, smiles and solidarity revealed confidence.

Because now we are a people enjoying God's grace.

Dear God, nobody knows the glories we've seen! We are truly a gay gathering! Glory! Hallelujah!

For I will leave in the midst of you
a people humble and lowly.

Zephaniah 3:12

Our confidence as a community does not prevent us from being a "humble and lowly" remnant of the people of faith.

Howard Warren is director of pastoral care for an Indianapolis AIDS agency and founder of Presbyterian ACT UP. He is a dear, older, white-haired gentleman who is defiantly gay and HIV-positive. He interrupted a committee hearing at a national church assembly when a man claimed that homosexuals had spread AIDS to Africa. "That's a lie!" Howard shouted. The chair threatened to have him removed. "Are you going to continue to interrupt?" she asked. "If that man continues to lie, I will!" Howard declared. Thankfully for all of us concerned for Howard's safety, the man did not lie again.

Later, Howard himself testified about how insulting it was to have time limits placed on our input, when we had so little access to church process. When his time was up, the chair hesitantly interrupted him. Not hearing her, Howard continued, and she seemed fearful he might not relinquish the floor. She spoke again and he said, "Huh?" She said, "You're time is up." "Oh, okay," he said almost meekly, "thank you for your time."

I smiled. Though we are a proud and feisty people, we are at heart a people humble and gentle.

We celebrate our soul as a community, spirited and gentle.

When he saw the crowds, [Jesus] had compassion for them, because they were harassed and helpless, like sheep without a shepherd. Then he said to his disciples, "The harvest is plentiful, but the laborers are few; therefore ask the [Sovereign] of the harvest to send out laborers into [the] harvest."

Matthew 9:36–38

Many lesbian and gay people are close to the Spirit of Christ, yet their spiritual resources are largely untapped. Other lesbians and gay men are hungry for purpose and meaning and hope, yet lesbian and gay Christians are not actively sharing our faith.

When we open our community of faith, selfishness and selflessness coincide. Selfishness, because we want more people in our spiritual community, sharing their spiritual gifts. Selflessness, because we are willing to change to accommodate new people and share our spiritual resources.

As we realize the mutuality of conversion, witnessing our faith seems less paternalistic and more transforming for all. We recognize that as our spiritual community expands, so does our faith.

Give us faith that others would like to share faith—ours and theirs—in your community, God.

Now the whole group of those who believed were of one heart and soul.

Acts 4:32

Remember the "good ol' days" when the gay community was of one mind? No? Neither do I. But it *seemed* that way.

Every city had a mother or father of the local movement. Reverend Troy Perry began a church. Then came the Stonewall Rebellion. Political and religious networks and community centers and congregations formed; urban neighborhoods became more clearly defined as gay.

Of course, we left off half our experience by being the "gay" rather than the "gay and lesbian" community. Males were more available and easier to organize. Whites were, too. Drag queens were pushed aside with transexuals and socialists as undesirable representatives. We were going to mainstream ourselves. It *should've* been easier to be of one soul then.

The truth is, we were always a diverse and often divided community. But there have been moments when we were of one heart and soul. When Harvey Milk was assassinated, we mourned together. When we observe pride day, we celebrate together.

The early church nostalgically remembered a time when it, too, was of one heart and soul. It, like us, has been looking for the same kind of unity ever since.

Touch our brokenness as a community, Healing Spirit. Make us no less diverse, but less divisive and divided.

Awe came upon everyone, because many wonders and signs were being done by the apostles. All who believed were together and had all things in common.

Acts 2:43–44

What an exciting but fearful time for the church! It was a new community where miraculous things happened, while facing religious and political opposition. Sound familiar?

Sometimes we get overwhelmed by the resistance we face, from families of blood to families of faith, from the scourge of antigay rights legislation to the pandemic of AIDS.

But miracles are happening all around us.

After my participation on a panel at a community center, a young man introduced himself. "You don't remember me," he began, "but when I was fourteen my father brought me in to talk with you." I remembered that his foster father wanted his gay son to meet some responsible gay adults.

The young man continued, "You were the first gay man I ever met. You became a role model to me, and I have never forgotten you. You have no idea how important you are to me." Imagine my joy! It felt like I, too, had a son. I was in awe.

We do not always know the miracles we perform by being who we are: gay, lesbian, Christian. We are not always aware of all we hold in common as a community: especially our youth, who look for the way we build for them.

Open my eyes to the signs and wonders being done by our community. Increase my awe-bility to be amazed.

Each of you must give as you have made up your mind, not reluctantly or under compulsion, for God loves a cheerful giver.

2 Corinthians 9:6–7

In saying the Lord's Prayer (Matt. 6:9-13), I alternate between "debts" and "trespasses." As I pray, "Forgive us our debts as we forgive our debtors," I try to let go of feelings that people owe me something because of what I have done for them. After all, God overlooks all that *we* owe.

If we discover we are no longer cheerful givers in a relationship, whether with a lover, friend, church, or organization, it is time to re-evaluate. If we repeatedly feel that they are indebted to us, or we find ourselves giving compulsively rather than as a glad duty, then maybe we need to consider if we are codependent, that is, too willing to give up our needs to meet theirs.

Ram Dass and Paul Gorman's book, *How Can I Help?*, explains that helping must be recognized as mutually beneficial, else it begins as paternalism and ends in burnout. That doesn't mean there must be some big payoff; rather, to paraphrase Paul quoting Jesus, it is *at least* as blessed to give as to receive (Acts 20:35).

May my giving be a blessing both for me and for others.

How great a forest is set ablaze by a small fire! And the tongue is a fire.

James 3:5-6

Many years ago I met a leader of a national lesbian and gay religious organization for lunch. She greeted me with horrible news: the lover of a leader of a comparable group had died, and the gay press suspected foul play. The journalist who called her said rumor had it that one killed the other in a sado-masochistic sexual encounter, and that the gay press was ready to expose it all. Stunned, we pondered what effects it would have, both on the individual and on our movement.

None of the story was true, except the part of the lover dying. The two were not only in different cities, they were in different countries at the time! The country in question ruled out foul play.

"How great a forest is set ablaze by a small fire! And the tongue is a fire. . . . With it we bless [God], and with it we curse those who are made in the likeness of God" (3:5-6, 9).

We curse the image of God not only by our profanity, but by our put-downs, innuendos, and gossip.

Holy Word, may my tongue bless rather than curse, spread the gospel rather than gossip.

Have nothing to do with stupid and senseless controversies.

2 Timothy 2:23

The initial spirit of expectancy that permeated the early church began to wane. The fulfillment of time signified by Jesus' anticipated return no longer seemed imminent. Churches turned to practical community concerns in later epistles, in this case, the problem of pointless controversies.

A contemporary version of this advice from an experienced missionary——possibly Paul——to young Timothy is: choose your battles. In any struggle, strategy counts as much as passion. The members of a national church task force on homosexuality, which I served on, had strong disagreements in hammering out a study and position paper. We indicated minor disagreements by saying, "I wouldn't die for it."

We need that kind of flexibility because not everything is worth dying for or even raising a fuss over. Many of us have an extra need to be in control because we feel so much of what happens to us is out of our control. Sometimes we need to remind ourselves to "chill out" and trust God's cosmic process.

So many things are important to me, God. Help me to discern which things are vital.

Do not give heed to everything that people say, or you may hear your servant cursing you; your heart knows that many times you have yourself cursed others.

Ecclesiastes 7:21

Ecclesiastes means "leader of an assembly." Thus this proverb arises from practical congregational experience.

In the mostly gay congregation I served, I unknowingly worked with a volunteer who was a very subtle drama queen. He would tell me something that someone had said behind my back——always portrayed negatively——and then report my response——also skewed negatively——to the person in question. I only learned this when I compared notes with a member with whom I had experienced unexplainable tensions.

We sometimes care too much about what other people think or say about us, and so we can be manipulated. This proverb offers perspective by reminding us that we also say things in the heat of the moment not intended for another's hearing.

The title of a book written by a female therapist has ministered to me, though I never read the book. *It's None of My Business What You Think of Me* has become a mantra when I worry about what someone thinks of me.

We are a sensitive people and would do well to take this proverb from Ecclesiastes to heart.

Help me listen for your blessing, O God, rather than another's curse.

You prepare a table before me
in the presence of my enemies;
you anoint my head with oil,
my cup overflows.

Psalm 23:5

The community to which God invites us includes enemies.
Those who oppose us want our groups out of the church.
We do not respond in kind, except to say their inclusion
should not be at the expense of our welcome. This is true
in the broader lesbian and gay community as well. Though
we want discrimination prohibited, we do not seek "special
rights" over others. In seeking justice, we show mercy.

Sometimes our "enemies" are members of our own family. The BBC televised a mini-series entitled *Oranges Are
Not the Only Fruit,* based on the novel. It's the coming-of-
age story of a young lesbian reared in a restrictive religious
environment. Though emotionally bruised by their rigidity
and an attempted "exorcism," she began to forgive them on
a return visit, graciously accepting their hesitant hospitality.
In finding a place in our families, many of us show similar
mercy.

You prepare a table for us in the presence of our opposition.
As you anoint us, may our cup overflow with your mercy.

A soft answer turns away wrath,
but a harsh word stirs up anger.

                    Proverbs 15:1

During a question-and-answer period of a church conference on homosexuality, I pointed out to a woman quoting
Paul against us that, ironically, the apostle would not have
allowed her to speak in church. Evaluating my presentation
in light of this one exchange, a minister told a friend that I
was going to have to lose my "bitter streak"!

At a national church assembly, a group of lesbians and
gay men were allotted a total of twelve minutes to offer a
one-sentence self-description followed by the refrain, "I
offer my gifts to the church." We were warmly received
with a standing ovation.

Later, after another negative vote on our issue, some of
the same group of lesbians and gay men staged an unwelcome, angry demonstration. Few felt good about it, including the protestors. The anger seemed to make everyone's
shame kick in, causing a backlash.

Clearly our gifts were more welcome than our anger.

We have a right to our anger. How to express it is the
strategic question.

Accept our anger as an offering of our passion for justice.
Guide us in directing and shaping our anger justly.

A cheerful heart is a good medicine,
but a downcast spirit dries up the bones.

Proverbs 17:22

The film *Sullivan's Travels* tells the saga of a movie director who wants to depict the pathos and suffering of life in a film. To prepare, he sets out to bum around the country as a homeless man, but ends up in a prison chain gang. The one relief for the prisoners is being invited to watch cartoons with a poor, African-American church, and he finds himself laughing at Mickey Mouse despite his sorrows. Laughter heals.

We value laughter in our community. It has been an antidote to pain, a means of gaining acceptance, a method of keeping perspective, a way of keeping healthy. We know that a gay party is likely to be just that——gay. We know laughter's therapeutic value: a friend with AIDS regularly watches cartoons to keep his immune system strong; a friend with breast cancer kept up the spirits of her caregivers by telling them jokes.

A scene in *Mary Poppins* demonstrates the lift that laughter brings our souls. The nanny takes the children to see a character, played by Ed Wynn, whose laughter makes him float.

Years later, on my way out of a mausoleum, I noticed where Ed Wynn's ashes were interred. His marker read, "Dear God, Thanks!" and it was signed Ed Wynn. In three words he caught the meaning of it all, and in a place of death, lifted my soul and put a smile on my face.

Dear God, thanks for cheerful hearts and happy laughter!

*"Those who withhold kindness from a friend
forsake the fear of the Almighty. . . .
In time of heat [my companions] disappear. . . .
You see my calamity, and are afraid."*

                                   Job 6:14, 17, 21

Being in community means being there in sickness as well as
health. With AIDS, the gay and lesbian community can truly
say, "Been there! Done that!" And we're still *doing that,* not
just for gay men, but for the whole AIDS community.

It's easier to deal with AIDS "out there" than "in here":
in my family, in my friends, in my lover, in my self. The
closer it gets, the more frightening.

Many of us have been deserted like Job. Those who
grieve are not easy to be with. Those who are sick remind
us of our own vulnerability. Those who may die remind us
of our loss. No wonder Job's friends abandoned him. It was
easier.

A former church member confided to a friend, "I used to
like going to church, but every week somebody else was
sick or in the hospital. It got to be too depressing."

Well, excu-u-use *me!* Who said life would be easy? Life is
not easy, life is community. Who's *he* going to count on? To
"withhold kindness from a friend" is to forsake an awesome
reflection of God. For Mother Teresa, holding a leper is
holding "Christ in a distressing disguise."

*Inspire us never to forsake your presence in the human soul,
All-Loving God.*

And whenever the evil spirit from God came upon Saul, David took the lyre and played it with his hand, and Saul would be relieved and feel better, and the evil spirit would depart from him.

1 Samuel 16:23

I've always felt compassion for Saul. Scripture says that the spirit of God was taken from him, and he was given an evil spirit. What if that ever happened to me? What if God withdrew the Spirit from me because I had failed as Saul to be the kind of leader God wants?

In some of the later passages about David and Jonathan, it seems almost as if Saul behaves like a jealous and jilted lover toward David. And certainly Saul is jealous of God's spirit now resting on David, and he feels bereft of the solace that David's music provided when the evil spirit came upon him. What was the "evil" spirit? Clinical depression? Mental illness? Disease? Complications of old age? Senility? Or was it unrequited love?

Our community has many people like Saul who suffer for such reasons. We cannot abandon them. As David did with music, we may find ways to alleviate their loneliness and anguish. If I became like Saul, I would want a ruddy, handsome young man like David to play his lyre for me.

Bless all who suffer anguish with those who offer solace, God of Saul and David.

There are both heavenly bodies and earthly bodies, but the glory of the heavenly is one thing, and that of the earthly is another. There is one glory of the sun, and another glory of the moon, and another glory of the stars; indeed, star differs from star in glory. So it is with the resurrection of the dead. What is sown is perishable, what is raised is imperishable. It is sown in dishonor, it is raised in glory. It is sown in weakness, it is raised in power.

1 Corinthians 15:40–43

Part of our community is no longer visible. They have crossed the threshold of death. This poetic passage describes an early Christian view of what that meant. Like a planted seed, the mortal, diseased, and weakened earthly body gives way to a blossoming heavenly body.

Paul was writing to those who could accept the ongoing life of the spirit, but stumbled on the resurrection of the body. Like Hebrews, Christians saw that the body was good. This influenced their belief that the ongoing soul had a body, though with a different kind of glory, as "star differs from star in glory."

So our fallen stars have simply gone beneath the horizon of our experience, where they behold the full glory of God.

Thank you, God, for eternally loving us, body and soul, in this glory and the glory to come.

LIBERATION

●
●
●
●

Afterward Moses and Aaron went to Pharaoh and said, "Thus says the . . . God of Israel, 'Let my people go, so that they may celebrate a festival to me in the wilderness.'"

Exodus 5:1

The emphasis in this verse has usually been on "Let my people go." The people suffered while enslaved in Egypt; God heard them and now intervenes to deliver them. Their salvation (another word for deliverance) becomes a central metaphor of the Bible. Later, Christians would experience themselves liberated from the bondage of the Law and of sin.

Lesbians and gay men may readily identify with such liberation. We have suffered the closet's confinement and prejudice, discrimination and abuse. Our pharaohs have ranged from the pope to the Joint Chiefs of Staff, from parents to ministers of our local congregations. And we seek deliverance from legalism and the label of "sin" for our love.

In the era of Vietnam War protestors, a church woman asked, "Why do they always have to be *against* something? Why can't they be *for* something?" A woman, who would come out a decade later, answered, "They're marching *for* peace."

What are *we* marching for? "Let my people go, so that they may celebrate a festival to me in the wilderness." We want the freedom to worship God in spirit and in truth.

Free us, God of Deliverance, that we might serve you!

Be gracious to me, O [Yahweh], for I am languishing;
O [God], heal me, for my bones are shaking with terror.
My soul also is struck with terror,
while you, O [Yahweh]—how long?

Psalm 6:2–3

A lesbian raped by her former boyfriend. A gay teenager thrown out of his family home. A gay man on the way to his car surrounded by bashers. A lesbian outed at work. A gay man learning his T-cell count has dropped. A lesbian diagnosed as having breast cancer. A fundamentalist Christian lesbian "damned" by scripture.

We downplay the many ways we are "languishing" while we wait for Yahweh's deliverance. How long, O God, before ignorance abates? How long, O God, before violence against us ends? How long, O God, before we're safe in our jobs? How long, O God, before there's an AIDS cure? How long, O God, before there's a cure for cancer? How long, O God, before the Bible is used to comfort rather than terrify?

"Turn, O God, save my life," the Psalmist continues. Literally, it reads "save my breath," referring to the breath of soul which Yahweh breathed into the first human creature.

Turn, O Yahweh, save our lives! Deliver us for the sake of your steadfast love! Only alive can we worship and serve you!

*The fear of others lays a snare,
but one who trusts in [God] is secure.*

Proverbs 29:25

There are many things I fear, but being "outed" is not one of
them. It's been so long since I came out, I forget the paralyzing
fear I felt lest someone find out or suspect.

At a workshop for lesbian and gay Christians, I acciden-
tally outed a participant to the full group. I didn't give her
name, nor her sexual identity. But I identified her work and
her employer in an attempt to be affirming, without thinking of the consequences of such a disclosure in that context. The look on her face made me realize my terrible
mistake. I forget how terrifying such revelation is.

Many years after the fact, an old friend in the church
asked me if I had told a minister that she was lesbian. I said
no; she said the minister indicated he had learned it from
me. Then I remembered that he had asked me if she was,
and I had told him that was the sort of question he should
ask her. Unintentionally, I had revealed the truth. (I subsequently learned how to lie justly in the face of such intru-
sive questions.) For years, this woman had carried rage at
me inside her born of her fear of exposure.

Lesbians feel especially vulnerable in a male-dominated
world. We all are afraid, and need the security of a God we
can trust.

*In my fear of others, help me rely on you, Steadfast Friend.
You will never put me to shame.*

How long, O [God]? Will you forget me forever?
How long will you hide your face from me?
But I trusted in your steadfast love;
my heart shall rejoice in your salvation.

                                              Psalm 13:1, 5

I have been told that babies sometimes cry when their parents leave them because, in an infant's limited perception, the parent's absence means their death.

I believe that we sometimes cry because, in our limited perception, God's absence means God is dead or doesn't exist.

In someone's absence, we have relied on certain "icons" of their presence. Photographs. A book that was a gift. A stuffed animal we nicknamed together. A shirt with the loved one's scent. A baseball glove. Our song. A place we liked to walk. A favorite deli. Stories of things that happened to us.

In God's absence, we may rely on the "icon" of God's presence in the Bible. In the tradition of the Eastern Orthodox churches, icons are images that serve as conduits of divine mystery and presence. Just as we have a kind of icon in a memento that reminds us of an absent loved one, so scripture may be a verbal icon that helps us know God's presence even when God seems absent.

Trusting God's steadfast love revealed in past events, the Psalmist was able to rejoice in a salvation yet to come.

I trust in your steadfast love, O God. My heart shall rejoice in your salvation.

*Then [Yahweh] said, "I have observed the misery of my people
who are in Egypt; I have heard their cry. . . . I know their sufferings, and I have come down to deliver them. . . . So come, I
will send you."*

Exodus 3:7–8, 10

The chief complaint against professionals in medicine, ministry, therapy, social work, and politics is an emotional distance, an aloofness, that makes patients, parishioners, clients,
or constituents feel as if they and their suffering are not being
heard. "Hello! Is anybody *in there?*" we cry.

Somewhere within these professionals is the compassion that led them to choose their vocations. But to keep
sane and avoid burnout, they have erected a wall to defend
against too much emotional pain.

But God can take our pain. God has the capacity to feel
everything as *we* feel it. That's why God would rather we
feel pleasure than pain, joy than sorrow. Yet God does not
abandon us no matter how we feel. Such compassionate
identification is the first act of liberation.

Moses was called to share in Yahweh's liberation, but
that also meant sharing divine compassion, suffering with
the oppressed. Those of us who have been desensitized by
suffering might rediscover our compassion in the sanctuary
of prayer.

*Open our hearts to the cries of others as your heart is open
to our cries, Sovereign God.*

Then Job answered:
"How you have helped one who has no power!
How you have assisted the arm that has no strength!
How you have counseled one who has no wisdom,
and given much good advice!"

Job 26:1–3

This is Job's sarcastic reply to Bildad the Shuhite, assigned by seminary humor to be the Bible's shortest person.

Bildad was offended that Job asserted his goodness in the midst of suffering that *surely* was the product of his sin. "How can a mortal be righteous before God?" Bildad pontificated earlier, comparing human existence to that of a "maggot" and "worm."

His speech sounds like the doctrine of original sin, the belief that Adam's sin meant we were all, as the rock song goes, "born to be wild." Our opponents sometimes echo Bildad, claiming that homosexuality is a product of the Fall, the first human sin that was believed to predispose us to sin.

The powerless in the church need empowerment, but instead are given bad advice by Christians who *just don't get it*. With Job, in the midst of our suffering, we affirm our integrity as gay and lesbian Christians.

Defying injustice, give me Job's confidence and impatience.

[God] said to Moses, "See, I have made you like God to Pharaoh."

Exodus 7:1

Many of those who became liberators in the gay and lesbian community "happened" to be in the right place at the right time. They weren't always sure they were the best choices, and our community was difficult to manage. As they pushed for acceptance in the church and in society, they met resistance, which made life harder on us all.

Moses did not feel up to the task of liberator. He had escaped to the wilderness because he had murdered an Egyptian beating a fellow Hebrew. He had no official authority and was a poor speaker. The Israelites were difficult to manage. Pharaoh proved resistant, and made life harder for the Hebrews. They complained, and Moses expressed doubts to God.

But God empowered him, making him "like God" to the powerful, intimidating authority of Pharaoh. A divinely inspired passion for justice empowers. Spiritual passion confronted political power.

A few folk balked when I used this scripture in a workshop exercise, resisting the pitting of power against power. But a churchman who worked in the field of corporate responsibility offered me an insight long ago. "I used to think our call was to give up power, like Christ," he said. "Now I believe that the modern Christian is called to sacrifice in quite another way: to use power responsibly to do justice."

God, in your passion for our liberation, make us powerful!

But I have understanding as well as you;
I am not inferior to you.

Job 12:3

Zophar takes a shot at Job's suffering, blaming Job's supposed stupidity. In his view, "secrets of wisdom" reveal how out-of-step Job is with God. But Job affirms his own understanding in this verse, a step toward liberation.

Our opponents may sport a knowing look as if they have some secret wisdom about us. Their pseudo-biblical, pseudo-intellectual wisdom is a dressed-up blend of ignorance and prejudice. It's liberating to affirm our own understanding.

John Wesley, the founder of Methodism, believed the conscientious Christian consulted four sources in making a decision: scripture, tradition, reason, and experience. Science is a blend of reason and experience.

Both experience and its product, science—even *biblical* science—are distrusted by many Christians. They fear that the Bible would come out the loser in any dialogue. But experience is what makes the Bible a classic: the recorded experiences of people of faith parallel ours today. And science and scripture answer different questions: how and why. Science explores process; the Bible explores meaning.

Science is confirming our understanding of how we came to be lesbians and gay men; our faith reveals why we are here.

Send your wisdom to us, O God, that we may know truth.

"If you continue in my word, you are truly my disciples; and you will know the truth, and the truth will make you free."

John 8:31

The Pharisees of Jesus' day, like the self-righteous Pharisees of our time, were very evangelical. That means they enthusiastically sought converts to Judaism, just as modern-day evangelical Christians zealously pursue converts today.

But Jesus was critical of those who believed they could be saved by following the Law of Moses. He accused the Pharisees of making "the new convert twice the child of hell as [them]selves" (Matt. 23:15) by placing the burden of the law upon them. We've seen lesbian sisters and gay brothers similarly burdened by well-meaning evangelical Christians who were antigay.

In today's scripture from John, Jesus addressed the legalistic evangelicals of his day. The fully redemptive truth was God's gracious love. That's why those who follow Jesus will enjoy a light burden, as Jesus invited: "Come to me, all you that are weary and are carrying heavy burdens, and I will give you rest. Take my yoke upon you, and learn from me; for I am gentle and humble in heart, and you will find rest for your souls. For my yoke is easy, and my burden is light" (Matt. 11:28–30).

Take from me my burden, Jesus, and give me rest.

Whenever Moses held up his hand, Israel prevailed; and whenever he lowered his hand, Amalek prevailed. But Moses' hands grew weary; so . . . Aaron and Hur held up his hands.

Exodus 17:11, 12

When I was leading a retreat for gay and lesbian Christians, a man gave me his business card. On the back of it was a rubber-stamped image of geese flying in formation, and I asked what it signified. He explained that his corporate division had elected this symbol of their work together.

Then he explained how geese work together. They fly in a V-shaped formation, aerodynamically cutting wind resistance. The others honk to encourage the leader. They take turns being the leader to share the effort. If one gets sick, two fly low with it until they are able to rejoin the flock. If two flocks meet, they merge into a larger V rather than compete.

I wondered why we don't work together as well. At the Iona monastery off the coast of Scotland, I learned that an ancient Celtic symbol of the Holy Spirit is the wild goose. It is that Spirit that helps us work together in this way.

In battle, when Moses lifted his hand, Israel began to win. When he rested his arms, Amalek looked victorious. When Aaron and Hur and Moses worked together, lifting their hands in blessing, they worked with those in the struggle for victory.

Liberation requires we do no less.

I lift hands of blessing on all who work for our liberation!

[God] said to Gideon, "The troops with you are too many for me to give the Midianites into their hand. Israel would only take the credit away from me saying, 'My own hand has delivered me.'"

Judges 7:2

Yahweh did not want the children of Israel to get haughty, for their deliverance was to be of God. So God tells Gideon to send home the fearful, and later, those who drank from a stream by cupping the water. The troops were cut from thirty thousand to three hundred, and yet God gave them victory.

Our troops in the gay and lesbian community have been cut, not by God, but by a variety of circumstances. Closets have kept our visible community smaller than we are. Those rendered additionally vulnerable because of their gender or color may be less able to help publicly. AIDS has taken an enormous toll among gay men, reducing the number of activists and diverting our attention to the pandemic. But all of these circumstances have only slowed, not stopped, our quest for rights.

Our troops have also been cut by recent surveys that question previous estimates of our population. Though the scientific method of these recent counts may be questioned, it doesn't matter whether our number is 10 percent or 2 percent of the population. Injustice against any is injustice against all. And the God of justice will liberate us, no matter how few or how many.

Keep us from being discouraged, O God of the remnant. We trust the deliverance that you have promised.

"Do not think that in the king's palace you will escape any more than all the other Jews. . . . Who knows? Perhaps you have come to royal dignity for just such a time as this."

Esther 4:13–14

Esther advanced in the court of King Ahasuerus without his knowing she was Jewish. She became queen. The evil prince Haman urged the king to destroy all Jews in the land. Mordecai got wind of Haman's plan, and here challenges Esther, his adopted daughter, to intervene with the king. Esther knew to do so risked both her station and her life.

We all know gays and lesbians——maybe ourselves—— in similar positions of power, prestige, and influence. From the Vatican to the *700 Club,* from the White House to city council, from corporate headquarters to the officers club, there are those who could intervene for us by coming out.

Mordecai does not threaten to "out" Esther, for he knows the workings of God's liberation and resists the temptation to play God. But he does challenge her and, through this scripture, all of us, to consider God's purpose in entrusting us with whatever positions of influence we have, whether it's as a bishop to a pope, or as a child to a parent.

God, you know I have been born for such a time as this. Help me make a difference in my corner of your commonwealth.

*When you have eaten your fill and have built fine houses and
live in them, and when . . . all that you have is multiplied, then
do not exalt yourself, forgetting . . . your God, who brought
you out of the land of Egypt, out of the house of slavery.*

Deuteronomy 8:12–14

There are many more cautions about wealth in the Bible than
about homosexuality. This text expresses fear that personal
success in the Promised Land will make people forget God's
salvation. They might think they no longer need God.

Four gay men who had fine homes in the exclusive hills
around Hollywood would readily testify of a need for God.

One became addicted to crack cocaine, lost everything,
but rediscovered his Higher Power in a Twelve-Step program.
Another had a lover who took his business and his house before God helped him recognize the codependent nature of
their relationship. A third also had a Malibu home and was
often on the *New York Times* bestseller list, but all this did
not offer the meaning that spirituality could, especially in facing his death. The fourth, feeling trapped in his home, sold it
and moved to a center for New Age spirituality.

Sometimes deliverance from the closet only leads to bigger closets from which we need another deliverance.

*Deliver me from spiritual amnesia when I am blessed, O
God.*

"It is easier for a camel to go through the eye of a needle than for someone who is rich to enter the kingdom of God."

Mark 10:25

The "eye of a needle" was the nickname of a gate in the city wall of Jerusalem that was so small, a camel had to be unloaded before it could pass through. The thinking in Jesus' day (and in our day) was that wealth could liberate one to do one's duty to God, but Jesus was not so naive. He knew that wealth too easily served our baser nature.

Money is not the only wealth that restricts our access to liberation. There is a story about a professor who wanted to study with a Zen master. The mystic invited him to tea, and after filling his cup, continued to pour. "Stop!" the professor cried, "No more will go in!" "Like this cup," the master replied, "you are filled with your own ideas and speculations. First empty your cup to learn about Zen."

Jesus told a wealthy man, "You lack one thing; go, sell what you own, and give the money to the poor, and you will have treasure in heaven; then come, follow me" (Mark 10:21). The verse says Jesus "loved him," but the man left sorrowful.

We have a lot of religious baggage. We carry much sexual freight. We are filled with presuppositions of spirituality. Jesus invites us to unload and empty ourselves to follow.

Free me to follow you, Jesus. Together, may all who are "wealthy" follow you to freedom.

Surely oppression makes the wise foolish,
and a bribe corrupts the heart.

Ecclesiastes 7:7

At the gay beach in Santa Monica one summer it was in vogue for men to take off their swim suits in the ocean and wear them around their necks while they swam. Assuming it legal, I enjoyed its sensual freedom. But when I came out of the water dressed, I was arrested by Los Angeles vice cops.

That morning I'd been appointed to a national church task force on homosexuality. Noticing my address, Yale Divinity School, the police took the opportunity to harass a gay seminarian. And though I was arrested in good company——with a writer for the *Opera News*——I felt devastated by the humiliation of it all.

Booked and fingerprinted, wearing only my swim suit, I read my Bible as I awaited my father to bail me out. Paul's letters from prison didn't make me feel any better.

The other man was in the city on business and knew no one, so he asked if I could help him. All I wanted was to save myself. I was stunned by my lack of compassion. I was embarrassed enough without having my father associate me with this *très* gay man. Reluctantly, I agreed.

My foolishness was not baring my skin, but seeking only to save my skin. The bribe was survival, which corrupted my compassion.

Deliver us from stepping on others as we run for freedom.

Does it seem good to you to oppress,
to despise the work of your hands
and favor the schemes of the wicked?

Job 10:3

Sometimes it seems like God is the oppressor. With every victory given our opponents and with every needless death, it feels like godlike powers are arrayed against us.

The *Star Wars* trilogy recognized that there is a "dark side" to "The Force," from which people can suck spiritual power to achieve evil ends. There is implicit racism in calling this the "dark" side, but the metaphor helps us understand the spiritual power of evil.

What we experience as God's abuse, or Satan's abuse, are human beings and human institutions who exploit spiritual power to selfish rather than selfless ends. The Bible tells the story of the spiritual struggle between God and these "demonic" forces.

Jesus represents God to us as a force so compassionate that it is willing to die for us on a cross. For the sake of redemption this force is willing to suffer evil so as to persuade rather than coerce us to be reconciled to God, to inspire rather than control our doing good.

God, grant us grace to confront those who exploit your power.

For our struggle is not against enemies of blood and flesh, but against the rulers, against the authorities, against the cosmic powers of this present darkness, against the spiritual forces of evil in the heavenly places.

Ephesians 6:12

When I served as a news reporter and then editor of a gay news magazine, I thought I was neglecting my "spiritual work" to do so. I had no idea the amount of spiritual warfare I would continue to witness in my new "secular" vocation. The vast majority of those who oppose us claim to do so in the name of God.

I interviewed the founder of Colorado for Family Values, which initiated that state's antigay amendment in 1992. He didn't know I wrote for a gay and lesbian audience. At one point, I played dumb and explained I wanted a fuller understanding of his group. "Outside your antihomosexual stance," I asked, "what family values do you promote?" His response was both naive and revealing: "Oh——none. This is our only issue."

"The spiritual forces of evil in heavenly places" could certainly describe the agendas of most groups like his, that purport to be promoting good when indeed they only bolster bigotry.

Deliver our world from wolves in sheep's clothing, who prey on rather than pray for the oppressed.

*Then Esther said in reply to Mordecai, "Go, gather all the Jews
to be found in Susu, and hold a fast on my behalf, and neither eat nor drink for three days, night or day. I and my maids
will also fast as you do. After that I will go to the king, though
it is against the law; and if I perish, I perish."*

Esther 4:15–17

A magazine survey reported that what men most fear in relat-
ing to women is being laughed at; what women most fear in re-
lating to men is being killed! As a woman, Esther shared that
vulnerability, even as a queen.

Queen Esther had two other reasons for her fear of inter-
vening with King Ahasuerus to save the Jewish people from
his edict of destruction. First, he didn't know that she was
Jewish. Second, the king's law forbade any visit without invitation. Unless the king extended his "royal scepter" in a
demonstration of welcome, it meant death.

Esther knew that, at heart, this was a spiritual struggle.
So she fasted and asked all of her people to fast, a spiritual
discipline that would have been accompanied by prayer.
She was then welcomed by the king and ultimately saved
her people.

At heart, we know that ours is a spiritual struggle, too.
Spiritual disciplines and the prayers of our community
strengthen us in our resolve to deliver our people.

Grant us courage to face the authorities of our day, O God.

Saul clothed David with his armor. . . . Then David said to Saul, "I cannot walk with these; for I am not used to them."

1 Samuel 17:38–39

The armor of an earlier generation may restrict the movements of a younger generation.

One of the first things I learned in ministry within our community is generational differences. Back then I was perceived as the young, militant, naive, idealistic, gay activist who was pushing too hard and too fast. In turn, I could not know the paralyzing fear of so many older men and women, the seductive privacy of the closet, their willingness to settle for so little, their seemingly counterrevolutionary patience.

Now I view some of the younger generation in the same way I was viewed, from the self-righteous arrogance of Queer Nation to the strident clamor of ACT UP. Yet I also look upon——and yes, even participate in——some of their "actions" with a private glee that someone is expressing my rage.

Young David couldn't move in King Saul's heavy and awkward armor. Without it, he defeated Goliath.

Liberation movements are led by succeeding generations. Old armor is not just outdated, it inhibits movement.

Give us grace to listen and follow as well as guide and lead.

Therefore take up the whole armor of God. . . . Fasten the belt of truth around your waist, and put on the breastplate of righteousness. As shoes for your feet put on whatever will make you ready to proclaim the gospel of peace. With all of these, take the shield of faith, with which you will be able to quench all the flaming arrows of the evil one. Take the helmet of salvation, and the sword of the Spirit, which is the word of God.

Ephesians 6:13–17

It may not be politically correct to use militaristic language to describe spiritual realities. But the intent of Paul's advice to the Ephesians was subversive: using the all too familiar images of war to speak of peace. Pieces of armor with names like "truth," "gospel of peace," and "word of God" are peaceful instruments of change. But zealots and crusaders and fanatics throughout the ages subverted this message of peace to that of war.

It may not be "P.C." to describe our efforts as lesbians and gay men as a war. But calling a war by any other name, as the United States attempted in Korea and again in Vietnam, does a disservice to its troops and veterans. We have been and are being wounded spiritually, emotionally, physically. The devastation of this war must be acknowledged. Some of us are walking wounded in need of tender, loving care.

Spiritual armor built for peacemaking rather than warmaking is our best defense in the ongoing struggle.

In the spiritual struggle, O God, grant us peace.

I mean, brothers and sisters, the appointed time has grown short; from now on, let . . . those who mourn [be] as though they were not mourning, and those who rejoice as though they were not rejoicing, and those who buy as though they had no possessions, and those who deal with the world as though they had no dealings with it. For the present form of this world is passing away.

1 Corinthians 7:29–31

Liberation changes the very form of this world! Whether deliverance from oppression, salvation from sin, or freedom from legalism, liberation transforms our experience of God's realm. Paul believed that Christians should therefore live *as though* the commonwealth of God was breaking into our world.

Coming up to the dance tent of a gay pride festival, I noticed the participants had stopped to cheer on two dancers. One was a very tall, black gay man. The other was a very short white boy, whom I knew to be ten, straight, but gay-friendly. The smiles, nods, and applause of the others signaled delight at their dance together. I spoke to the boy's father, a church member: "Looks like your son has captured your fantasy, to have every gay man's eyes on you!" He laughed and agreed.

For a few moments, in the dance, they lived the commonwealth of God. Color didn't matter, nor gender, nor age, nor height, nor sexual orientation. The present racism, sexism, ageism, sizeism, heterosexism had passed away.

Keep that commonwealth coming, God! Make us ready!

For this reason I remind you to rekindle the gift of God that is within you through the laying on of my hands; for God did not give us a spirit of cowardice, but rather a spirit of power and of love and of self-discipline.

2 Timothy 1:8

The "gift of God" did not come to Timothy only through the gift of the Spirit through the laying on of Paul's hands. It came as a "sincere faith, a faith that lived first in [his] grandmother Lois and [his] mother Eunice and now . . . lives" in Timothy (1:5).

Though it would have been far better if women and men had shared equally in writing scripture and handing down tradition, it is also true that women informed, influenced, and inspired the Christian faith we have today. Women were among Jesus' disciples. The church throughout history, while admittedly viewing women as subordinates, gave women places of influence the surrounding cultures often did not.

This is also true of lesbian women and gay men. While the church's tolerance varied, we found roles to play in religious orders, in teaching, and in leadership. Undoubtedly we played a role in the very formation of scripture. Invisible roles do not mean we were not involved. We inherit our spirit of courage, power, love, and self-discipline in part from these silent partners of our tradition.

For our invisible ancestors of faith, we give you thanks!

And [Jesus] answered them, "Go and tell John what you have seen and heard: the blind receive their sight, the lame walk, the lepers are cleansed, the deaf hear, the dead are raised, the poor have good news brought to them. And blessed is anyone who takes no offense at me."

Luke 7:22–23

Go and tell anyone who has any doubt that our spiritual power comes from God: those who thought they'd never have a lover, now do; those who never understood homosexuality, now do; those for whom life seemed an out-of-body experience are now embodied; those considered unclean are now welcome; those who never heard the gospel, now have; those buried in closets are now raised; those with poor self-esteem have self-worth. And blessed is anyone who takes no offense at us.

John the Baptist sent his disciples to——in a sense—— examine Jesus for ordination. "Are you the one who is to come, or are we to wait for another?" they asked (7:20). Jesus had had a rough day, the text says, curing people "of diseases, plagues, and evil spirits" and giving sight to the blind (7:21). Instead of saying "Read my lips!" he said, "Read my works!"

Those who read *our* works and take no offense at us will be blessed by our presence and our ministry.

Holy Liberator, thank you for our gift of healing, the personal experience of liberation.

"Mortal, can these bones live?"
> Ezekiel 37:3

A gay staff member in the church put up a sign on the bulletin board that read, "Anyone who doesn't believe in the resurrection of the dead should be here at quitting time." It's true, we often do come alive when we leave the weariness of our work behind.

My brother couldn't believe it when I chose church work as a profession. "I couldn't think of anything more *boring* to do!" he said, thinking of all the dreary worship services he'd endured. It's true, Sunday brunch is the carrot at the end of the stick for many worshipers.

Ezekiel dealt with the weary/dreary question. In a vision, God took the prophet to a valley of dry bones and asked, "Mortal, can these bones live?" Then God told him to prophesy to the bones, saying they will live, that God will bring them out of their graves. "I will put my spirit within you, and you shall live," God said (37:14).

The closet was and is a living death. Those who have been raised from it know new life is possible. That should inspire us to come out again: out of old patterns that make work or worship boring.

You have put your Spirit within me, Holy One. Inspire me to live!

*This day shall be a day of remembrance for you. You shall cel-
ebrate it as a festival to [God], throughout your generations
you shall observe it as a perpetual ordinance.*

Exodus 11:14

As the Jews celebrate Passover in remembrance of their deliverance from Egypt, so we celebrate gay and lesbian pride
month, week, and day, as a remembrance of our deliverance
from spiritual and societal bondage.

A straight minister invited to deliver the sermon at a gay
pride worship service approached me for advice. "I've always been taught that pride was a sin," he said, perplexed.

I explained that I believe shame, not pride, is more of an
issue for people today. False pride, or *hubris*, may itself be
an expression of deeply felt shame, the need to puff oneself
up because of low self-esteem. Current theories link shame
to many of our personal and social ills. Then I told him that
one cannot apply a concept of the sin of pride to a marginalized people like us who have always been taught that we
should be ashamed of ourselves.

Isak Dinesen wrote in her book *Out of Africa,* "Pride is
faith in the idea that God had when [God] made us." Lesbian and gay pride simply expresses "faith in the idea that
God had when God made us."

*We celebrate our faith in your idea in making us, Creator
God. We pray others will share our faith and our pride.*

Then the prophet Miriam, Aaron's sister, took a tambourine in her hand; and all the women went out after her with tambourines and with dancing. And Miriam sang to them:
*　"Sing to the [Sovereign], for God has triumphed gloriously."*

Exodus 15:20–21

When the narrator of *Zorba the Greek* asked Zorba to teach him to dance, it was an incarnation, or embodiment, of the protagonist's new freedom. Having lost a financial investment, he was free to leave. Having lost his spiritual investment in the book he was writing on the Buddha, he was free to embrace a more embodied spirituality.

Miriam led the women in a dance inspired by their deliverance from oppression and slavery in Egypt. They had just crossed the Red Sea on dry land and watched the waters come down on Pharaoh's armies, who had been giving chase. Now they were free and on their way to the Promised Land.

Jesus knew the dance of freedom, too. The Christian Acts of John, not included in the Bible, recorded Jesus issuing an invitation to his disciples after their last supper together: "Let us dance." The disciples dance in a circle around Jesus while singing a joyous song responsively. "Glory be to thee, Word!" Jesus sang, and the disciples sang "Amen." The Bible only records them staidly singing a hymn! (Joseph Campbell, *The Power of Myth*.)

Dancing God, teach us to follow Miriam in the dance! Teach us to dance our liberation in our laughing, loving, living, singing, and serving!

Weeping may linger for the night,
but joy comes with the morning.
You have turned my mourning into dancing.

Psalm 30:5, 11

When I first contemplated accepting my sexuality, I anxiously thought long into the night about its effect on my soul. By the next morning I felt more confident in my freedom.

When I began searching for someone to love me, I spent many a night searching, hoping, despairing. But every morning I was certain there was someone out there for me.

When I came out to my folks by letter, they phoned and I heard my mother weeping, and I felt grief. The next morning, I felt peace at my decision.

When I came out in a big way at seminary by arranging for Troy Perry to speak, I slept the night before in a fetal position in physical *angst.* I awoke feeling born anew.

When I learned in seminary that friends were consoling my roommate about being placed with a gay man, I felt forsaken. A night's sleep refreshed me for the task of making other students more comfortable with me.

Sleep is an underrated gift of God and an undervalued source of spiritual healing. Sleep offers a sanctuary to work things out, transforming tears to joy and grief to dance.

Praise to you for the blessing of sleep and rebirth!

"Hosanna!
Blessed is the one who comes in the name of the Lord!"

Mark 11:9

What a day of pride! Yet a day of humility, too, for Jesus rode
into Jerusalem on a donkey and was heralded by everyday people, not local officials or dignitaries. But it was a moment of
kairos——a spiritual turning point. And it was so powerful
that, as Jesus said to the religious fundamentalists objecting to
the revelers, "If these were silent, the stones would shout out"
(Luke 19:40).

  "Blessed is the one who comes in the name of the Lord!"
This is how I praised God for my first encounter with a gay
Christian minister, Bill Johnson. This is how I praised God
for my first encounter with a lesbian and gay Christian
church, the Universal Fellowship of Metropolitan Community Churches. This is how I praised God for my first Christian boyfriend, Stan Schobert. If I had not cried out with joy,
church walls would have screamed!

  That's why the religious organizations get extra applause
and shouts in lesbian and gay pride parades, so the pave-
ment beneath them doesn't bellow!

Hosanna! Blessed are all those who re-present you, God!

The stone that the builders rejected
has become the chief cornerstone.
This is [God's] doing;
it is marvelous in our eyes.

Psalm 118:22–23

The Gospel of Mark quotes this passage in relation to Jesus (Mark 12:10). The Psalmist seeks entrance to the temple, and is told by the gatekeeper that only those who are fit may enter. The Psalmist replies that God has confirmed her worth by liberating her when others rejected her.

Two lesbians stand at the gate of my own church. Janie Spahr was told by a higher church court that, though ordained, she was unfit to serve as a pastor because she is in a covenant relationship with a woman. The same court told Lisa Larges that her declaration of her sexuality disqualifies her from ordination. Both have incredible stories of liberation to tell. Yet will the gatekeepers hear it, and affirm them with the choral blessing of this Psalm? *"Blessed is the one who comes in the name of the [Sovereign]!"* (118:26.)

Carl Jung's saying is proving true again: "Religion is a defense against the experience of God."

"Save us, we beseech you, O [Sovereign]! O [God], we beseech you, give us success!" (118:25.)

But Paul shouted in a loud voice, "Do not harm yourself, for we are all here."

Acts 16:28

Paul and Silas are beaten and jailed for delivering a young female slave from those who were exploiting her psychic powers. Midnight finds them praying and singing hymns to God, when an earthquake opens the prison doors and unfastens all the prisoners' chains. The jailer awakes. Knowing the penalty is death for allowing an escape, he intends to take his own life. But Paul shouts, assuring him no one has escaped.

Paul's generosity of spirit prompts the jailer to ask about the gospel, and he is converted, caring for their wounds and feeding them.

The chair of the committee guiding my preparation for ministry opposed my ordination because I was gay. Years later, on a visit to the church I served in a non-ordained capacity, he asked more about the gospel we proclaimed. His son had come out to him. In our dialogue that followed, I invited him to serve on the board of my ministry.

Our liberation is not complete until we free those who imprison us. Through prayer and singing, God will give us the grace to prove redemptive even to our captors, and proclaim the gospel of the integrity of spirituality and sexuality.

God of Mercy, we pray for the liberation of our captors rather than their harm. Grant us grace to be gracious.

TABERNACLE

Then the cloud covered the tent of the meeting, and the glory of [God] filled the tabernacle. . . . Whenever the cloud was taken up from the tabernacle, the Israelites would set out on each stage of their journey.

Exodus 40:34, 36

The tabernacle was a portable, tentlike sanctuary for Yahweh, the God of Israel. Worship was truly a moveable feast, because Yahweh was leading the Israelites, newly freed from Egyptian slavery, to the Promised Land. God led them by cloud by day and by a fire within the cloud by night.

The tabernacling experience serves as a wonderful metaphor for our encounters with God, the One who told Moses, "I will be what I will be." God and God's activity cannot be fixed in time or place. Karl Barth described the theologian's task as a painter trying to capture on canvas a bird in flight: once painted, the bird is somewhere else. We know how coming out is an ongoing metamorphosis.

As with the performing arts, our worship, our response to God, is also provisional, achieving spiritual harmony even as it disappears. An order of worship is a skeleton; it has no flesh and blood until we "perform" it for God.

Both God and we are on-the-go. We take comfort that God tabernacles with us in our quest for the Promise.

Lead on, O God eternal. Your tent shall be our home.

*But when Christ came as a high priest . . . through the greater
and perfect tent, . . . he entered once for all into the Holy Place
. . . with his own blood, thus obtaining redemption.*

Hebrews 9:11–12

In Christ, we worship in a "greater and perfect" tent, or
tabernacle. Christ is at once high priest and final sacrifice of
atonement, at-one-ment, which welcomes us to God's
bosom. The exquisite, vaulted ceilings of cathedrals can
only hope to remind us of this greater and perfect tent.
Their priests, in celebrating the Eucharist, only reenact a
sacrifice made once and for all by Christ, both priest and
sacrifice.

Mahatma Gandhi said it depends on our attitude whether
or not we gain something by entering cathedrals or
churches. The church's bad attitude toward us may beget
our bad attitude, limiting our receptivity. But God has provided an alternative tabernacle, as Gandhi wrote, "Churches,
mosques and temples which cover so much hypocrisy and
humbug and shut the poorest out of them seem but a mock-
ery of God and [God's] worship when one sees the eternally
renewed temple of worship under the vast blue canopy
inviting every one of us to real worship" (Mohan-M-al-a [A
Gandhian Rosary], compiled by R. K. Prabhv [Ahmedabad,
India: Navajivah Publishing, 1949], p. 44).

Help me find you in whatever tabernacle I worship, O God.

Again Jesus spoke to them saying, "I am the light of the world. Whoever follows me will never walk in darkness but will have the light of life."

John 8:12

Some Christians have a sense of "having arrived" when they believe in Christ. The self-assurance of the Christian bumper sticker "I FOUND IT" is rebutted by the Jewish bumper sticker "WE NEVER LOST IT." I believe that Jews often have a better sense of spirituality as an ongoing pilgrimage than Christians, who think of it as a "done deal." And religious Jews often have a better understanding of communal deliverance than Christians, who tend toward individualism in their salvation; thus the "I" of the one sticker becomes the "we" of the second.

Like the cloud by day and the fire by night that led the Israelites through a wilderness, so, for Christians, Jesus Christ serves as a light to be followed. As written in Hebrews, "Jesus Christ is the same yesterday and today and forever" (13:8). But Christ illumines new understandings of ourselves, our sexuality, and our spirituality, revealing yet new frontiers on our way.

Christ Jesus, lead me with your light through this day and through life's shadows.

Do you not know that you are God's temple and that God's Spirit dwells in you?

1 Corinthians 3:16

The "you" here is plural, and refers to the community of believers. God chooses to dwell, or tabernacle, with the people of faith. The church is the new tabernacle or temple. But the church is independent of a structure——after all, worship was held in believers' homes. The church is the community of faith.

A gay church member who had housed and fed and supported a homeless gay youth asked me why the church had not done anything for the young man. I said, "You're watching out for him. And you're the church!"

When we complain about the church, we are also complaining about ourselves. If the church is homophobic, it may be because not enough of us are doing our part to overcome prejudice. If the church is not ministering to lesbians, gay men, bisexuals, transgenders, and persons with AIDS, we also have failed to fulfill our ministry.

And, more broadly, we have to get over our "edifice complex," so that we look for God's Spirit among us rather than within an institutional structure.

Bless us with your Spirit dwelling within and among us, making us holy.

Or do you not know that your body is a temple of the Holy Spirit within you, which you have from God, and that you are not your own? For you were bought with a price; therefore glorify God in your body.

1 Corinthians 6:19

The "you" here is singular, addressed to the individual Christian. In my upbringing, this scripture was used to remind us of what we shouldn't do with our bodies. That is how Paul begins describing a sexual ethic that comes less from law than from our affiliation with Christ. What we do with our bodies is important because we are a temple for the Spirit as members of Christ's Body. Just as we can't imagine Christ doing anything sexually exploitive, we can't use our part of his body for such sin.

For the same reason, Paul continues, couples should not ordinarily refrain from lovemaking, though he wishes everyone was single like him. Though his guidance is preceded by what we shouldn't do, it's followed by what we should do.

In a body-affirming spirituality, to "glorify God in your body" means to enjoy our bodies, others' bodies, and the body of creation as sacred gifts. We are not afraid to touch, but we do so carefully. We are not afraid to look, but we avoid profaning the sacred. We are not afraid to love, but we do so devotedly.

I belong to you, O Christ. May I glorify God as your Body.

How lovely is your dwelling place,
O [God] of hosts!
My soul longs, indeed it faints
for the courts of [Yahweh];
my heart and my flesh sing for joy
to the living God.

                    Psalm 84:1–2

Throughout the Bible, Yahweh's dwelling place was redefined, from the tabernacle to the temple, from creation to
the community of believers. However experienced, it may
be recognized by certain marks of character found in Psalm
84. It is lovely, causing longing and joy. "Even the sparrow
finds a home . . . where she may lay her young, at your al-
tars" (84:3). A happy place to live, it empowers, and it welcomes prayer. "For a day in your courts is better than a
thousand elsewhere" (84:10). It offers justice, symbolized
by the sun. It offers protection, symbolized in the shield.
And "no good thing" is withheld, providing reason to trust.
And it is there that God lives.

   I have seen many tabernacles throughout my travels:
Mother Teresa's home for the dying in India, the determina-
tion of the Nicaraguan people, a green wooden cross on a
hill in Santa Barbara, a Philadelphia gathering of lesbian and
gay Lutherans, a retreat of persons with AIDS and their caregivers near Detroit. And many other places. The more we
look for God's dwelling, the more we see it.

How lovely is your dwelling place, O God of Love!

Come to [Jesus], a living stone, though rejected by mortals yet chosen and precious in God's sight, and like living stones, let yourselves be built into a spiritual house, to be a holy priesthood, to offer spiritual sacrifices acceptable to God through Jesus Christ.

1 Peter 2:4–5

The solemn way in which her church worshiped made a friend, growing up, think that the urnlike chandeliers in the sanctuary contained cremated remains of former members! But for me, that church was a place of solemn joy. Its stained glass cast rainbows on the people; its red brick walls, even in silence, echoed eloquent sermons of justice.

Knowing that a true tabernacle is where God lives, and sensing that God wants us to choose life, many gay men and lesbians have avoided the church as we might a mausoleum. But 1 Peter tells us to come to Jesus as "living stones," letting ourselves "be built into a spiritual house." Churches who welcome us realize that we bring resurrection and life. We offer "spiritual sacrifices acceptable to God through Jesus Christ."

Build us into your dwelling place, Holy God, that others may have life and have it more abundantly.

For freedom Christ has set us free. Stand firm, therefore, and do not submit again to a yoke of slavery.

Galatians 5:1

This scripture was forever transformed for me when Tari Lennon, a pastor, preached on it during an interfaith service for human rights, a service held at Los Angeles' Greek Theater to voice religious opposition to an antigay initiative on the California ballot in 1978. I cannot read this text without seeing her animated interpretation before fifteen hundred souls seated in the outdoor amphitheater.

She spoke of her own "yoke of slavery," her fear that demonstrating her solidarity for gay rights might imply she was a lesbian to the prejudiced. And she spoke of the church's "yoke of slavery" to a new sexual legalism contrary to the freedom from the law Paul proclaimed to the Galatians.

Our own yoke of slavery to which we must not submit is an ideological legalism that sets in stone what it means to be gay, lesbian, and politically or spiritually correct. Broadening people's awareness accomplishes more than shaming them into conformity.

For freedom you have set me free, O Christ. Deliver me from any yoke of slavery.

For you were called to freedom, brothers and sisters; only do not use your freedom as an opportunity for self-indulgence, but through love become slaves to one another.

Galatians 5:13

To follow the command to "love your neighbor as yourself," quoted in verse 14, the Galatians are not to be irresponsible or insensitive to one another in their freedom. Becoming "slaves to one another" means to consider another's needs as superior to one's own.

Thus gay men who don't know why lesbians want to be called lesbians should just "get over it" and call them by the name they choose. People with HIV disease who want to be called persons living with AIDS rather than AIDS patients have that right. Black friends who now want to be called African-Americans need no justification.

Even more personally, if we take someone's number and say we're going to call, the person has every right to expect we will do so. If we plan to meet someone or to help someone, we have an obligation to fulfill. Whether or not we're HIV-positive, we engage in safer sex. And whether we like it or not, we have to be responsible to our community for our behavior.

Though liberated, we tabernacle with one another as a community in a wilderness. We must get along to survive.

Keep us from both legalism and license, that we may love one another.

When the people saw that Moses delayed to come down from the mountain, the people gathered around Aaron, and said to him, "Come, make gods for us, who shall go before us; as for this Moses, the man who brought us up out of the land of Egypt, we do not know what has become of him."

Exodus 32:1

How quickly they forget! At the base of Mount Sinai, after the ten plagues, the deliverance out of Egypt, the crossing of the Red Sea——Moses should have gotten a little more respect, not to mention Yahweh!

I met a gay man who spoke of how his gay congregation had "saved" his life when his longtime lover died. Then he told me he had fallen in love with a prison inmate who, upon his release, ripped him off. Nonetheless, he had decided to leave his entire estate to this young man, thinking it would help him. I thought, how many more could he aid if he left it to his church to finance a program to help gay inmates!

Insecurity in the wilderness makes us easy targets for false gods, whether of the human or material variety. Lonely for God, we worship what we have. Aaron took the Israelites' jewelry and molded a golden calf, which they worshiped. Hindsight makes us see how stupid that was, but we ignore our own idols: television, alcohol, bars, tricks, muscles, money, drugs, cigarettes, celebrities, and so on.

O God, deliver us from worshiping anything less than you.

Jesus said to him, "Away with you, Satan! for it is written, 'Worship the Lord your God, and serve only [God].'"

Matthew 4:10

During his forty-day fast in the wilderness en route to God's commonwealth, Jesus was tempted as the Israelites were during their forty years wandering in the wilderness en route to the Promised Land: to worship something other than God.

The personification of evil in the Bible, the devil, took Jesus to a high mountain not unlike Mount Sinai and showed him "all the kingdoms of the world and their splendor" (4:8), promising them to Jesus if he would worship evil. Jesus refused. Tradition holds that Jesus later suffered betrayal at the hands of a disappointed Judas for not becoming a political messiah.

The film *Jesus of Montreal* accurately translates this into our contemporary milieu. The impoverished actor who plays Jesus in an avant garde Passion play is tempted to sign a contract for megabucks and stardom. But it risks the soul of his craft.

Our own deprivation makes us hungry for political power. We may be tempted by both friends (Judas) and foe (evil) to achieve our goals by any means necessary. But what kind of people would we become? Jesus opted for spiritual power to announce God's commonwealth, the persuasive rather than coercive power of love.

Away with you, all who tempt me from the love of God!

The whole congregation of the Israelites complained against Moses and Aaron in the wilderness.

Exodus 16:2

Of course, we would never do such a thing!

A primary cause for burnout among the leaders within our community is our failure to support them. They hear from us when we're angry, or annoyed, or vaguely uncomfortable with their or their organization's work. They rarely hear from us when we're happy, or grateful, or generally satisfied with their efforts. Often, we take the good for granted.

This is a problem with our culture. Only watch television news to get the picture. But it is more pronounced in oppressed communities. The anger that should be directed at the opposition is leveled at one another. Poor communities reflect this in higher crime rates and more acts of violence.

What's particularly insulting about the Israelites' complaints against those who led them out of Egyptian bondage is that, in their hunger, they actually begin pining away for "the good old days" of oppression when they "ate [their] fill of bread," saying they would have preferred to die there!

We wouldn't go that far, would we?

To you God, the great sustainer of all life, we pray for those working for our liberation, that they may be satisfied.

"One does not live by bread alone,
but by every word that comes from the mouth of God."

Mark 4:4

Tempted to turn stones to bread, Jesus quoted Deuteronomy's reference to the hunger of the Israelites in the wilderness. Jesus reminded his tormentor that, though basic survival is a human instinct, it is not enough to satisfy us.

Hostages taken in the Middle East have confirmed this. Though given food barely adequate for survival, many spoke of their hunger for words: words of memory, words of their internal voice, words of conversation with captors and fellow captives, words of prayer. Terry Waite, the envoy of the Archbishop of Canterbury abducted in his heroic effort to negotiate the release of hostages, said that during his years of captivity what sustained him was remembering the words of the Anglican Book of Common Prayer.

Quite another kind of "hostage," Tom Boomershine teaches the telling of biblical stories so that the punch of their original oral transmission is not lost in their reading. He developed this method in order to emotionally and spiritually survive a bad accident that left him bedridden with impaired eyesight for more than a year. He couldn't read, nor watch television, so he tried telling biblical stories aloud from memory. He discovered new life in himself as he found new life in the Word.

We bless these words to the nourishment of our bodies, and
we bless your Word to the nourishment of our Body. Amen.

[Yahweh] said to Moses, "I am going to rain bread from heaven for you, and each day the people shall go out and gather enough for that day."

Exodus 16:4

"Give us this day our daily bread," Jesus urged his disciples to pray.

The Israelites were given bread enough for the day. If they did not trust God's providence, and gathered more than their daily requirements, what was left over turned to worms. The bread was called manna, and it may have been a naturally occurring edible substance produced by insects and found on certain trees in the wilderness. The text explains the term "manna" is derived from the question "What is it?" (16:15) in Hebrew. To them it was bread from heaven, a gift from God.

In workshops, I have passed around a jar in which I invited participants to place an index card on which they've written what is their manna in the wilderness, their daily bread that has kept them going on their spiritual journey. The collective input reveals diverse sources of nourishment that we may share with others. They may be naturally occurring resources, but they are gifts from God.

Give us this day our daily bread. Thank you for the manna in our wilderness!

The Israelites also wept again, and said, "If only we had meat to eat! We remember the fish we used to eat in Egypt for nothing, the cucumbers, the melons, the leeks, the onions, and the garlic; but now our strength is dried up, and there is nothing at all but this manna to look at."

Numbers 11:4-6

Well, we'd probably get tired of manna, too.

Those among us who have sacrificed a lot to come out—giving up a spouse, children, parents, a home, an inheritance, or a job—may indeed wonder if it was worth it. We may nostalgically remember the luxuries the closet afforded us, just as the Israelites fondly remembered their days enslaved. We might feel lonely, or poor, or underemployed.

As a tasty respite to manna, God sent quail, on which the Israelites ate themselves sick. The good thing that came out of it was that Moses, exasperated, decided to share leadership with seventy others, saying, "Would that all [Yahweh's] people were prophets, and that [Yahweh] would put [God's] spirit on them!" (11:29).

If we all became leaders, we might dwell less on the past and see the future more clearly. Not just our future, but the future of generations to come who need the Promised Land.

Would that all of us were prophets, blessed with your Spirit!

Taking the five loaves and the two fish, he looked up to heaven, and blessed and broke the loaves, and gave them to the disciples, and the disciples gave them to the crowds. And all ate and were filled.

Matthew 14:19–20

I read this the morning after I had learned that my life savings had been lost in a bad investment. It just "happened" to be the next story as I was reading through Matthew during my morning prayers. Half-smiling, half-chagrined at the irony, I didn't quite know what to make of it.

I noted the story began with Jesus withdrawing by boat "to a deserted place by himself" (14:13). It ended with him dismissing the crowds, and afterward, "he went up the mountain by himself to pray" (14:23). A few verses later he'd be walking to them on stormy seas, reaching out to Peter sinking in the chaos, and saying, "You of little faith, why did you doubt?" (14:31).

The meaning of it all never came absolutely clear to me. Oh yes, it's easy to make connections with my experience, but I distrusted them. Rather, the story simply comforted me.

In our hunger and in our loss, Jesus takes a few words of scripture and blesses them, and it is sufficient.

Dear Jesus, thank you for bringing the Word out to where I am, blessing me as I am.

Jesus said to them, "I am the bread of life. Whoever comes to me will never be hungry, and whoever believes in me will never be thirsty."

John 6:35

A politically correct lesbian and gay congregation took offense at my preaching on this chapter from John in which Jesus offers his body as the bread of salvation and life. (Later it would become the chapter, "Welcoming Embodiment," in my book, *Come Home!*) There were some who didn't like the Christ talk. There were some who didn't like its apparent exclusiveness. There were others who didn't like Jesus being male.

I wanted to tell them what my sometimes bumbling Baptist pastor used to say, "Go by what I mean, not by what I say."

My intent was to demonstrate how God welcomed our embodiment by becoming flesh in Jesus Christ. Somehow I failed to communicate, or they failed to accept, the spiritual metaphor and its radical implications. In Jesus Christ, God hallowed all flesh by tabernacling with us in human flesh. In offering his body to us as "manna in the wilderness" (6:49), God dwells in us, and we in turn embody God.

Feed us with your manna, that we might become bread for others, Holy Word.

Do not neglect to show hospitality to strangers, for by doing that some have entertained angels without knowing it.

Hebrews 12:2

The allusion is to Abraham and Sarah, who demonstrated hospitality to strangers, sojourners who turned out to be God and two angels, and to Lot, who protected two of the same strangers from gang rape when they visited Sodom.

There are Christians who have shown hospitality to us as strangers and have realized our sacred worth. There are other Christians who have proven to be inhospitable as the citizens of Sodom in their desire for our spiritual humiliation.

There are lesbians and gay men who have welcomed our gay religious groups and our congregations into their communities, affirming our value. There are other lesbians and gay men who have been inhospitable, ignoring us, wishing we would go away, or expressing hostility.

Hospitality makes all the difference. Considered a mere courtesy in our culture, hospitality was a vital (in the sense of life-giving) virtue to ancient people tabernacling in a wilderness, as hospitality still is today in the Middle East. If more in the church and the gay and lesbian community practiced it, both would be revitalized and less in danger of fire and brimstone.

Inspire me to demonstrate the welcoming hospitality that I would wish to be offered, O Spirit who tabernacles with us.

"Go from your country and your kindred . . . to the land that I will show you. . . . I will bless you . . . so that you will be a blessing."

Genesis 12:1–2

When Abraham and Sarah heard this challenge from God, they were not oppressed. They had just settled down. But the invitation to move on came anyway.

Just when we've settled down or settled in, we've had to move on to be blessed. Sometimes it meant leaving families, friends, hometowns, or rural communities to be ourselves. We grieve letting go of the familiar just as we fear the familiar may not prove friendly to the "stranger" within us.

Many of us have had to "go from" our church to affirm who we are. That doesn't mean that we cannot affirm whose we are as God's children and our right to the spiritual heritage of several millennia of people of faith found in the Bible.

Others of us have had to "go from" gay ghettos or congregations because of circumstance or because we have chosen a less intense and more diverse community experience. We're no less part of a community that transcends boundaries. Coming out we are blessed so we may prove a blessing for others. Despite its unsettling qualities, we sense we must go from to go to our destinies.

Spirit of restlessness, in your call to journey toward the unfamiliar, we pray for blessings that we might be a blessing.

For all who are led by the Spirit of God are children of God.
Romans 8:14

When I led a segment on spirituality for an AIDS-buddy training program, my intent was to open up the volunteers' understanding of spirituality. Most had preconceived notions of spirituality as dogma and judgment, so it bothered some.

I would ask two questions of them: What in your belief system prompted you to volunteer as an AIDS buddy? And, What is your spiritual support group? I urged them to respond with creativity.

What prompted them to volunteer, I believe, revealed their core spirituality: anger at injustice, compassion for those hurting, love for a friend or family member who had died of AIDS, belief in human value, and so on. These things made them feel connected to someone they had never met and were their spiritual resources.

People were creative in naming their spiritual support groups, from the expected "home church" to the unexpected "women's tennis group." Considering this question made volunteers aware of whom they could depend on when the going got rough.

To me, these volunteers were led by the Spirit and were children of God, no matter how they described their commitment.

Bless all who are led by your Spirit to do what is right. Give them the inheritance promised your children.

Jesus said, . . . "I am the way, and the truth, and the life."
                                                      John 14:6

I attended a gay and lesbian pride week interfaith worship
in which the Jewish organizer asked the Christian groups
not to mention the name of Jesus. The Christians complied
by contributing material that was not uniquely Christian,
while the form of worship was a wonderful Pride Seder that
paralleled the Passover Seder, the observance of the central
event of Jewish history: the deliverance from Egypt.

Jesus Christ is the central event of Christian history. Not
to be able to mention his name or quote his words made
the worship less than interfaith. Acceding to the request
may have been done out of deference to the service being
hosted by the synagogue, which was, ironically, held in a
Quaker meeting house. But I'd been to joint services in a
temple before that made no such requirement.

It's true that the New Testament reflects an anti-Jewish
bias, since the early church was revolting against its parent
faith. This gave "sacred" sanction to the church's long history of persecuting the Jews.

As well, Christian claims of being "the only way" are out
of sync with a religiously pluralistic society. But it is also
true that for Christians, Jesus is our way, our truth, and our
life. Jesus is our cloud in the tabernacle who leads us
through the wilderness.

*Christ Jesus, forgive us, the church, for using your name to
reject others rather than to follow God.*

Say to those who are of a fearful heart,
"Be strong, do not fear!
Here is your God. . . .
[God] will come and save you."

Isaiah 35:4

"Take heart, it is I; do not be afraid."

Mark 6:50

Once I preached on how the world changes around us. Even standing still, we continue to "move" through the wilderness. The closing of the nearby Safeway gave me the title for the sermon: "When There Is No Safe Way."

But our fears of such change seem petty compared to those of my closing story. Friends, Christian singers Jim and Jean Strathdee, took their children to Nicaragua. When their plane was forced by weather to stay overnight in El Salvador, a Salvadoran woman and a Guatemalan woman expressed fear that they'd be murdered by death squads if they deplaned. As comfort and protection, the Strathdees elected to stay with them on board. The airline officials shut the power off, leaving them in darkness to watch the storm. It was Halloween, and their kids, who had disliked missing the fun back home, thought this was a cool way to spend it, singing in the shadows.

That night, the Strathdees embodied God to the fearful women. They were Christ, assuring his disciples as he came to them in a storm, "Take heart, it is I; do not be afraid." That is how God comes to us and comforts us in our fear——in one another, as we tabernacle together in the wilderness.

I will take heart, for it is you, God; I need not be afraid.

"Therefore I tell you, do not worry about your life."
                                          Matthew 6:25

A friend from Chicago dropped in unexpectedly one Sunday, and realizing I was on my way out the door, came right to the point of his visit.

He had been trained in seminary but dropped out of the church when he realized being gay made him unwelcome. What brought him back to his spirituality was a Twelve-Step program he embraced after admitting his alcoholism. He lived in a house with several gay men, one of whom was a Christian who had AIDS. They became fast friends.

While my friend was at work one day, a verse came to him from the text surrounding today's scripture. His intuition told him to go home to this friend with AIDS. As he walked in the friend's room, he quoted, "Consider the lilies of the field." Without missing a beat his friend continued, "they neither toil nor spin, yet I tell you, even Solomon in all his glory was not arrayed like one of these!" —— as if they had been thinking of the same scripture. They sat and talked, and within hours his friend died. If my friend had not listened to that inner voice, if scripture had not linked them in a mystical way, the man would have died alone.

Having told the story he came to tell me, my friend said good-bye. What a stunning gift!

I will try not to worry about my life or my death, trusting in your eternal love and providence, Holy God.

"Ask, and it will be given you; search, and you will find; knock, and the door will be opened for you."

Luke 11:9

The Quest is a classic metaphor for the spiritual life. Seeking meaning, purpose, passion, and fulfillment for life sets us on a heroic adventure. Jesus' words here have less to do with day-to-day needs than ultimate ones.

What has given direction to many lesbians and gay men is the quest for rights in our society. What has given purpose to many lesbian and gay Christians is the quest to open the church's door wider, so that more may enter.

A gay man told me that he and his lover were welcomed into a largely straight congregation. His lover had AIDS and wanted to reclaim his spirituality in a church that was more inclusive than the one in which he'd been reared. The pastor befriended them and happened to share with them a private dream he had for the church. He wanted the church's heavy wooden doors, which seemed to shut people out, replaced with glass ones, symbolizing a more welcoming congregation.

The final request of this man's lover as he was dying was to have donations made in his memory to the church for the purpose of fulfilling this dream. The doors have been installed and dedicated in this man's memory.

To those who quest for an open church, these new glass doors represent a kind of Holy Grail.

Bless all doors that lead to you, O God. Bless all who enter.

"I will not leave you orphaned; I am coming to you. In a little while the world will no longer see me, but you will see me; because I live, you also will live."

John 14:18–19

Jesus is presented very tenderly by the "beloved disciple" John. This is the Jesus of reflection, since this gospel was the last of the four written. This is the mystical Jesus, since John was a visionary. This is the gospel less of chronos, as in chronology, than of kairos, God's appointed time, because John was concerned more about faith than fact.

It is this tender and mystical Jesus of reflection and faith that comforts us: "I will not leave you orphaned; I am coming to you." That's why the world can't see him; that's why people of faith can.

How can we improve our vision of Jesus?

We use the same paths to know a lover. Begin with conversation, reflecting on Christ's words in scripture. Then touch, reaching out tenderly to Christ's Body in believers and in the stranger. Pray together, in silence and in words, welcoming Christ's presence and being present to Christ's Spirit. Begin to trust Christ's love that says, "because I live, you also will live." Then, in Christ's embrace, we will know God's tenderness.

Christ Jesus, may I open my awareness to your tender and yet passionate embrace, so that I may know the love of God.

I love you, O [God], my strength.
[Yahweh] is my rock, my fortress, and my deliverer,
my God, my rock in whom I take refuge.

                                        Psalm 18:1–2

A lesbian urban planner once told me that if she was to design a church for our community, she would make it of stone and make it look solid. "We experience so much transiency in our lives, we need something we can count on," she said.

When I advise a church on beginning a ministry within the gay and lesbian community, I encourage them to plan a stable program that can be sustained for a period of time, hiring someone with stamina. As we learn we can depend on it, we'll eventually respond to a specialized ministry.

Like the Psalmist, we need solid, dependable "rocks" in our lives that we can trust to be there.

The rocks may be literal. On a retreat, a new gay friend took me for his favorite hike within a nearby national park. Our destination was a rock on the edge of a mountain lake. On this rock, he told me, he had often poured out his heart and soul to God. As we sat eating trail mix and freshly baked cookies, we swapped stories of our spiritual and sexual struggles. The rock was comfortable and seemed friendly. It did not shrug us off, nor take offense at anything we said.

I understood why the Psalmist compared God to a rock.

I love you, God, my rock, my strength, my deliverer!

"Do not put the Lord your God to the test."

Matthew 4:7

The devil tempted Jesus to risk his own life so that God might come to the rescue. Jesus had nothing to prove. And he didn't want to try God's patience with a foolish prank like jumping off "the pinnacle of the temple" (4:5).

I don't believe anyone is beyond God's patience or beyond God's grace. But some wildernesses are of our own making, and in them we suffer without purpose. They probably come from some damage to our psyches along the way, which is why it is all the more vital for us to hold on to God's love.

I led a memorial service for a gay alcoholic who set fire to her apartment in an attempt to kill herself. Horribly burned, she died three days later. When I invited her friends to tell of their feelings during the service, anger mixed with grief. One friend from a Twelve-Step meeting she attended seemed to speak for everyone when she said, "I am so angry that she didn't believe we loved her. She wouldn't trust our love."

Eliminating unnecessary wildernesses in our lives is a healthy step, spiritually and otherwise.

Tabernacle with me, Sovereign God, by leading me out of any wilderness that proves unredemptive.

Beloved, do not believe every spirit, but test the spirits to see whether they are from God; for many false prophets have gone out into the world.

1 John 4:1

"Beware of false prophets, who come to you in sheep's clothing but inwardly are ravenous wolves. You will know them by their fruits."

Matthew 7:15–16

The wilderness is full of spirits. Discernment is crucial. We hear their whispers: *Maybe it was better in slavery. Here's a better God. Let's go our own way. Here's an easier path. Go ahead—they'll never know. Everything is hopeless. There's nothing wrong with this picture. One time won't hurt. Why am I doing this?*

1 John insists that to be of God, the spirit must affirm "that Jesus Christ has come in the flesh" (4:2), and a few verses later insists that love is the fruit of anyone from God. In Matthew, Jesus said that discernment may be made by judging the fruit, good or bad.

There is a network of groups whispering to some of us, *"It was better in Egypt,"* that paradoxically takes its name from the exodus. The groups claim to change, or render celibate, homosexual people. But do they have a body-affirming spirituality? Don't they inhibit, restrict, and limit love, both human and divine? Aren't their fruits damaged?

Holy Spirit, I pray for the gift of discernment, that I may follow your tabernacle and not get lost.

Therefore thus says the [Sovereign], the God of Israel, con-
cerning the shepherds who shepherd my people: It is you who
have scattered my flock, and have driven them away, and
you have not attended to them.

Jeremiah 23:2

A mother of a son dying of AIDS called for support. She
could not go to her minister because of his antigay sermons. She feared telling anyone, lest it get around her small
town. Another mother of a son who died of AIDS was horrified when her pastor used the funeral to condemn the son
and his parents to hell. She has now become an advocate
for us.

These "pastors" are but two of the "shepherds" who
seek to drive us away and refuse to attend to us. We know
others.

In Jeremiah, God promises judgment of these shepherds.
God also promises to personally "gather the remnant" of
God's flock. For Christians this refers to Jesus, who is the
"good shepherd" who lays down his life for his sheep (John
10:11), bringing "other sheep not of this fold" (John 10:16).

Finally, God promises: "I will raise up shepherds over
them who will shepherd them, and they shall not fear any
longer, or be dismayed, nor shall any be missing, says the
[Sovereign]" (Jer. 23:4).

We pray for the sheep who have been scattered and driven
away, that they may return to you, Good Shepherd.

And I will save the lame
and gather the outcast,
and I will change their shame into praise
and renown in all the earth.
At that time I will bring you home.

Zephaniah 3:19–20

Home. That's what it's all for, isn't it? The wandering in the wilderness is to lead us to a new home, a real home, where shame dissolves into praise. The outcast is welcomed, a common biblical theme——something we wouldn't know by listening to those who oppose us!

Yet the wandering in the wilderness is to accomplish more. Not only will it lead us to a real home, but it will help us create a real home, for God and for one another. That's the essence of tabernacling.

Among those we have to provide a real home for are our own outcasts: those with physical or mental disabilities. We all have physical and mental limitations, yet we cast away those on the "more so" end of the spectrum, maybe out of fear that "they" could be "us"——much like our opposition on the Kinsey scale of sexual orientation does. But "they" are as much "us" as we are, and we will be God's instruments, transforming shame into praise, if we learn that and welcome them home.

We pray for our own physical and mental limitations that deny access to lesbians and gay men with disabilities.

For we know that if the earthly tent we live in is destroyed, we have a building from God, a house not made with hands, eternal in the heavens.

2 Corinthians 5:1

As a very small child, the only "earthly tent" I knew was the circus. There I got a balloon. Over the days that followed, the air seeped out, and I was saddened by my first conscious experience of mutability. My mother offered to stuff it——maybe kidding, maybe serious. But I declined.

Life is tabernacling. When the circus is over, when the breath has seeped out, when the Spirit in the cloud has moved on to another place, it's time to go on to another tent.

Paul, who provided for himself by tentmaking, was concerned with our "earthly tent" or tabernacle. For him, death is folding up this tent and receiving a new one, "eternal in the heavens."

This body, that body, this tent, that tent——all are places that God chooses to dwell or tabernacle with us forever.

See us through the wilderness, awesome and loving God, and bring us home to you.

HOLINESS

See, I have set before you today life and prosperity, death and adversity. . . . I have set before you life and death, blessings and curses. Choose life so that you and your descendants may live, loving . . . God, obeying [God], and holding fast to [God]; for that means life to you.

Deuteronomy 30:15, 19–20

The God who gave us life wants us to choose life as an act of holiness. Holiness means being set aside for a sacred purpose. Holiness means harmony within the community. Holiness means wholeness, integrity within the self. Holiness will bring us life and well-being.

Just as there are guidelines for "safer sex," there are guidelines for "safer spirit." But, just as the rules for safer sex may not cover all circumstances, neither do the rules for safer spirit. Ultimately, what is good for the body is good for the spirit, what is good for the spirit is good for the body, since they find integrity in "soul."

Soon after the children of Israel were liberated from Egyptian oppression, as God tabernacled with them in the wilderness, God gave Moses the Covenant of the Law by which Israel would be governed. Now, on the threshold to the Promised Land in Deuteronomy, Moses urges the Israelites to choose life by following God's Law so they may live long in the land.

I choose life, Creator God, the life you have given me as a gay man/lesbian woman.

*You shall love the Lord your God with all your heart, and with
all your soul, and with all your might.*

Deuteronomy 6:5

*Moreover, the Lord your God will circumcise your heart and
the heart of your descendants, so that you will love the Lord
your God with all your heart and with all your soul, in order
that you may live.*

Deuteronomy 30:6

To know us is to love us. We've said this to many people
hesitant to welcome lesbians and gay men. We're confident
that if they really knew who we were inside, that they
would appreciate our integrity and give thanks for our gifts.

To know God is to love God. The Bible says this to all of
us who may feel hesitant to welcome God into our lives.
The biblical writers are confident that if we really know
who God is inside, then we will appreciate God's integrity
and give thanks for God's many blessings.

The first verse from Deuteronomy urges us to love God
with all we've got: our will (heart), our vitality (soul), our
passion (might). The second verse assures us that God will
transform (circumcise) our hearts to do so.

Just as we want others to give us a chance, we need to
give God a chance.

*As you know us and love us, God, help us know you and love
you.*

*You shall not take vengeance or bear a grudge against any of
your people, but you shall love your neighbor as yourself. . . .
The alien who resides with you shall be to you as the citizen
among you; you shall love the alien as yourself, for you were
aliens in the land of Egypt.*

Leviticus 19:18, 34

One might wonder why so many Christians who quote Leviticus 18:22 and 20:13 skip over these verses in chapter 19 that
Jesus himself highlighted in the second great commandment!

Xenophobia is the answer. The same people who hate or
fear us hate and fear a lot of people different from them.
They love their neighbor insofar as the neighbor is like
themselves. They love the alien insofar as the alien adopts
their lifestyles, values, and language.

The gay Christian poet W. H. Auden once wrote, "Remember the gift, the one from the manger; it means only
this, you can dance with a stranger." But most Christians
have forgotten that Jesus constantly reached out to the outcast.

The church is afraid of the stranger, within or without,
and the religious right capitalizes on this fear.

While exorcising our own xenophobia, we must capital-
ize on the church's faith.

*Dear God, you are our neighbor, you are the alien in our
midst. Teach us to love you rather than fear you.*

[Jesus said,] "'You shall love the [Sovereign] your God with all your heart, and with all your soul, and with all your mind, and with all your strength. . . . You shall love your neighbor as yourself.' There is no commandment greater than these."

Mark 12:30–31

Isak Dinesen said it another way. Having defined pride as "faith in the idea that God had, when [God] made us," she adds a later corollary: "Love the pride of God beyond all things, and the pride of your neighbor as your own."

Learning to love ourselves expresses our faith in God's idea in creating us lesbian and gay. As we take pride in ourselves we begin to affirm the pride of God and of others. Not undue pride, but the pride due them. Those who enjoy little self-pride are the ones most likely to devalue others.

Rabbis of Jesus' day were frequently asked how they would summarize the law of Moses while standing on one foot, and their response would have been similar to Jesus' answer.

What's unique is how Jesus *redefined* both law and neighbor. The law was made for humankind, not the other way around. And the neighbor included not only the resident alien, but enemies.

In your holy presence, Sacred God, I feel more sacred. The holiness in me reverences the holiness of others.

"In everything do to others as you would have them do to you; for this is the law and the prophets."

Matthew 5:12

Jesus here turned into a positive what other teachers of his time had said in the negative: Do *not* do to others what you would *not* want them to do to you.

Until we love ourselves properly, as Martin Luther encouraged, we may "feel better about ourselves" by putting down other categories of people. One of my big disappointments coming out as gay was discovering that the oppressed, who presumably would know better, easily fall into oppressive behavior. Though more sensitive to our own racism, for example, gay men and lesbians can behave as racist as the rest of the society. People of color, who might also know better, may be as homophobic. And all of us may be hesitant to share what little power we have.

Jesus transformed others' prohibition into positive action: "Do to others as you would have them do to you."

It's not enough to refrain from racism. If we want people of color to support our rights, then we must support theirs, *whether or not* they do so for us. The Golden Rule, expressed in most religions, does not make our behavior dependent on how others act. Rather, it's based on how we want to be treated.

Help me to do for others what I would like them to do for me.

The city and all that is in it shall be devoted to [God] for destruction.

Joshua 6:17

In war, the enemy is depicted as infidels who are less than human. The irony is that war makes all of us behave as infidels who are less than human. "Holy wars" are not holy. In Joshua, the Israelites believed that God ordained their taking the land of Canaan, so the destruction of Jericho was to be a holocaust, or burnt offering, to God ("devoted to [God] for destruction").

When millions of Jews, gay men, political dissidents, Gypsies, and religious minorities were murdered in Nazi death camps, those trying to give meaning to the meaningless called it the Holocaust. As do many Jews, I prefer calling it the "Shoah," which is Hebrew for annihilation. It's time we stopped confusing human sin with a sacrificial offering to God that is redemptive.

But I do believe that in all senseless, catastrophic suffering, those who suffer may serve as redeemers by the way they respond. The citizens of Hiroshima, who lost almost half their population to the atomic bomb dropped on this date in 1945, have created a shrine for peace on the site.

We have created a shrine for love in our own shoah: the AIDS Quilt. The panels give "faces" to those that many in society would prefer to regard as less than sacred and as less than human.

On this day, we remember all who have suffered and died at the hands of human sin and human neglect.

"Blessed are those who hunger and thirst for righteousness, for they will be filled."

Matthew 5:6

"Blessed are you who are hungry now, for you will be filled."

Luke 6:21

Matthew was concerned for our souls, Luke was concerned for our bodies. Jesus, whom they quote, was concerned for both. That's why he fed the multitudes that came to hear him talk. That's why he gave spiritual meaning to the last supper he shared with his disciples.

Jesus viewed human life as an integrity of body and spirit. A disciple does not need to deny her hunger to follow Jesus. A disciple does not need to deny his holiness when eating a meal.

Why then do people assume that we have to deny our sexuality to follow Jesus? And why do people think that holiness can't be associated with a sexual encounter?

Jesus warned his disciples to beware of the "leaven" of the self-righteous Pharisees that could spoil faith. We, too, must beware of the leaven of self-righteous Christians that spoils our faith.

He also said the commonwealth of God was like leaven a woman hid in a loaf that made the bread rise. Within the ordinary, we may find the sacred. Even within our lovemaking.

Thank you God, for bread and body, for leaven and lovemaking.

The law of God is perfect,
reviving the soul;
the decrees of God are sure,
making wise the simple;
the precepts of God are right,
rejoicing the heart.

Psalm 19:7–8 (Inclusive Language Lectionary)

The Psalmist gives us a set of criteria for discerning a law that is truly of God. If it doesn't give us hope, offer wisdom, and rejoice the heart, it's not of God.

There are many laws that don't fit the Psalmist's criteria which are not necessarily bad, just human. Traffic laws, for example, may not send our spirits soaring, or clear our brains, or make our hearts happy.

Laws that would restrict our rights do not meet the criteria, since they weary the soul, further ignorance, and grieve the heart. These would not be of God. What would fit the criteria would be a gay rights law. Think how that would revive our soul, enlighten the ignorant, and rejoice our hearts! That would be of God.

Deliver us, God of Righteousness, from those who substitute human prejudice for your eternal, loving law!

Then Aaron shall lay both his hands on the head of the live goat, and confess over it all the iniquities of the people of Israel, and all their transgressions, all their sins, putting them on the head of the goat, and sending it away into the wilderness.

Leviticus 16:21

I believe that the greater dilemma we pose for the church is that we affirm our integrity as sexual-spiritual beings within the community of faith. Christians' initial reaction may be that of homophobia, but ultimately they respond to us out of their erotophobia——as Carter Heyward names it——their fear of sexuality. We become the scapegoat for their anxiety.

Examples: Church members ostracized a woman who blew the whistle on a clergyman's sexual abuse of female parishioners. A pastor led a fight against the ordination of gays and lesbians while having multiple heterosexual contacts with parishioners. A pastor who tried to force a gay-affirming ministry to "change" homosexuals later admitted that he struggled with his own homosexual feelings.

The priest of the Israelites projected the sins of the people onto a goat, which was sent into the wilderness. This "excommunication," or exile from the community, meant certain death without the resources of food and water.

The principals change, the principle remains.

Bring healing to those frightened by our affirmation of the holy integrity of sexuality and spirituality, O God.

And Samuel said,
Has [God] as great delight in burnt offerings and sacrifices,
as in obeying the voice of the [Sovereign]?
Surely, to obey is better than sacrifice.

1 Samuel 15:22

The penance I offer for a sin is far more burdensome than doing the right thing in the first place. First and foremost, I cope with a depreciated self-image. I confess to God, and pray for the best. I make amends to any whom I might have hurt. I fix what can be fixed. I try to learn from the experience. I go on with my life, but I wish I could undo it, and I think how much better it would have been if I hadn't done it. After all the trouble, I wonder why I sin.

But I'm grateful I have God when I do.

A lesbian with a drug and alcohol problem told me once that she wished she had a belief system. She wanted so much to have a Higher Power to trust, to believe, to forgive. She had previously viewed religion as a crutch for people who didn't want to take responsibility for their own lives, but now she saw it as liberation.

In the many years since our conversation, I've realized that spirituality is, in reality, for those who *want* to take responsibility for their lives.

Thank you for forgiveness that sets us apart, that makes us whole and holy, Merciful God.

[God] has told you, O mortal, what is good;
and what does the [Sovereign] require of you
but to do justice, and to love kindness,
and to walk humbly with your God?

                                        Micah 6:8

Many denominations name both homosexuality and homophobia as sins, but only ban ordination for those who practice the
"sin" of homosexuality. The inconsistency of the policy reveals
their goal is discrimination rather than holiness.

Things may not change quickly. Church historian Martin
Marty has pointed out that the church as an institution is
becoming skewed toward the right every year largely because of a single phenomenon. When conservatives come
to power, they ruthlessly ax progressive leadership. When
liberals come to power, they tend to allow conservative
leadership to stay.

Holiness means separation from the surrounding culture,
to be set apart for a holy purpose. What's wrong with the
church is not that it's exclusive——after all, being set apart
requires boundaries of belief and practice. What's wrong is
that it's exclusive of the wrong kinds of behavior. Instead of
excluding lesbians and gay men, it should exclude unjust,
unkind, and self-righteous behaviors.

We can purify the church by making sure that justice,
kindness, and humility become the criteria for membership
and leadership, not sexual orientation.

Purify your church from unholy, unjust practices, O Holy
One.

"You know that my father David could not build a house for the name of the [Sovereign] his God because of the warfare with which his enemies surrounded him."

1 Kings 5:3

"But God said to me, 'You shall not build a house for my name, for you are a warrior and have shed blood.'"

1 Chronicles 28:3

In the first tradition, King Solomon explained that his father, David, could not build God's temple because he was preoccupied with enemies who kept him engaged in combat. In the second tradition, King David explained that his son, Solomon, would build the temple because of the blood on his hands from war.

Those of us who are not in gay-welcoming churches are so preoccupied with our struggle, we may have difficulty creating a sanctuary for God among us. And the ways we "frame" God will always be provisional, because our hands are not clean of the struggle.

That's why those communities of faith that welcome us have an awesome responsibility in building sanctuaries for God. That's why we must look to these oases of freedom to discover what it means to be a lesbian or gay Christian unfettered by oppression.

Master Builder, instruct us in the structure of your new sanctuary. Give us the dimensions of your grace.

"I am not worthy to have you come under my roof; but only speak the word, and my servant will be healed."

Matthew 8:8

For me, the most moving element of Catholic mass is the prayer offered before receiving Holy Communion: "Lord, I am not worthy to receive you, only say the word, and I shall be healed."

As Moses did not feel worthy to enter the Promised Land, as David did not feel worthy to build God's temple, so we may not feel worthy to receive Jesus into our lives.

A Gentile centurion asked Jesus to heal his beloved servant, but said the words of today's verse when Jesus offered to come. Jesus is "amazed," remarking, "In no one in Israel have I found such faith" (8:10). Then, to the centurion, he said, "Go, let it be done for you according to your faith" (8:13). And the servant was healed in that moment.

Jesus is willing to come to our homes. He will heal from a distance, if we feel unworthy. But he prefers to make us worthy by entering our homes, blessing them as sanctuaries for all.

Bless my home, my workplace, and my self as sanctuaries for your presence, as sanctuaries for healing for all who enter.

And he entered the temple and began to drive out those who were selling and those who were buying in the temple, and he overturned the tables of the money changers and the seats of those who sold doves; and he would not allow anyone to carry anything through the temple.

Mark 11:15–16

"No business as usual!" we shouted in antiwar demonstrations against corporations profiting from the Vietnam War. "No business as usual!" ACT-UP demonstrators say in the AIDS era during actions directed at everything from pharmaceuticals to pharisees. "No business as usual!" Jesus implied in a demonstration removing commerce from the temple grounds, shouting, "My house shall be called a house of prayer for all peoples!"

Using uncivil means to reveal an uncivil business finds its roots in Jesus and the prophets who preceded and followed him. As Jesus purified the temple, so we seek the purification of the church and other social institutions.

Howard Warren was virtually a one-man demonstration one year at a national church gathering, holding up a sign with the word "SHAME" written on it beneath a pulpit where someone was preaching. I doubt anyone remembers who was preaching or what words were spoken, but everyone will remember the Word enfleshed by his courageous demonstration against the church's unholy, antigay attitude.

We bless all those who choose to ACT UP rather than simply act out their oppression.

Jesus said, "I came into this world for judgment so that those who do not see may see, and those who do see may become blind."

John 9:39

The Pharisees were blinded by their inability to see from another's perspective. The man who had been born blind believed Jesus could not have given him his sight if he wasn't from God. Wanting to see Jesus in their own way, the Pharisees dismissed the blind man's view with, "You were born entirely in sins, and are you trying to teach us?" (9:34). They pettily saw Jesus as someone who broke the Sabbath law by "working," or healing the man on the day to be kept holy.

Jesus came into the world to confirm the view of those of us on the margins of society who question purported authority and the status quo. We are considered blind sinners by those who benefit from the way things are. For "our own good," they would arrogantly teach us. But Jesus came into the world to bless us with a vision of how things ought to be. Since it varies from the way things are, we are rendered visionary and established authorities are rendered visionless.

Thank you, Jesus! They questioned my vision, but you confirm and consecrate it.

"And ought not this woman . . . be set free from this bondage on the sabbath day?"

Luke 13:16

How we, too, would appreciate being set free on the sabbath!

On the sabbath, Jesus set a woman free from an invisible burden that bent her back for eighteen years. The leader of the synagogue whined that there were six other days when people could be healed. Jesus pointed to his hypocrisy, explaining that he would untie an animal to give it water on the sabbath——so how much more should this woman be set free.

On a Sunday, a preacher might deliver a sermon on the equal rights of women or on civil rights for lesbians and gay men. The president of the church council may whine that there are six other days when politics could be done. The preacher might point out the hypocrisy of preaching good news that does not set people free.

Holiness is wholeness, harmony within an individual or within society. Healing a person or a society is a proper task for a holy day.

Deliver us from the burdens that bend our backs, Jesus, so that with this woman we may rise up confidently to praise God.

"The sabbath was made for humankind, and not humankind for the sabbath."

Mark 2:27

In the scripture that follows this text, Jesus becomes angered at the hardness of heart that prevents an affirmative response to his question, "Is it lawful to do good or to do harm on the sabbath, to save life or to kill?" He is about to heal a man with a withered hand.

But in the passage preceding today's verse, he is not doing anything nearly as laudable. His disciples are simply picking grain to eat on the sabbath, and he defends their action to the Pharisees. Clearly he wanted to make the point that religious law was intended to benefit, not paralyze, human beings. Not only the sabbath but the whole law was made for humankind, not the other way around.

Holiness emerges from doing, not don't-ing.

A Babel tower of regulations will not allow us to climb into your heaven, God. Forgive the babble of Christian legalism.

Jesus said to them, "Isaiah prophesied rightly about you hyp-ocrites, as it is written, 'This people honors me with their lips, but their hearts are far from me; in vain do they worship me, teaching human precepts as doctrines.' You abandon the com-mandment of God and hold to human tradition."

Mark 7:6–8

Jesus would be the first to question those who uncritically equate the human traditions found in scripture with God's commandments. He would also freely critique the precepts that have evolved since the Bible. He readily discerned what was closest to the heart of God in both his own scrip-ture and tradition. Surely he'd do the same today.

Since the church is the Body of Christ, then the church must not only be involved in such critical review but must be the leader in discerning what scriptures and what tradi-tions are mere human custom and which are closest to the heart of God.

Biblical scholarship does not question biblical authority; rather it values God's Word in scripture highly enough to discern it, filtering out words of lesser authority. Then the Word is out.

Holy Spirit, guide my heart closer to God, so that the Word comes out as I meditate on the words of the Bible.

If any harm follows, then you shall give life for life, eye for eye, tooth for tooth, hand for hand, foot for foot, burn for burn, wound for wound, stripe for stripe.

Exodus 21:23–24

"You have heard that it was said, 'An eye for an eye and a tooth for a tooth.' But I say to you, Do not resist an evildoer. But if anyone strikes you on the right cheek, turn the other also."

Matthew 5:38–39

Jesus reinterpreted scripture. What was intended as a restraining order——take *no more* than an eye for an eye or a tooth for a tooth——is not close enough to God's command, according to Jesus. God, who marked Cain lest someone kill him for his murder of Abel, wants us to turn the other cheek.

This does not mean we cooperate with evil. Rather, it means that we do not let the deeds of evil people make us into people like them. We don't spread lies when our opponents spread lies. We don't work to exclude others from the church when they work to exclude us. We don't become bashers of straight people when they bash us.

Being set apart for a holy purpose requires the ultimate resistance that Jesus talked about: a refusal to let the opposition hook us or push our buttons. After all, if they hook us, they're in control.

Make us holy by delivering us from behaviors we deplore, Sacred Spirit.

"The [Human One] has come eating and drinking, and you say, 'Look, a glutton and a drunkard, a friend of tax collectors and sinners!'"

Luke 7:34

Compared to the rigorously ascetic John the Baptist, Jesus enjoyed earthly pleasures. He also referred to himself more earthily as "Son of Man" (better rendered as the "Human One") rather than use the more heavenly designation "Son of God," as followers would later call him.

The evangelical Pharisees and the legalistic lawyers (who interpreted the Law of Moses) attacked Jesus for his lifestyle, just as many evangelical and legalistic Christians attack us for our "lifestyle."

A lesbian was asked to resign as director of a council of churches because of her "lifestyle." She was wonderfully naive enough to think, at first, that the board was concerned about her living in an upper-middle-class neighborhood when her work was primarily among poorer people. Soon she caught on that what they objected to was her female partner!

There are as many lesbian and gay lifestyles as there are Christian lifestyles. Yet others condemn us by painting us with one brush, as if we all lived the same way.

I would rather be condemned with Jesus than condoned by the church.

Rainbow Maker, thank you for a spectrum of lifestyles, a holy rainbow of promise.

*You shall not lie with a male as with a woman; it is an abom-
ination. . . . If a man lies with a male as with a woman, both
of them have committed an abomination; they shall be put to
death; their blood is upon them.*

                                             Leviticus 18:22, 20:13

It is an understatement to say that finding God's Word within
these words is extremely difficult for us. But the spiritual principles underlying these mistaken applications may still be true
for us. The Holiness Code, of which these laws are part, advo-
cated separateness ("set apart") and integrity as goals of holiness.

Separateness demands that our church separate itself
from the homophobia and bigotry of the surrounding culture.

Our church's integrity requires that we question laws
such as this one from Leviticus that are based on an ancient
Israelite worldview: that there are categories of creation
that may not be mixed up. If the church no longer practices
kosher laws and mixes up different kinds of food at every
church potluck, then the church cannot bind us who "mix
things up" sexually.

Christian integrity requires that we put Christ in the mix,
and remember that the law was made for us, not us for the
law. Such integrity demands that anyone who confesses
Jesus as Sovereign is welcome in the church.

Jesus, may your Word guide us in reading the Bible's words.

For this reason God gave them up to degrading passions. Their women exchanged natural intercourse for unnatural, and in the same way also the men, giving up natural intercourse with women, were consumed with passion for one another.

Romans 1:26–27

When we first discovered we were gay, most of us would have probably preferred finding the exchange window of heaven to return our natural homosexual orientation for a heterosexual one. Life would have been easier.

Paul and other biblical writers did not know today's distinction between sexual orientation and behavior. They, like many heterosexuals today, assumed everyone was born like them, and that homosexual behavior involved some choice contrary to one's natural inclination.

Paul associated the phenomenon with idolatry. How then do we account for *Christians* who are lesbian, gay, or bisexual? Clearly, Paul is wrong. Reason and experience (and science, their product) contradict his understanding.

Ironically, Paul's own teaching contradicts his judgment. His letter to the Romans is devoted to the principle that we are not made holy by conformity, but by faith in Jesus Christ. We cannot be saved by behaving heterosexually, only by following Christ.

Christ Jesus, give us the faith to follow you, rather than the idolatrous god of heterosexuality.

But [Jesus] said to them, "Not everyone can accept this teaching, but only those to whom it is given."

Matthew 19:11

The church is quite capable of setting aside or re-interpreting Jesus' teaching on divorce, from which this verse comes. But the exceptions Jesus described in the verses that follow are eunuchs, those made so by others, those who chose it, and those so born. That covers all possible ways that we might be homosexual, doesn't it? And wouldn't that cover bisexuals and transgenders, too?

Yesterday's eunuchs would be roughly our equivalent today as outcasts and as non-procreationists. So Jesus may be indirectly speaking up for us. Ironically, heterosexual Christians quote this scripture not against divorce but against us: "For this reason a man shall . . . be joined to his wife, and the two become one flesh" (19:5). But Jesus said this wasn't for everybody.

That's the more important aspect of this scripture text. Jesus clarifies that one saying doesn't fit all. Guidelines to holiness are just that: guidelines.

Open our ears to the sayings intended for us; help the church take the beam out of its own ear before speaking into ours.

"Truly I tell you, it will be more tolerable for the land of Sodom and Gomorrah on the day of judgment than for that town."

Matthew 10:15

It was centuries after Christ that the sin of Sodom and Gomorrah became associated with sexuality. Jesus uses the cities several times as comparisons to towns refusing to welcome his disciples or to receive his message. He clearly believed the sin of Sodom and Gomorrah was inhospitality.

The broader church will be called to account for its inhospitality to Jesus' lesbian and gay disciples. And it will be judged for failing to receive our message of spiritual-sexual integrity.

And the hospitality of the gay and lesbian community will be lifted up as an example: the ear willing to listen to someone's troubles; the arms lifted to offer a consoling embrace; the home opened to someone who needed a place to stay; the dinner party that didn't exclude someone in grief or in trouble; the center that helped homeless youth regardless of sexual orientation; the agency that broadened its efforts to all communities affected by AIDS; the church that gladly welcomed the spectrum of sexualities.

Our inhospitality will *also* be judged. So be careful.

May all who are strangers be to me as Christ, O God.

The [Sovereign] spoke to Moses, saying: Command the Israelites to put out of the camp everyone who is leprous, or has a discharge, and everyone who is unclean through contact with a corpse; . . . they must not defile their camp, where I dwell among them.

Numbers 5:1–3

Proposals to quarantine people with HIV disease have come from fearful, ignorant, and often hateful people, many of whom claim to be followers of Christ. Now it is commonly known that the general population poses more of an infectious threat to PWA's than the other way around. Only fear and wanton ignorance still keep some people at a distance.

Holiness is not about separating ourselves from one another in this way. The ancient Hebrews sent the diseased from their midst because they knew of no other way. But Jesus went out to lepers, was touched by a woman with a discharge, touched the eyes of the blind, and raised the dead. Jesus corrected ancient practice, calling us to follow.

A friend once told me that if he had AIDS, he would be willing to live alone in a plastic bubble to protect himself from opportunistic infections. When he later tested positive for HIV antibodies, he instead surrounded himself with an invisible bubble of secrecy.

Isolation, whether as the church, in a gay ghetto, in a closet, or even in a disease, while keeping us safe, will not make us holy.

Keep me from quarantining people in my life to keep safe.

"Listen to me, all of you, and understand: there is nothing out-side a person that by going in can defile, but the things that come out are what defile."

Mark 7:14

Some Christians believe limiting their perception of the world is a way to holiness. My fundamentalist cousin won't have a television in her home. My sister signed an agreement not to see movies when she briefly attended a Christian college. The Catholic church only allows its imprimatur on books that ab-solutely conform to doctrine, and it has a movie rating system. Christian bookstores and book catalogues resist carrying gay-positive titles.

I enjoy seminaries because it's easier to be a Christian where my perceptions are reinforced. But my faith seems more authentic facing the realities of everyday life and doubt. A Lutheran writer critiqued my style of ministry within the gay community: "There's no distance there." In response, an agnostic friend told me, "But that's your unique gift."

Jesus was criticized for not keeping himself holy in the old-fashioned ways. He and his disciples did not "baptize" their hands before eating. Jesus used the occasion to illus-trate that it's not how you eat, but how you act, that keeps you holy. By correlation, it's not what you know about the world; what matters is what comes from your heart in re-sponse.

Within my heart, Holy Spirit, transform the cries and crises of this world into deeds of kindness and mercy.

*For why should my liberty be subject to the judgment of some-
one else's conscience? If I partake with thankfulness, why
should I be denounced because of that for which I give thanks?*

1 Corinthians 10:30

Admittedly, the apostle Paul wrote this while advising care
that our behavior as liberated Christians does not hurt the
consciences of those less free. And yet, it is a truth we need
to write on our hearts as lesbian and gay Christians.

Strolling in a park with a lover, I noted a heterosexual
couple walking arm in arm. Wishing I could do that with
my lover, a slight flash of anger illuminated the many times
we have to restrain our impulses to do what is natural for
us.

My lover and I are looking for a church in a new city, and
we've decided it has to be a church where we feel comfortable holding hands or putting an arm around each other.

We need to flaunt ourselves more. No matter how much
we do so, we will never come close to the frequency by
which straights flaunt their sexuality in society and the
church.

And we need to give thanks to God for lesbian love and
gay love, because it's appropriate to thank God for the gift,
and because it serves as a reminder that our love is holy.

*Thank you for the love that once dare not pray its name! We
bless it and call it holy.*

[Christ] has abolished the law with its commandments and or-
dinances, that he might create in himself one new humanity
in place of the two, thus making peace, and might reconcile
both groups to God in one body through the cross, thus putting
to death [their] hostility through it.

Ephesians 2:15–16

Paul wrote about Gentiles and Jews being made one in Christ
Jesus, but he could have been writing about gays and straights.
The law of compulsory heterosexuality has been abolished, for
it is by God's grace in Christ Jesus that we are reconciled with
God and with one another.

A dividing wall of hostility, earlier mentioned, has been
brought down. This was the wall of the temple separating
the section for the Jews from the section for the Gentiles.
Our dividing wall of hostility is the closet wall.

Holiness is harmony. Paul was concerned for such holiness in this letter to the church at Ephesus. The blending of
Gentiles and Jews, the uncircumcised with the circumcised, was crucial to the early church's integrity.

People sometimes say that homosexuality will split the
church. The truth is, *homophobia* is more likely to cause
schism. Looking to Christ will help us overcome ancient fear
and hostility. For Christ is "our peace" and our unity (2:14).

Christ Jesus, as you've done before, unite us with your cross
and with your peace.

Work out your own salvation with fear and trembling; for it is God who is at work in you, enabling you both to will and to work for [God's] good pleasure.

Philippians 2:12

The paternalism of our opposition "being burdened for our souls" is often galling. Don't they realize that it's *our* souls on the line, and therefore we're more likely to have worked out our salvation with humility before an awesome God?

In *Uncommon Calling* I described how Huck Finn worked out his salvation in fear and "a-trembling." Halfway down the Mississippi River, his conscience convinced him that helping a runaway slave was wrong. Sunday school taught him better. So he wrote a letter to Jim's owner and felt "all washed clean of sin." Then he remembered when Jim saved his life, when he cared for him in sickness, when he let him sleep through his watch on the raft, how he would call him honey and pet him and do everything he could for him. Huck looked at the letter, thought of Jim, and then ripped it up, saying, "All right, then, I'll go to hell!"

Sometimes with the inspiration of a lover like Jim, we all make Huck Finn choices to do what we believe to be right, even if it flies in the face of religious upbringing. We must trust that God is at work within us, and that God's grace is sufficient even if we get it wrong.

God, grant me the grace to take risks for your commonwealth!

By contrast, the fruit of the Spirit is love, joy, peace, patience,
kindness, generosity, faithfulness, gentleness, and self-control.
                                                    Galatians 5:22

The mother of a son who died of AIDS wrote his gay congregation of her transformation when she came to "save"
him. She wrote that she brought her Bible, but no food for
the pantry. She brought her Bible, but the neighbor brought
an afghan for his chills. She brought her Bible when they
went to church, but the members gave him the hugs and
kisses that he needed. Then she realized in the six months
she had been with him, she had been so busy holding onto
her Bible she had never held *him!*

   She now hugged him. Finally she wrote, "The God my
son knew so well was not the God I had heard so much
about or the God I was striving so hard to introduce Bob to.
I came that day, many months ago, to save my son; and
praise God and your community! *My son saved me!"*

   What comes from the heart is vital, Jesus said. Love, joy,
peace, patience, kindness, generosity, faithfulness, gentleness, and self-control are marks of holiness. And holiness is
the fruit of the Spirit.

Holy Spirit, sanctify my life, that I may live up to your
promise by acting out your faithfulness to others.

Create in me a clean heart, O God,
and put a new and right spirit within me.

Psalm 51:10

Though saved and made holy by God's grace, God's unmerited mercy and favor, we may still grow in grace. Early Christians called the process sanctification.

A rabbi was asked by the *Los Angeles Times* for his opinion of the "born again" movement of Christianity. He said that he thought of himself as born again every day. Each day served as an occasion to start afresh in the spiritual life.

Every day we may pray for God to create new and steadfast hearts within us. "This is the day that the [Sovereign] has made; let us rejoice and be glad in it," the Psalmist also wrote (118:24). And Paul, urging that we not "accept the grace of God in vain," wrote, "now is the day of salvation!" (2 Cor. 6:2.)

A Buddhist mystic who was said to have attained nirvana was asked what was left in his life to achieve. He replied, "I have also arrived in this city, but I have not seen its every corner."

Though we have been blessed with God's salvation, we have yet to see all of its dimensions.

Create in me a clean heart, O God, and put a new and right spirit within me!

THE CALL

●
●
●
●

Consider your own call, brothers and sisters: not many of you were wise by human standards, not many were powerful, not many were of noble birth.

1 Corinthians 1:26

Nor were many of us called to do "grand" things that would get us on the evening news or *Phil Donahue*.

We are often unaware that the smallest act of hospitality, generosity, or love may have reverberations in the world. On the AIDS Quilt I found the panel of a friend, Chris Chlanda, whose act of hospitality affected my entire denomination. When we were both students at Yale, he arranged a dinner so that I could meet John Boswell, who was then working on his book *Christianity, Social Tolerance, and Homosexuality*. As a result, I arranged for the Presbyterian Task Force to Study Homosexuality, on which I served, to meet with Boswell, and his research influenced our positive recommendations.

I daresay Chris's life was filled with many such occasions that gave the world a better future. Even in ordinary circumstances with ordinary resources, our call to make a difference provides extraordinary results.

Spirit of God, may I consider everyday opportunities as calls to help you bring in your commonwealth of love.

The [Sovereign] spoke to Moses, saying: Speak to Aaron and say: No one of your offspring throughout their generations who has a blemish may approach to offer the food of his God.

Leviticus 21:16–17

Just about everyone who serves in ministry today would be disqualified by the Levitical code's stringent requirements for priesthood! Any physical or moral imperfection meant rejection. And women need not apply!

Small wonder that when Christianity opened the doors wider to ministry, there were still some debates about who was qualified. The first letter to Timothy permits "no woman to teach or to have authority over a man" (2:12), maintains slaves as second-class citizens of faith (6:1), but argues against those who would "despise [Timothy's] youth" (4:12).

The daughter of friends who are a clergy couple was playing with a doll in the bathtub. "This one's having a baby," she said. Playing along, the mother asked, "Is it a boy or a girl?" "Neither," the little girl answered. "It's a minister!" She viewed the pulpit as gender-free.

But there are those for whom women and gays represent undesirable sexuality in the pulpit, while, ironically, handsome male pastors with charisma enjoy successful careers in the church. Our call challenges the supposed asexuality of ministry.

May I draw on the powers of the earth and of my body to minister to your Body, O Christ.

But the [Sovereign] said to Samuel, "Do not look on his appearance or on the height of his stature, because I have rejected him; for [God] does not see as mortals see; they look on the outward appearance, but [God] looks on the heart."

1 Samuel 16:7

In a television program called *Crossroads,* two attractive, personable, and well-dressed men visit a small town, each claiming to be an angel of God. To discern which is from God, the townspeople have them engage in a staring match. A circle is drawn around the perimeter of their spiritual struggle. Whoever blinks or looks away will clearly be of the devil.

A little girl, unaware of what is going on, runs into the circle. The spiritual powers knock her down, and one turns to catch her as she falls. The dilemma remains: some believe the one who turned away is of Satan; others believe that since he is the only one who cared about the little girl, he is of God.

Appearances are deceiving. We know this in a community so driven by appearance. Charming, good-looking, well-dressed women or men may or may not be good to us or for us. The same is true of ministry. Those who minister to us may not be immediately recognizable as angels, or even as "ministers."

Just as the Spirit kept Samuel from anointing the wrong son of Jesse as king of Israel in today's scripture, she helps us discern who is ordained to minister to us.

Teach me to look inside a person's heart for your Spirit.

*But Moses said, "O my Lord, I have never been eloquent, nei-
ther in the past nor even now that you have spoken to your servant; but I am slow of speech and slow of tongue."*

Exodus 3:10–11

*"When they bring you before the synagogues, the rulers, and
the authorities, do not worry about how you are to defend
yourselves or what you are to say; for the Holy Spirit will teach
you at that very hour what you ought to say."*

Luke 12:11–12

A lesbian who teaches public speaking advised me that the key
to communication is that the audience like you. That's why a
panel of lesbian and gay Christians simply speaking of their
lives to church congregations is very effective at informing
minds and transforming hearts——the goal, it seems to me, of
communication.

Moses is endearing as he admits the limits of his verbal
competence to God. While such confession would not im-
press a political leader like Pharaoh, it touches the heart of
truly spiritual people. So it is not necessarily a liability when
our expertise is limited to our personal experience.

The Spirit will teach us what we are to say to the church.
But the Spirit also helps us prepare through meditation on
scripture and reading gay-friendly interpreters of the faith.

Open my lips, Holy One, so that they may declare your Word!

*"Woe is me! I am lost, for I am a man of unclean lips, and I
live among a people of unclean lips; yet my eyes have seen
[God]!"*

Isaiah 6:5

I had a boyfriend who just couldn't get the blending of spirituality and sexuality. He heard me preach Sunday morning, and
enjoyed partying with me Sunday night. But it bothered him
that the same lips that preached God's Word could drink a beer
or kiss him.

His respectful awe of God's Word was appropriate. Isaiah felt this awe at his calling, for he knew he was both mortal and sinful. A seraph, a kind of angel, touched his lips
with a live coal from the altar to purge him. God asked,
"Whom shall I send, and who will go for us?" And Isaiah
replied, "Here am I; send me!" (6:8).

I, too, am a person of unclean lips. I'm aware of that
whenever I say something hurtful or hateful. But having a
beer and kissing someone are not defiling in and of themselves. It's what comes out of my heart that matters.

In lovemaking, we must be careful not to call unclean
what God has called clean.

Here we are, Lord, send us!

Then Gideon said to God, ". . . I am going to lay a fleece of wool on the threshing floor; if there is dew on the fleece alone, and it is dry on all the ground, then I shall know that you will deliver Israel by my hand, as you have said."

Judges 6:36–37

Many of us have heard the old adage about "putting our fleece before the Lord" without knowing its origin in this challenge from Gideon. God did as requested, but just to make sure, Gideon also asked for the reverse: dry fleece, wet ground. God gave him irrefutable proof of his call to action.

Rarely are we given empirical evidence of God's call to serve. The more mystical of us may be more certain, but when the going gets rough, any of us may doubt our spiritual vocation.

God's calls in the Bible are frequently accompanied by signs and wonders. But think of Esther, Ruth, Jonathan, or Timothy, who had no miracles. They only happened to be in the right place at the right time on the right side with the right intentions——and they fulfilled God's will.

Moments of *kairos*——spiritual opportunities——are rarely accompanied by visions or special effects or a swelling orchestral score. True, the more dramatic ones were recorded in scripture or in church history. But without the less fantastic ones, the church could never have been the *ecclesia*, the *called* community.

Call me, God. I will listen, watch, wait, and act.

"Who is on [God's] side? Come to me!"
                                    Exodus 32:26

What follows in the text is the bloodiest ordination in history. Aaron had let the people "run wild" (32:25) and Moses called the people who would serve God. The sons of Levi gathered, and Moses instructed them to put on their swords and "go back and forth from gate to gate throughout the camp, and each of you kill your brother, your friend, and your neighbor" (32:27). When this had been done, Moses announced, "Today you have ordained yourselves for the service of [God]" (32:29).

This bizarre episode in the history of the people of faith may be the unspoken scriptural basis for the periodic bloodletting of national church governing bodies! Their scapegoats are often us. "Homosexuality is the reason the church can't get it together," some say. Others announce, "The peace, unity, and purity of the church are dependent on ridding ourselves of homosexuals."

All who are ordained in a church that does not welcome us have blood on their hands. The more sensitive and informed among them are aware of this and work for change.

Holy God, we pray for the day when ordination will no longer be a violent or vile act of exclusion in churches that reject us.

"My grace is sufficient for you, for power is made perfect in weakness."

2 Corinthians 12:9

Ironically, those of us who were not ordained by mainstream churches may have more power not being co-opted by the church. We may not carry the official sanction of the church, but we have *referent* power, that is, spiritual power derived from our meaning-full position unjustly excluded. We may not have the official rights afforded clergy, but that also means we are not responsible to church authority. This is especially helpful for those in the Roman Catholic church, which can silence voices that disagree.

Being marginalized by the church gives us greater power and perspective and freedom to question its authority and injustice. God's call to the church may be made manifest in our weakness.

God gave Paul this answer when the apostle prayed for "a thorn . . . in the flesh" to be removed. Speculation on this "thorn" has included homosexuality. Whatever it was, it made Paul aware of God's power perfected in his vulnerability.

Our own thorn in the flesh is the church's heterosexism. Within us, through God's grace, it blossoms into a vigorous freedom.

Called to freedom, may we manifest the power of your grace in our vulnerability, Christ Jesus.

When they had crossed, Elijah said to Elisha, "Tell me what I may do for you, before I am taken from you." Elisha said, "Please let me inherit a double share of your spirit."

2 Kings 2:9

The prophets in the Bible rarely enjoyed official status, but lived on the margins of society, better able to critique it. Elijah and Elisha both were forced to hide from the authorities from time to time. People did not like the truths they were called to proclaim.

For Elisha to ask for a double share of the spirit that rested on Elijah was an awesome request. But after Elijah's mystical departure, Elisha picked up the mantle he left behind. It was an outward sign of the passage of spiritual power from one to the other.

A church in Rochester, New York, was denied the services of a lesbian pastor by its parent denomination. That community of faith then decided instead to employ Janie Spahr as a "lesbian evangelist," to preach the gospel to the whole church. Every member, from age six to eighty, embroidered a line or two on a stole for her to wear when celebrating Communion on her missionary journeys.

This collective "mantle" represents more than a passage of spiritual power from a prophetic congregation to a prophet. It is a gift of spiritual power to all of us.

God, give me a double share of your Spirit, that I may proclaim your truth!

Now the boy Samuel was ministering to [God] under Eli. The word of [God] was rare in those days; visions were not wide-spread. . . . Samuel was lying down in the temple. . . . Then [God] called, "Samuel! Samuel!" and he said, "Here I am!"

1 Samuel 3:1, 3–4

A disproportionate number of us heard God's call when we were very young. Many of us were or are active in youth programs and church school. The congregation I served had more than its fair share of lesbians and gay men who attended parochial schools, Bible colleges, seminaries, or special training programs for lay ministries.

When I travel, I meet many helping professionals who happily do what they do, but tell me they had originally intended to enter the ministry. A happy "complaint" I hear from the mostly gay Metropolitan Community Church is that "too many" want to be professional or lay ministers!

Now that there are congregations open to us, some of us are hearing God's call when we're as old as Eli. Many of the older generations were prevented from even imagining a vocation as a minister or priest.

Just as God's call to serve is no respecter of sexual orientation, it is no respecter of age.

Speak, Sovereign, for your children of all ages are listening!

Many Samaritans from that city believed in him because of the woman's testimony.

John 4:39

Jesus "astonished" his disciples by speaking to a woman. Equally astonishing was that he revealed his messianic identity to her, a woman from the hated people of Samaria. She had been drawing water from a well and ran to tell others from her city, becoming the first Christian evangelist.

In their conversation, Jesus had offered her "living water" that would "become in [her] a spring of water gushing up to eternal life" (4:14).

Many of us who experience or proclaim the good news forget to return to the well. The gospels provide us with living words from Jesus that quench our spiritual thirst. We may also use them to water the dry places in our lives, transforming the wilderness into a watered garden.

And we may bring our people back to the well to meet Jesus, as the Samaritan woman did.

Dear Jesus, you call us to serve you, but not without giving us water for the journey.

Jesus said to [the Samaritan woman at the well], "You are right in saying, 'I have no husband'; for you have had five husbands, and the one you have now is not your husband."

John 4:17–18

After my autobiographical book *Uncommon Calling* appeared, a nongay minister took me aside at a national church gathering to offer his reflections. He told me that he thought the book was good, except that I reinforced the notion that gay men are promiscuous.

"How so?" I asked. He said, "You talk about several different relationships in the book. I know you said they ended because of things like homophobia, but this would just reinforce my congregation's view of homosexuality."

I replied, "You mean to tell me that straight people don't go through several relationships before they find the right person?" By the heterosexual divorce rate, I could have added that straight people are as bad at finding the "right" person as we are!

Jesus didn't seem to care that the Samaritan woman had had five husbands and was now living unmarried with another. He did not tell her to "Go, and sin no more." He offered her living water that might quench her apparent thirst for love.

Jesus, you know us inside and out, past and present. Give us living water to quench our thirst for love.

*But Rahab the prostitute, with her family and all who be-
longed to her, Joshua spared. . . . For she hid the messengers
whom Joshua sent to spy out Jericho.*

Joshua 6:25

One of the earliest debates in the Metropolitan Community
Church was whether a congregation should accept the offerings of a hustler or prostitute. Was the money somehow "de-
filed" by the way it was earned, a defilement that lingered with
the money when it was offered to God?

Rahab, a prostitute, offered sanctuary and hospitality to
spies that Joshua had sent to Jericho. She played a central
role in the Israelites' defeat of the city, which they gave as
an offering to Yahweh. Hanging a crimson cord from her
window alerted the conquerors which family to save. She
then joined the lineage that led to King David and ultimately
to Jesus.

That the question of accepting money from a prostitute
can even be raised reveals how negatively we view sexuality. We don't ask if anyone else's offering is tainted. To
MCC's credit, it's possibly the only church that can honestly
discuss a topic like this!

*Forgive us for unfairly judging the offering of another. Bless
all of our gifts to your service, O God.*

"As for yourselves, beware; for they will hand you over to councils; and you will be beaten in synagogues; and you will stand before governors and kings because of me, as a testimony to them."

Mark 13:9

George Lynch was outed on the way to answering a call to ministry. An unbalanced mother broke into her son's apartment and found letters from George supporting the integration of his faith and his sexuality. She sent the letters to George's seminary, who in turn sent them to the committee overseeing his preparation for ministry. Spiteful church leadership not only wanted him thrown out, but even refused him a transfer to a more accepting committee.

Now he serves his denomination as a volunteer for its peacemaking program and as chair of a committee overseeing clergy. But he himself is denied opportunity to serve in the professional ministry.

As angry as this story may make us, it is but one of thousands that I have heard, and one of tens of thousands that we have heard collectively. As Jesus warned, our calling puts us in danger. But it also calls the church to repentance for the lives it has damaged and destroyed. Jesus continued, "And the good news must first be proclaimed to all peoples" (13:10). That means the Lavender People as well.

Call forth our anger, God of great passion, that our fire may purify, not destroy, the church.

"Look well, for you shall not cross over this Jordan. But charge Joshua, and encourage and strengthen him, because it is he who shall cross over at the head of this people and who shall secure their possession of the land that you will see."

Deuteronomy 3:27–28

Many of us who are called to serve will only see the Promised Land from a distance, as Moses is here informed by God. Yet as Reinhold Niebuhr wrote, anything worth devoting your life to requires more than a lifetime to achieve.

Discouraged by recent events within the church and by continued resistance within society, it occurred to me I'd been in our movement twenty years. Then I realized that twenty was only half of forty, the number of years the Israelites journeyed to the Promised Land. So maybe, I told myself, I should wait a little longer.

Marj Adler, a dear friend once involved in the women's movement in the church, asked me what I thought the future held. It dawned on me that my longevity in the movement was both blessing and liability. I've witnessed slow, incremental change, so I'm not as disillusioned as newer activists by setbacks. But I've also seen how slowly pulpits have opened to women and people of color long after church approval of their ministry. Even when we "win," full acceptance will take generations.

O Great Deliverer, give us a glimpse of the Promised Land with which to encourage those who follow.

I pray that the God of our Lord Jesus Christ . . . may give you a spirit of wisdom and revelation as you come to know [God], so that, with the eyes of your heart enlightened, you may know what is the hope to which [God] has called you.

Ephesians 1:17

Human wisdom and divine revelation combine to enlighten our hearts to God's hope for us. We don't check our brains, our bodies, nor our experience at the door when we enter church.

We hear the hope to which God calls us in scriptures read aloud, interpreted in the sermon, and sung in anthems and hymns. We feel it in the waters of baptism and taste it in the bread and wine of Communion. We see it in the church's art and architecture, and in the ballet of those leading worship. We inhale its fragrance in the burning of incense. *The hope to which God has called us* is no mere idea, it is a bodily sensation. It is sensual.

Roman Catholic tradition includes marriage as a sacrament. I believe that lovemaking is a sacrament that communicates *the love to which God has called us.* That love is not "Platonic," that is, without eros, distant, of the mind and not the body. Rather, the love to which God has called us is embodied, passionate, touching, healing, and intimate.

The hope to which God has called us *is* the love to which God has called us. It is a pleasure, even if we are called to suffer for it.

God, who is love, reveal the hope to which we are called in the love to which we are called.

"The Spirit of the Lord is upon me,
because [God] has anointed me
to bring good news to the poor.
[God] has sent me to proclaim release to the captives
and recovery of sight to the blind,
to let the oppressed go free,
to proclaim the year of [God's] favor."

Luke 4:18–19

We are not called to proclaim a burdensome message. It enlightens the heart rather than making it heavy. It's good news to the poor, release to the captives, sight to the spiritually impaired, freedom to the oppressed. It's a new era!

We hear Jesus' call as our own, just as he heard the call of this scripture from Isaiah as his own, reading chapter 61 to his home congregation. Interestingly, he is as selective with scripture as anybody, and stops short of finishing the second verse: "to proclaim the year of [God's] favor, *and the day of vengeance of our God.*" Jesus leaves the vengeance out, a sure clue that those who want to bring it back do not proclaim his gospel.

Christ Jesus, thank you for the unbearable lightness of proclaiming your gospel! Blessed be.

The spirit of the Lord God is upon me . . .
to comfort all who mourn; . . .
to give them a garland instead of ashes,
the oil of gladness instead of mourning,
the mantle of praise instead of a faint spirit.

Isaiah 61:1, 2–3

We are not fully aware of our own heaviness and grief in the AIDS crisis. Many of us have few tears left, and we greet the news of the death of yet one more friend with the numbness that our psyches bless us with when we can take no more. As Holly Near sings, we are a gentle but angry people. Beneath often placid surfaces, we are angry and anxious.

What saddens me most is that I cannot feel as deeply for each friend as I would have felt if the death were an isolated event. My lover and I have talked about this, a little envious of those for whom losing a friend to AIDS is a new, life-changing experience.

Lesbian and gay Christians might hear God's call "to comfort all who mourn" visibly or invisibly. We could bring flowers to the living, not just the dead; offer oils for massages, not just last rites; and praise the efforts of caregivers, not just lament over AIDS.

Bless all who mourn, God of the dead and of the living.
Transform our faint spirits into blessings of praise.

Do not fear, for I have redeemed you;
I have called you by name, you are mine.
When you pass through the waters, I will be with you;
and through the rivers, they shall not overwhelm you;
when you walk through fire you shall not be burned,
and the flame shall not consume you.

Isaiah 43:1–2

Responding to our call to serve God does not mean safety. It means that God will be with us. We will still pass through rivers and walk through fire, but we will not be overwhelmed nor consumed.

As I wrote the last sentence, the arrogance of it struck me. I know a woman who lost her faith when her husband suffered a stroke that left him a child mentally. I know another woman who withdrew from God when her husband died young, leaving her with three children to raise alone. There are burdens that seem too great to bear, and it's better not to judge another's experience. Some people *are* overwhelmed or consumed.

I am only reiterating what God promised in Isaiah. God's stated intention is to be with us through every crisis, not so much as protection as guide. A daily prayer time has been the best way for me keep that guide in view. But when prayer doesn't seem to help, I simply trust I'm God's.

You have called me by name, and I am yours. You have redeemed me, and I have nothing to fear.

I can do all things through Christ who strengthens me.

Philippians 4:13

My mother phoned and asked me to include this verse in my book. Her only explanation was that the verse strengthened her.

I thought back on her life, and I realized it must have helped her through unbearable crises. Her mother's death. My sister's divorce. Her husband's first bout with cancer. Her younger son's coming out. Losing her teaching career at a "Christian" school because of my coming out. Her oldest son's long illness. My father's death. My moving away. Her unbearable loneliness missing my dad.

I am grateful that my mother and my father never shielded us from life's crises. They never abandoned us either, neither literally nor figuratively. They were there for us, even when they didn't understand. And they were willing to learn. All because they loved us. That's how I learned God was neither overly protective nor about to leave me.

And they were fundamentalist, Bible-believing Baptists.

I can do all things through Christ who strengthens me.

It was not because you were more numerous than any other people that [God] set [God's] heart on you and chose you—for you were the fewest of all peoples. It was because [God] loved you.

Deuteronomy 7:7

Gay men and lesbians are a minority. Lesbians themselves seem to be a minority within the gay community. Lesbian and gay Christians are a smaller minority still. Lesbian and gay Presbyterians or Baptists or Catholics or United Methodists, and so forth, are minorities within minorities. There is no way we could imagine that God picked us because we're big or powerful or influential.

Yet God uses minorities. The Israelites' national deity was the God of all nations, thus Israel was to be "a light to the nations" (Isa. 42:6). Christians were a minority sect within Judaism, yet were called to proclaim Christ to every nation (Matt. 28:19).

God loves underdogs. That's why we love God. God is with us, for us, and cheers us on. To the majority culture, to the gay community, to the church, we may look like the lowest ranking team. But to God, we're headed for the world series.

Cheer us on, dear God! You make us sure that we're champions!

Now there are varieties of gifts, but the same Spirit.
1 Corinthians 12:4

We don't all have the confrontational nature of militant protestors. We don't all have the emotional fortitude of a primary caregiver. We don't all have the ability to speak or write about the lesbian or gay experience. We don't all have the financial resources to give generously to gay community centers or lesbian organizations.

But we all have the ability to do something rather than nothing. It may be as simple as serving on a committee, baking cookies for a fundraiser, building a booth for a pride festival, or serving as a monitor for a pride parade. We all have gifts to offer.

Two close Christian friends got into a dispute about a gay rights demonstration. One felt the other was not doing her duty if she wasn't out there on the front lines. The other supervised volunteers for a gay center and felt that was her calling. The difference interrupted their friendship for months.

There are varieties of gifts within our community, but the same Spirit inspires them all. It may be appropriate to challenge ourselves and one another, but none of us is in a position to dictate another's contribution.

Thank you, Holy God, for sanctifying the gifts we place on the altar of our community's liberation.

*But when God . . . called me through [God's] grace, . . . I did
not confer with any human being, nor did I go up to
Jerusalem to those who were already apostles before me.*

Galatians 1:15–17

Paul, who wrote much of the New Testament, explained to the
Galatians that he did not become an apostle of Jesus through ordinary human channels. He was not one of the twelve disciples
who followed Jesus and later became the apostles. Nor did he
go to them immediately for confirmation of his extraordinary
conversion and call to proclaim the gospel to the Gentiles.

We may not have received our call to serve God through
ordinary human channels. We were not necessarily part of
the church's "in" crowd. Or, if we were, we knew our sexual identity might exclude us in their eyes. We may not have
sought, nor been offered, confirmation of our call to proclaim the gospel to anyone, let alone to lesbians and gay
men.

We do not need the confirmation of the church to perform our ministry. Paul waited fourteen years to have his
call confirmed by the apostles. Then he had the audacity to
confront a prime church leader, Peter, about hypocrisy!

We share Paul's boldness in asserting God's call of us and
confronting Christian hypocrisy.

Give us Paul's boldness to assert our call, Christ Jesus.

"I came that they may have life, and have it abundantly."

John 10:10

Jesus said he came so that we might have abundant life, life beyond measure.

The Christian life was usually presented to me as a life of duty, obligation, responsibility, soberness. Christians didn't "live it up." While others partied on New Year's Eve, we prayed the new year in. While others took trips on weekends, our church obligations kept us home. While other churches at least served real bread and wine for Communion, we got wafers and grape juice.

And yet, even within such constraints, there was a certain pleasure to it all.

I wrote an article entitled "Spiritual Pleasures" for the newsletter of an AIDS agency, encouraging readers to draw upon their spiritual resources. However, the editor retitled the piece "Spiritual Comfort in the Time of AIDS." We sometimes think of spirituality as a last resort of comfort rather than a first resort of abundant living, or pleasure.

In my last book, *Coming Out to God*, a couple of prepublication readers for my Presbyterian publisher balked at my use of pleasure as a spiritual good. But my prayer life is pleasurable, or I wouldn't be doing it. Even the staid Westminster Catechism says that our chief purpose is to glorify God and enjoy God forever.

Pleasure me, God of sensational creation! Caress me to life with your presence.

Peter said to him, "You will never wash my feet." Jesus answered, "Unless I wash you, you have no share with me."

John 13:8

On a personal retreat at Pendle Hill, the Quaker center near Philadelphia, I met Lyle Jenks. Lyle was very interested in my ministry with gays and lesbians on the campus of the University of Pennsylvania. Later that evening, he asked if he might wash my feet as a sacrament of our spiritual friendship.

I did not expect the gesture to touch my inner self so deeply. The sensuality of the experience was heightened by its spiritual intent. I felt loved and cared for in a way that neither a simply spiritual nor a simply sensual contact could achieve. I felt moved to wash his feet, too, and we have remained bonded since, keeping in touch over the years.

In Jesus' day, the dusty roads made footwashing the first order of hospitality. It was a sensual pleasure with a spiritual intent. In his insistence on washing the disciples' feet, Jesus expresses a wish to touch us that deeply, as God in human flesh, to bond with us intimately and be friends.

"Lord, not my feet only but also my hands and my head!" *(13:9.)*

Comfort, O comfort my people,
says your God.
Speak tenderly to Jerusalem.
                    Isaiah 40:1–2

Sometimes spiritual pleasure takes the form of comfort, comfort we are called to take for ourselves and comfort we are called to offer others.

In a prayer, a lesbian minister compared God to a warm and comfortable quilt. For me, a cat purring on my lap has made me spiritually content. A gay friend finds spiritual tenderness in a lover's eyes.

Prophets like Isaiah were called to challenge the comfortable and comfort the afflicted. Some of us who are comfortable need to be challenged to fulfill our call. But much of the lesbian and gay community is presently in such a state of affliction that we need to hear comfort more than challenge, affirmation more than confrontation.

God's Word to us tenderly comforts us and calls us to comfort one another.

Blanket me with your tender loving care, Loving God. Help me to share your Comforter with others.

As [Jesus] was walking in the temple, the chief priests, the scribes, and the elders came to him and said, "By what authority are you doing these things? Who gave you this authority to do them?"

Mark 11:27–28

I work from Garrison Keillor's maxim that it is easier to obtain forgiveness than permission.

A senior gay church leader was in intensive care after a major heart attack. Since many of us have been denied access into I.C.U.'s to see lovers or friends because we weren't "immediate" family or clergy, a friend and I bussed from New York City to New Jersey without certainty we'd be able to see our friend. We informed the nurses' station we were ministers, though we didn't add that the church had never seen fit to ordain us. Smiling wryly, a nurse said, "Go ahead. He's had a lot of ministers this weekend."

When I resigned a position with my church, clearing the way for ordained leadership rather than my lay leadership, a friend made me wince by saying, "Oh good, now we'll get a real minister." Even within the gay community, my lack of credentials made some question my authority.

Our authority is God-given. When the church is able to affirm it, it still will be God's gift.

You are our ultimate authority, Holy God. Vindicate us!

"Let your light shine before others, so that they may see your good works and give glory to your [God] in heaven."

"You are the salt of the earth; but if salt has lost its taste, how can its saltiness be restored?"

Matthew 5:16, 13

Later, in the same Sermon on the Mount, Jesus seems to contradict himself when he says that in giving alms, we are not to "sound a trumpet," nor let our left hand know what our right hand is doing (6:2–4).

We are not called to let our light shine before others for our own glory but as a witness to God's glory. This is difficult without sounding unduly prideful. Yet, for the sake of both the lesbian and gay community and the church, we could witness how wonderful it is when sexuality and spirituality work together in our lives.

Similarly, as we become more accepted in both our church and our community, we could remember that we are "worth our salt" if we keep in mind our unique slant on life that questions a disembodied spirituality and a despiritualized sexuality.

We are called to illumine life and keep it tasteful.

Let my light so shine before others that they may see your glory at work in me!

I therefore, a prisoner in the [Sovereign], beg you to lead a life worthy of the calling to which you have been called, with all humility and gentleness, with patience, bearing with one another in love, making every effort to maintain the unity of the Spirit in the bond of peace.

Ephesians 4:1–3

We tend to be overachievers. We so want people to like us that we go out of our way to do the right thing. We so want people to respect us that we work extra hard at whatever we do. We so want people to pay attention to us that we do extra-dramatic things——popular or antagonistic.

Some of us need to chill out!

But there is one area in which we are called to remain or become overachievers. Paul described it as he sat imprisoned for his faith. Leading "a life worthy of the calling to which [we] have been called" is not easy, because we've been called to unite sexuality and spirituality, the church and the lesbian and gay community "in the bond of peace."

As much as I or we may speak in "we-they" language, the church is "us." Whether inside or outside structures, the church is always the community of believers from which neither we nor they can be excluded. We share "the one hope of [our] calling," as Paul wrote in the very next verse.

Bless us with visions of unity and ministries of peace.

"So have no fear of them; for nothing is covered up that will not be uncovered, and nothing secret that will not become known. What I say to you in the dark, tell in the light; and what you hear whispered, proclaim from the housetops. Do not fear those who kill the body but cannot kill the soul."

Matthew 10:26–28

We have passed through fire that did not consume us and many waters that could not quench our love. We have reason to claim Jesus' words to the disciples as words given to us.

We are called from fear, for all closets of the church will be emptied, and the Word that is hidden in scriptures will be made known. God whispers that Word to us in the intimate lovemaking of our meditation, and we proclaim it, flaunting God's Word to the world.

The laws that denied us our bodies have been rolled away with the stone closing Jesus' tomb. Out of closets of death our souls have been raised with Christ, undefeated and victorious.

The Word is out. God's Word is out. Christ is the Word. The Word is Love.

Let us bear the Word, in words and deeds, ever grateful for our high calling in Christ Jesus our Lord.

COMMUNION

Therefore, since we are surrounded by so great a cloud of witnesses, let us also lay aside every weight and the sin that clings so closely, and let us run with perseverance the race that is set before us.

Hebrews 12:1

We are not alone. That is the central message of spirituality. The Bible tells us of a "blest communion" who shared the same faith, doubt, and trouble we experience. And we know of many friends no longer visible to us who are yet somehow present, encouraging us to "therefore lift your drooping hands and strengthen your weak knees" (12:12).

Our community has been reporting more and more experiences of contact with those who have passed. Scott Rogo, a friend who was a parapsychologist, told me that this is common for a community that has experienced much death. The boundary between death and life seems more fluid, and visits from the other side are welcomed.

Denise Eger, a rabbi, told me one such story. A close friend of her lover was dying of AIDS. In the middle of the night, Denise awoke feeling a friendly presence in the room. Later they learned the friend died at that hour.

"O blest communion, fellowship divine; we feebly struggle, they in glory shine; yet all are one in thee, for all are thine. Alleluia! Alleluia!" (From the hymn "For All the Saints.")

There is one body and one Spirit, just as you were called to the one hope of your calling, one [Christ], one faith, one baptism, one God and [Creator] of all, who is above all and through all and in all.

Ephesians 4:4–6

Growing up, my Baptist church fostered anti-Catholic sentiment. Yet my mother read Catholic writers, introduced to her by nuns who cared for her mother in a Catholic hospital. In high school, I visited the church of a Catholic friend. As we drove there with his family, his mother pointed out a Protestant church, commenting, "We all worship the same God, just in different ways."

As ecumenical as we were in seminary, church divisions were important to us earnest young zealots. After seminary, I met people who moved from church to church on the basis of geography and program rather than theology, and I wondered if the separations were only the product of church leadership.

Because of such divisiveness, the National Council of Churches never celebrated Communion together——that is, until Council representatives did so visiting a Metropolitan Community Church in San Francisco. MCC thereby witnessed how its members, coming from different traditions, could blend into one communion. Yet the Council would ultimately resist MCC's membership!

Forgive us, O God, for keeping Christ's body broken. Heal us.

There is no longer Jew or Greek, there is no longer slave or free, there is no longer male and female; for all of you are one in Christ Jesus.

Galatians 3:28

If there is no longer male and female in Christ Jesus, it does not matter to God which gender we love, which gender we are, or which gender we believe ourselves to be.

Divisions of race, nationality, class, gender, and sexuality drop away in this vision of the communion of the church. Worldwide Communion is observed in October to embody this understanding. For the occasion I once drew a globe encircled by people of all colors holding hands, but with one person hidden by a closet door.

National Coming Out Day in the United States is also observed in October. Coming out is the unique sacrament that we offer the church. As with Communion, in which we give thanks for Jesus giving himself to us, we may give thanks for those who vulnerably offer themselves to others in the communion of coming out.

In Christ's communion, there are no closets.

Help us find our voice, Christ Jesus, so we may join your chorus praising God.

"The glory that you have given me I have given them, so that
they may be one, as we are one, I in them and you in me, that
they may become completely one, so that the world may know
that you have sent me and have loved them even as you have
loved me."

John 17:22–23

Coni Staff, an MCC minister, is also a physical education coach
at a school. She knows the importance of teamwork, and con-
tributes her team-building skills to demonstrations at our Presbyterian church gatherings.

At a church assembly considering a controversial sexuality report, she coordinated the protest that followed its defeat. We silently carried a human-sized cross through the
seated delegates, hammered nails into it, then encircled the
delegates and sang Holly Near's "We Are a Gentle, Angry
People." Because she had worked with church leadership in
organizing the protest, we had security guards helping us
rather than resisting us, and we enjoyed the privilege of the
floor. As a result, hundreds of delegates and visitors and national staff joined our demonstration.

In *The Spirit and Forms of Love,* Daniel Day Williams
wrote that belonging is a primary characteristic of love.
Jesus belonged to God, and he prayed that we would belong to God and to one another through him. As we work
together as a team in the awareness of that unity, God's
glory is revealed.

We pray that we may be one, even as you are one, Holy God.

*Then Jesus cried again with a loud voice and breathed his last.
At that moment the curtain of the temple was torn in two, from
top to bottom.*

Matthew 27:50–51

Jesus lived and died so that we may be one with God. That is
the meaning of atonement: to make "at-one" God and us. This
is the story of the Bible. God walks with us in the innocence of
Eden, saves us through the waters of the flood and now of baptism, delivers us from oppression, tabernacles with us through
the wilderness, writes the Law first in stone and then on our
hearts, leads us to the Promised Land and God's commonwealth, dwells as one of us in Jesus Christ, and now communes
with us through the Holy Spirit.

The curtain that separated the Holy of Holies——where
God was said to dwell——from the rest of the temple is no
longer necessary. The curtain that only the high priest
could pass through no longer separates us from God. In
Christ, God now dwells within us.

Etty Hillesum, a young Jewish woman who faced the
horrors of the Holocaust, understood God's accessibility.
She wrote of impending imprisonment, "There will always
be a small patch of sky above, and there will always be
enough space to fold two hands in prayer" (*An Interrupted
Life* [New York: Simon & Schuster, 1985], p. 190).

*All that really matters, God, is that we protect a sanctuary for
you in ourselves and in others.*

For [Christ] is our peace; in his flesh he has made both groups into one and has broken down the dividing wall, that is, the hostility between us.

Ephesians 2:14

The "dividing wall" was the wall in the temple separating the areas where Jewish men could worship and where Jewish women and Gentiles could worship. Paul writes in Ephesians that this dividing wall of hostility has been destroyed by Christ. Those who had feared Jesus would destroy temple customs were absolutely right.

Jews and Gentiles lived very different lifestyles. There was distrust and animosity between them. Jews viewed Gentiles as idolators who had given in to their lusts and baser natures. Gentiles viewed Jews as self-righteous and arrogant. Jewish Christians wanted to keep Gentiles out of the early church unless they first became Jews. Even then there was still distrust.

If Christ could overcome the division between Jews and Gentiles in the early church, Christ can overcome the division among sexual orientations in today's church. Those who fear Christ will destroy the church's customs are absolutely right.

Christ Jesus, Cornerstone of the church, rise again and shake off unnecessary walls that divide your people.

[Jesus] said to them, "Come away to a deserted place all by yourselves and rest a while." For many were coming and going, and [the disciples] had no leisure even to eat.

Mark 6:31

Most of us have busy days in which we try to accomplish as much as we can. Many of us have hectic lives in which we are trying to achieve and experience as much as possible. We struggle daily with the many public and personal hindrances to being at rest. Some of us are running from death's grip. We are in a hurry to leave our mark on the world, a legacy.

In the midst of running for our lives, we need to rest in God. As Saint Augustine prayed, "All hearts are restless, Lord, until they rest in thee."

People tend to take shallow breaths. When excited, afraid, or anxious, our breathing becomes more shallow. Meditation begins with taking deeper breaths, which slows our breathing and body rhythms. This reduces stress and opens our bodies to healing and to at-one-ing with God.

To imagine taking God in with each breath is to begin to feel the presence of God in everyday things. Communion is not limited to bread and wine. To the attentive heart, communion occurs in breathing and resting.

And remember, in the spiritual life, there is no finish line.

God of peace, give me rest in your arms of mercy.

"Abide in me as I abide in you. Just as the branch cannot bear fruit by itself unless it abides in the vine, neither can you unless you abide in me."

John 15:4

I've been told that some plants do better in pots. I suppose that's true of some of us who are "potted" in closets. But I believe that most of us prefer to sink our roots deeper and raise our branches higher than pots would allow. Whatever our preference, we need nutrients to grow.

A friend with AIDS was compelled every couple of days to sit with an IV-drip delivering necessary medication to keep him healthy. Asked if this was a burden, he explained that, first, he might die without it, but that, second, it offered him an opportunity to relax and read.

Our vitality and the quality of our gifts similarly depend on "sitting with" Christ, drawing on Christ's resources. That means relying on the mystical Christ who speaks to us through the pages of scripture, as well as the Body of Christ, the church. That church may be a welcoming congregation, or a gay Christian support group, or a network of supportive Christians.

Abide in me, Christ Jesus, as I abide in you.

"Martha, Martha, you are worried about many things; there is need of only one thing. Mary has chosen the better part, which will not be taken away from her."

Luke 10:41

Jesus care-fully chided Martha when she asked him to persuade her sister Mary to help her with her many tasks hosting Jesus. Mary chose to commune with Jesus.

Hospitality itself may distract us from communing with our guests, as we want everything to be "just so." "Proper" hospitality may seem so demanding that it inhibits us from inviting people into our homes. Or, our fastidiousness might prove intimidating and inhospitable to a guest, who may be afraid of mussing the bathroom or eating with the wrong fork.

Just as some of us are fussy about the appearance of our home——how the dinner table is set and the gourmet quality of what we serve——many of us are fastidious about worship. It has to be a "certain way" for us to experience God.

But we deny ourselves the presence of the Guest when we let a different liturgical style inhibit our communion with others. And we resist others' hospitality when we let our own rules of worship get in the way.

Christ Jesus, deliver me from distractions. I choose to sit at your feet and listen.

"Jerusalem, Jerusalem . . . how often have I desired to gather your children together as a hen gathers her brood under her wings, and you were not willing!"

Luke 13:34

When I counsel a lesbian or gay Christian about reconciling sexuality and spirituality, I first explain that the Bible has little to say on the subject——a handful of verses that may or may not have to do with homosexuality. The biblical writers did not know our contemporary distinction of sexual orientation and behavior. They believed that everyone was created heterosexual. The ancient Hebrews believed that the man's seed was a small baby, so to spill it anywhere but a womb was a kind of murder.

I explain that there were periods of church history in which homosexual Christians were tolerated and even elevated to high rank. Today's antigay statements of some churches result from new dialogue about homosexuality. There is a broad spectrum of opinion on the issue within the church, from acceptance to rejection.

Finally, to cut through all that, I simply ask, "If Jesus were here right now, what do you think his response to you would be?" Frequently, the answer comes, "I think he would give me a hug."

Somehow, despite the church's prejudice, we've gotten it right. A tender, gentle Jesus wants to gather us like a mother hen into a warm and cozy communion.

Blessed are you, Mother Jesus, for you gather us as your children.

"Peace! Be still! . . . Why are you afraid? Have you still no faith?"

Mark 4:39, 40

Worship in some Quaker traditions is primarily characterized by communal silence. If someone is moved to speak during the profound quiet, the words seem to carry more import. The shared stillness offers powerful, spiritual healing.

Other churches seem uncomfortable with silence in worship. Services are filled with words: read, spoken, sung. Intentional silences are brief and rare, and may suggest someone has "missed a cue."

When Quakers who practice silence in worship gather for business, they break into silence as conflict increases. As one gay-positive but pacifist national fellowship of Quakers discussed gays in the military, the silence was almost deafening!

The noise of our lives and of our conflicts sometimes is better addressed with silence. Not manipulative silence. But silence of the heart to ponder the larger picture.

In a boat, Jesus' disciples were frightened by a storm at sea and annoyed that Jesus could sleep through it all. His words commanding calm and faith may be directed to all the storms we face.

Heart within: Peace! Be Still! Be still and remember God. Have you still no faith?

But Jesus came and touched them, saying, "Get up and do not be afraid."

Matthew 17:7

The disciples were awed by Jesus' transfiguration on the mountaintop, revealing his divine nature. His touch relieved their fears in this scripture.

Touch is a form of communion. It is a response to life's awesome nature: The hug of joy at the covenant ceremony of lovers. The gentle caress of a loved one. The pat on the back to say "well done" or "well said." The reassuring touch of a friend in a doctor's waiting room.

The day before his death, I spent an afternoon by my father's hospital bedside. Though unable to communicate or open his eyes, my dad knew I was there, because he responded to my giving him water. I shaved his face, combed his hair, and held his hand. There was not much to say.

A few days before the death of a friend, I wet washcloths and cooled his face repeatedly, trying to help bring his temperature down. Conversation was difficult for him, but the cool touch soothed his restless angst.

If only we could be awed more often into touch by a person's ultimate worth before they meet their ultimate destiny! All of us would be less afraid.

Touch me, Jesus. Deliver me from fear.

Enough for me to keep my soul tranquil and quiet,
like a child in its mother's arms,
as content as a child that has been weaned.

                    Psalm 131:2 (Jerusalem Bible)

The courts assigned a juvenile offender to a therapist. Session after session, the child spent his time playing with items in the counseling office, resisting interaction. Frustrated, the therapist told the child he was going to recommend the courts assign another counselor.

"But I like you!" the boy exclaimed. Surprised, the therapist asked why. "Because you're the only grown-up that leaves me alone."

Sometimes God is the only friend who leaves us alone, not in the sense of abandonment, but by allowing us to be ourselves in God's presence.

If we are closeted with others, we need not be closeted with God. And if we're out, we don't have to be "model" lesbian and gay Christians in God's presence.

Enough for us to keep our souls tranquil and quiet in our mother God's arms.

Mother God, hold us in the luxury of your lap of unconditional love.

"For where two or three are gathered in my name, I am there among them."

Matthew 18:20

Providence provided a group of us who were trying to figure out what it meant to be gay, male, and Christian. We coalesced into a group, covenanting to meet biweekly in different participants' homes for three months. For the second three months, we agreed to meet every week.

We shared our stories, crises, and achievements. We worshiped and prayed together. We learned from one another and enjoyed mutual spiritual support. We did for one another what Jesus would have done for us. We became the Body of Christ. Jesus was among us.

One stopped coming early on, distracted by work and a busy life. Another left angrily, disappointed that we couldn't be all he wanted. But the rest of us stayed because we needed this form of communion.

My earlier search for sexual intimacy may have been, at heart, a quest for the full-bodied communion with other gay men that this spiritual intimacy bestowed.

Lead me to others with whom I may enjoy your presence, O Christ.

"So when you are offering your gift at the altar, if you remember that your brother or sister has something against you, leave your gift there before the altar and go; first be reconciled to your brother or sister, and then come and offer your gift."

Matthew 5:23–24

Mutual forgiveness is the key to communion.

Though we may understand that mutual forgiveness creates communion between people, we may not be aware that mutual forgiveness is needed even between us and God. We cannot be "cheerful givers" at God's altar while we are angry at God. We may need to forgive God for not being all that we expected. We may need to forgive God that we were created different and thereby targets of prejudice and hate. We may need to forgive God for not protecting us from God's followers. We may need to forgive God for not preventing AIDS.

Jesus told his followers to forgive others when praying for forgiveness (6:14–15) and to forgive another seventy times seven, in other words, countless times (18:22).

There are some reconciliations that may not be possible this side of God's kingdom, or commonwealth. But as forgiveness is possible, as reconciliation becomes plausible, we enter into the communion that God intends. Forgiveness releases us *as much or more* than those we forgive.

God of mercy, help me forgive others' trespasses as you forgive mine.

"Should you not have had mercy on your fellow slave, as I had mercy on you?"

Matthew 18:33

Jesus told the story of a king who forgives a slave a debt only to discover that the slave later imprisons a fellow slave who owes him money. Jesus thus illustrated God's forgiveness in relation to human mercy.

Those whose God is merciless tend to be merciless toward themselves or others. A merciless god is false, whether of religion, self, work, sex, acquisitiveness, addiction, compulsion, and so on. Those whose God is merciful but who behave mercilessly either inadequately experience God's forgiveness or insufficiently express gratitude for God's mercy.

Possibly the most moving lyric of the musical *Les Misérables* is when the unwed mother sings she thought God would be forgiving. Having experienced no mercy at human hands, she experienced God as merciless. Lesbians and gay men have often been subjected to a merciless god by the church. That's why we may eschew religion and sometimes God.

Those of us who know God's mercy may help the church better understand, interpret, and share that mercy. Then, with regard to the church, we would avoid acting like the slave in Jesus' parable who is shown mercy but proves unmerciful.

May my patience with others reveal your mercy toward me, God.

"[God] is God not of the dead, but of the living."

Matthew 22:32

My lover, who is HIV-positive, wonders about the possibility of my having another lover should our life together be cut short by AIDS. We are aware of an eternal quality of our love that goes beyond the present.

Religious leaders asked Jesus about marriage in heaven, but they were not interested in the dilemma my lover and I might face. They wanted to put Jesus' belief in the resurrection to the test. They presented a hypothetical question about a woman who is successively widowed seven times. "Whose wife will she be?" they asked.

There is no marriage in heaven, Jesus responded, saying they knew "neither the scriptures nor the power of God" (22:24). Then he pursued their disbelief in the resurrection of the dead by reminding them of God's self-declaration to Moses as the God of Abraham, Isaac, and Jacob. How could this be, Jesus questioned, if they were not still living? Luke's gospel adds, "for to [God] all of these are alive" (Luke 20:38).

This expression of confidence in the resurrection from our ultimate spiritual authority reassures us all. And though there may be no marriage in heaven, I believe God will embrace our earthly covenants, for, as Jesus said, whatever we bind on earth will be bound in heaven (Matt. 18:18).

Thank you, God, for your life-giving covenant and our life-giving covenants.

"If they do not listen to Moses and the prophets, neither will they be convinced even if someone rises from the dead."

Luke 16:31

Jesus told the parable of a rich man who failed in life to help a poor man named Lazarus, a beggar at his gate. In death, the poor man is comforted and the rich man suffers. The rich man asks Abraham to send the poor man to warn his brothers lest they share his fate. Abraham explains that if they listened neither to the lawgiver Moses nor the prophets, they wouldn't listen to anyone risen from the dead.

The story foreshadows those who would refuse to believe a resurrected Jesus. Unlike the other Lazarus that Jesus raised, this Lazarus remained in the bosom of Abraham.

We have been raised with Christ. Our old selves and self-perceptions have been shed in closets as we emerge as lesbian and gay people, as lesbian and gay Christians. And yet, though figuratively raised from death to life, other Christians resist believing our resurrection and our warnings. They would keep us begging at the church's door.

Bless those wealthy in religion with an awareness of their spiritual poverty, Creator of empty tombs.

"Blessed are those who mourn, for they will be comforted."

Matthew 5:4

Our communion includes those who have preceded us in life and in death. The fact that we mourn someone's death reveals the wonderful gifts we received at her or his hands. To comfort ourselves we use good words of sympathy and good words about the person's life. "Eulogy" comes from the Greek word for "good words." We eulogize someone in death, publicly expressing gratitude.

We don't have to wait till someone's death to offer eulogies. We may say good words about others now. A spiral of thanksgiving unites us as our thanks are welcomed with a smile that in turn lifts our spirits.

Comfort then takes on the double meaning that Jesus intended in today's verse. Not only is it consoling, it empowers the eulogized.

There are many good words for us in the Bible that console and strengthen us. Jesus, the Word made flesh, is the best "good Word" of all.

By your Word, comfort all who mourn.

"I am the resurrection and the life. Those who believe in me, even though they die, will live, and everyone who lives and believes in me will never die."

John 11:25-26

What we do today for lesbians and gay men will live beyond us. We will live in the legacy we leave behind in our fields, in our culture, in our church, and in Christ. Our communion not only reaches to those who have preceded us, but to those who will follow.

Some of us are content with this. Others of us want more, a kind of personal immortality. This is something I want for loved ones even more than for myself. If *I* love them this passionately, then surely God loves them more and will find a way to renew a relationship with them after death. We are called to trust in God and in Jesus.

In today's scripture, Jesus comforted Martha in her grief over the death of Lazarus, reminding her that those who find their life in him will never die.

The One who has loved us into being and loved us into becoming is trustworthy. There is no other god whom I would trust more in facing death.

My God in life and death, call me with Lazarus from death to renewed communion with you through Christ in your Spirit.

"Do not let yourselves be troubled. Believe in God, believe also in me. . . . And if I go and prepare a place for you, I will come again and will take you to myself, so that where I am, there you may be also."

John 14:1, 3

Those of us who have had the joy of moving into a home with a lover have a taste of what it will be like to move in with God. We also know that when we love, the form and content of the home we make together is not as important as being near the beloved.

A gay friend, who served as minister of a country church in Appalachia, told the story of a fellow preacher who took issue with a translation of John 14:2: "In my Father's house there are many rooms . . . " In defense, my friend pointed out that the original Greek text justifies this translation. The country preacher replied, "You mean to tell me that after all these good people have had to put up with here on earth, that when they get to heaven, they have to settle for a *room!?*"

Some of us have felt blessed just to have a room to ourselves to spend a few precious moments of intimacy with a lover. And though we may prepare our own rooms or homes carefully and elegantly, we know loved ones are what make it a home.

So it is with heaven.

Christ Jesus, keep my heart from being troubled, trusting God and trusting you.

Then their eyes were opened, and they recognized [Jesus], and he vanished from their sight. They said to each other, "Were not our hearts burning within us while he was talking to us on the road, while he was opening the scriptures to us?"

Luke 24:30–32

On a flight, a lesbian minister was handed a note from another passenger. In it, this sister passenger explained that she had visited her grandmother that week and found her looking up a word in the dictionary: lesbian. She had seen the word in a newspaper article about the minister's controversial work. The granddaughter recognized the minister on the plane from the photo accompanying the story.

No, the passenger wrote, she didn't use the occasion to come out to her grandmother. But now she felt safer doing so on her next visit to her hometown. She thanked the minister for being out there for all to see.

Just as the resurrected Jesus opened the scriptures to the travelers to Emmaus in today's verse, so we who are raised from closets open the scriptures and the dictionaries for other travelers as to what it means to be "lesbian" and "gay." To those who are lesbian and gay, we also reveal what it means to be "Christian," and we may serve as Christ in their midst.

May we warm others' hearts as we embody the word "lesbian" or "gay," and the Word, Christ.

"Death has been swallowed up in victory."
"Where, O death, is your victory?
Where, O death, is your sting?"

1 Corinthians 15:54–55

During a conference for religious AIDS volunteers in Fort Worth, Texas, a man living with AIDS stood up to tell of the healing his AIDS diagnosis had brought him. Reared as a Nazarene, a very conservative Christian church, he had not darkened the doorway of a church for a long time because he was gay. He moved from his hometown and his family rather than tell them of his homosexuality.

But his AIDS diagnosis prompted him to reclaim his church, his family, and his hometown. He risked coming out to them as a gay man with AIDS, and much to his surprise, his church, his family, and his hometown welcomed him with open arms. Movingly, he declared that his AIDS diagnosis resurrected a quality of life long dead. Quantity of life now was less important.

Eternal life for early Christians was more about quality than quantity. The sting of death——sin and law——no longer overshadowed their lives. They enjoyed Christ's victory over sin, law, and death in abundant life.

Though we have walked through the shadows of death, we fear no evil, God, for you are with us.

*"This is my body that is for you. Do this in remembrance of
me. . . . This cup is the new covenant in my blood. Do this, as
often as you drink it, in remembrance of me."*

1 Corinthians 11:24, 25

Howard Wells was one of the early gay activists at Union Theological Seminary in New York City. He fell in love with a man
who soon ended the relationship. Howard was devastated. His
obsession for the man, Pat, alarmed him, and he turned to therapy to explore his infatuation.

Infatuation is more desire than love, a desire to possess
the qualities of another. The unavailability or denial of the
other can make a person crazy with desire. The writings of
Carl Jung led Howard to a resolution of his obsession: to incorporate the qualities he loved in Pat into himself.

Wells also concluded that observing Communion may reflect the disciples' desire to incorporate Jesus' qualities by
symbolically ingesting his body and blood. Though early
Christians were mistakenly accused of cannibalism, the
principle is comparable. Cannibals eat the part of a victim
associated with the virtue they want.

Communion, then, may be experienced as an intaking of
the qualities of Christ. And, unlike the sacrifices in the temple that could only be eaten by priests, Christ's sacrifice
feeds us all.

*May your flesh and blood unite with mine, Christ Jesus, so
your love may live in me.*

*"For truly I tell you, whoever gives you a cup of water to drink
because you bear the name of Christ will by no means lose the
reward."*

Mark 9:41

Before I walked in Atlanta's lesbian and gay pride parade, I was
warned of a Baptist church along the route. One year, departing worshipers shouted Bible verses at marchers. The next
year, some carried antigay placards, but the United Methodist
church across the street staged a counter demonstration,
telling the marchers they'd be welcome in that church.

Now, as we passed the Baptist church to our left, we saw
ministers accompanied by police officers sitting on its
steps, as if defending the doors of the church. The congregation had been dismissed early.

On the right, the United Methodists were distributing
cups of water to the marchers, warmly greeting us. "Whoever gives you a cup of water because you bear the name of
Christ will not lose the reward," Jesus said. We may not have
known we bore any resemblance to Christ, but these Christians saw Christ in us. Their reward was that we saw Christ
in them.

*Christ Jesus, thank you for transforming water to wine in the
communion of pride day!*

[Jesus said:] "I was hungry and you gave me food, I was thirsty and you gave me something to drink, I was a stranger and you welcomed me, I was naked and you gave me clothing, I was sick and you took care of me, I was in prison and you visited me. . . . Just as you did it to one of the least of these who are members of my family, you did it to me."

Matthew 25:35–36, 40

The church into which I was to welcome gays and lesbians had a long history of helping the homeless. Our increasing gay membership gave us the volunteers and the money to do more for them in the form of a sack lunch program. We purchased the ingredients, first with our money, then assisted by government grants. Volunteers packaged them, often during Sunday coffee hour. I would give out as many as twenty lunches per day.

When we ran low on lunches, I would pass along the word among the street people to come for a lunch only in an emergency. It speaks well of them that this would temporarily reduce the level of requests. One day I told a young man as I gave him a lunch to let others know that we were running low. A few minutes later he returned, emptied his pockets of thirty cents, and placed it on my desk. "This is to help out your lunch ministry," he explained.

His spontaneous generosity stunned me. The "least of these" helping the "least of these" revealed that we each helped Jesus unawares.

Bless "the least" who help "the least" with an awareness of your presence!

"Remember those who are in prison, as though you were in prison with them; those who are being tortured, as though you yourselves were being tortured."

Hebrews 13:3

Our communion includes many in jails and prisons. Some of us have broken legitimate laws. Others are incarcerated because of illegitimate laws prohibiting homosexual acts between consenting adults. Still others are imprisoned unfairly because of police harassment. In some countries, the imprisonment and torture of homosexuals is commonplace.

A gay church member had felt unable to fulfill his call to the ministry. Then he learned that gay inmates of the Los Angeles County Jail were denied access to its worship services. This inspired him to lead our congregation to create a jail ministry that exists to this day.

Whenever I volunteered to help lead a worship in jail, I did so in fear and trembling. First, I feared that I couldn't speak meaningfully to the inmates. But second, I could imagine myself being in their place.

Imagining ourselves in their place is the first step toward remembering those in prison in our prayers and in our actions.

We pray for those in prison, that we may be one with them.

[The king said,] "The wedding is ready, but those invited were not worthy. Go therefore into the main streets, and invite everyone you find to the wedding banquet."

Matthew 22:8–9

One week after a Des Moines church voted overwhelmingly to welcome lesbian and gay members, the children led the service. As I watched children given the chance to grow up in an open congregation, tears came to my eyes, joyful for them, grieved for the rest of us who were not given the opportunity.

One class dramatized the story of today's scripture, a parable of Jesus. A king had invited friends to a wedding banquet, but the friends refused to come and even killed the servants sent to fetch them. The king, in turn, destroyed the murderers and invited strangers to the wedding. But one who failed to show respect by wearing the proper attire was bound and thrown "into the outer darkness, where there will be weeping and gnashing of teeth" (22:13). As the children enacted the killings, and as the poor girl was thrown out of the church for wearing the wrong dress, I wondered about the children's perceptions of God!

Many if not most lesbians and gay men left the church in youth, at a time when we thought we might be caught figuratively wearing "the wrong dress" and thrown out of church and heaven by an angry God. Yet the story is about those who either reject or fail to show respect for God's invitation to communion. We are instead the strangers invited when the friends refuse.

We choose you, O God, even as you have chosen us.

*"For I know that my Redeemer lives,
and . . . at the last . . . will stand upon the earth;
and after my skin has been thus destroyed,
then in my flesh I shall see God,
whom I shall see on my side."*

                                        Job 19:25–27

If Job——who lost family, friends, wealth, health, and standing
in his religious community——is able to affirm this, then surely
we can. Through scripture we commune with Job and find we
have many things in common: loss, condemnation, and suffering. Now we can assert with Job that our Redeemer, our Vindi-
cator (as the text is better translated), will come and stand with
us. Though we die, we shall see God.

In the final communion, Job is one person I would like
to look up. I still have many questions about why the good
suffer, while the merciless enjoy prosperity. Many of the
rest of us do, too.

And if God prepares "a table before me in the presence
of my enemies" as Psalm 23:5 would have it, does that mean
the final communion will include Job's condemning friends
and our own opposition? Only God could be that forgiving.

*God of mercy, teach me to forgive so heaven won't seem like
hell.*

"Why do you look for the living among the dead?"

Luke 24:5

The angels put this question to the women when they came to the tomb to anoint the crucified body of Jesus. We may ask ourselves the same question as we approach churches whose spiritual life seems dead.

A recent survey among United Methodists revealed that "courage" and "imagination" are among the traits least desired in their pastors, indicating, analysts say, a communion that wishes to maintain rather than advance, a sure prescription for decline.

On a church sign, a sermon title blended with the offering of Communion: "The Bottom Line, An Idol Communion." Though I realized that the sermon title ended with "Idol," I pondered what an idol communion might be. A friend had recently said she believed the church got so caught up in who was there that we failed to notice who was missing. An idol communion, I thought, makes an idol of those gathered, mistaking good feelings of togetherness as ultimate rather than as a small taste of what is still to come.

A former minister, broken by the church because of his homosexuality, once passed me Christ's broken body, moving me to tears as in him I felt Jesus' brokenness, which was intended to open up the communion of faith.

An idol communion inevitably leads to an idle communion, one in which we fail to enter into the brokenness of Jesus Christ, who brings us all together.

Christ Jesus, only say the words, and we will be able to receive you in one another.

Beloved, let us love one another, because love is from God; everyone who loves is born of God and knows God.

1 John 4:7

In many gay urban areas, Halloween is a "high holy day" second only to pride day. We celebrate each other's craft and creativity by parading ourselves in as little or as much costume as possible. Yet underneath our masks we all share human feelings and impulses.

Similarly, though we have different ways of expressing our sexuality, we share being gay and lesbian. And though we have diverse ways of expressing our spirituality, we are all spiritual people. Though we who are Christian have various ways of expressing our faith, we all follow Christ.

Scientific research has suggested that we speak of homosexualities rather than a single phenomenon called homosexuality, because of diverse origins and expressions. I believe, as well, we might speak of spiritualities rather than spirituality, because of diverse origins and expressions.

What unites the cosmic communion is love rather than conformity. In their best expressions, all spiritualities and all sexualities are paths that lead to love and ultimately to God, for "God is love" (4:16).

Bless us with loving sexual and spiritual communions, God of love.

COMMONWEALTH

·
·
·
·

So then you are no longer strangers and aliens, but you are citizens with the saints and also members of the household of God, built upon the foundation of the apostles and prophets, with Christ Jesus himself as the cornerstone.

Ephesians 2:19

Paul addressed this to those who had formerly been "aliens to the commonwealth of Israel, and strangers to the covenants of promise, having no hope and without God in the world" (2:12). These words were spoken to Christian converts at the time of their baptism.

Along with many other saints throughout history, we have been alienated from the church. The church has viewed us as strangers. We wondered if God's promises included us. When we doubted, we felt hopeless and abandoned by God.

"But now in Christ Jesus you who once were far off have been brought near" (2:13). We are not aliens, but citizens of God's commonwealth. We are not strangers, but we are the church. We are not without foundation, for we have the prophets, apostles, saints, and most centrally, Christ Jesus. And we share the common spiritual wealth of scripture.

"Jesus loves us, this we know, for the Bible tells us so." We are all saints, and this is our day.

For all of us saints, O God, we give you thanks! Alleluia!

Give the king your justice, O God.
　　　　　　　　　　　　Psalm 72:1

With patience a ruler may be persuaded,
and a soft tongue can break bones.
　　　　　　　　　　　　Proverbs 25:15

The commonwealth to which we are heir is as much the body politic as it is the Body of Christ. We pray for justice, but with patient lobbying and careful voting we persuade those in power.

In accepting an award on behalf of the *Los Angeles Times* from a gay Christian group, the paper's representative charged those gathered at the award banquet to address as clearly and forcefully as possible the biblical issues raised by fundamentalists. This would give the media a better chance to present a balanced view, as well as take the heat off them for doing so.

Sympathetic legislators, judges, and lawyers in many states have desperately sought biblical and church precedence for repealing antigay laws, supporting our civil rights, and advocating our marital rights.

This could be our unique political calling as lesbian and gay Christians. By supplying the media and our elected representatives with sound biblical scholarship and theological reasoning, we can diffuse the arguments of those who would legislate antigay "morality" in the name of Christ.

Give rulers your justice, O God. May we find our political voice to make it so.

"Give your servant therefore an understanding mind to govern your people, able to discern between good and evil; for who can govern this your great people?"

1 Kings 3:9

King Solomon prayed for wisdom to discern good from evil so that he could govern his people. In a democracy, this could be the prayer of every citizen.

"Ignorance of the law is no excuse," we say. Ignorance of the issues is also no excuse. We would do well to be "wise as serpents" (Matt. 10:16) in taking time to discern the issues and the candidates, voting our conscience. Especially when there are coordinated efforts to refuse or abrogate our rights from self-proclaimed religious groups, we who are lesbian and gay Christians need to establish and proclaim our understandings of the issues.

On election day 1984 in Nicaragua, we met an eighty-year-old woman running through her barrio past our group of observers to get to the polls. Upon her return, she gave us a "thumbs up" sign, proudly displaying that her thumb had been dipped in red ink, the symbol that she had voted. This was her first time voting, she explained, because now she had choices.

Now we also have choices, and we should share her enthusiastic commitment to vote.

Give your citizens an understanding spirit of discernment in the voting booth, and the spirit to vote.

One who rules over people justly,
ruling in the fear of God,
is like the light of the morning,
like the sun rising on a cloudless morning,
gleaming from the rain on the grassy land.

                                        2 Samuel 23:3-4

The beauty of an ideal ruler is reflected in this psalm fragment claimed to be the last words of King David. The heart of this saying asserts that a ruler governs justly when he or she does so in awe of God.

"Can We Be Good Without God?" asked Glenn Tinder in a 1989 article in *The Atlantic,* which became the book *The Political Meaning of Christianity.* Facing the cynicism of our day, it would seem improbable that, cut off from our spiritual roots, we could be good. Tinder wrote that a Christianity that values the individual, but recognizes our propensity toward evil and then critiques society by standing over against it, keeps us accountable to God.

If we recognize the governed as sacred to God, we behave differently. If we believe in God, we govern more justly. If we have no higher power, injustice only "happens" when we get caught publicly: Watergate, Iran-Contra, junk bonds, savings and loan scandals, welfare or medicare fraud.

If those who govern recognized our sacred worth and walked humbly with God, we would never have to worry about equal rights.

Sovereign of all nations, we pray for the gleam of joy as justice rises on all lands.

The human mind may devise many plans,
but it is the purpose of [God] that will be established.

Proverbs 19:21

Many seek the favor of a ruler,
but it is from [God] that one gets justice.

Proverbs 29:26

When invited to address the lesbian and gay group in the United Church of Canada, I learned more of that church's decision to permit the ordination of lesbian and gay ministers. According to members of Affirm, the favorable vote came not because their strategy was superior to that of the opposition, nor simply because it was the right thing to do. Rather, their opponents were so vociferous, unseemly, and reactionary that few others wanted to be associated with them!

Relying solely on our own political strategies, we fail to take into account God's providence. And defensively preparing our case, we sometimes forget that letting our opposition present their weak and often meretricious case may ultimately work to our advantage. Hating the sin but loving the sinner glides from their lips, but their actions reveal disdain and ignorance of *who we are.*

The best-laid strategies are enriched by God's justice and purpose in the face of our opponents' benightedness.

Establish your purpose, God, and give us justice.

From that time Jesus began to proclaim, "Repent, for the king-
dom of heaven has come near." . . . Jesus went throughout
Galilee, teaching in their synagogues and proclaiming the
good news of the kingdom.

Matthew 4:17, 23

A minister attending a workshop for clergy on opening the
church to lesbians and gay men observed, "Not long ago we
were condemning homosexuality from our pulpits. Now we
are approaching a proclamation that it is okay. Where's the repentance?" In other words, came the clarification, why isn't
the church first confessing its sin publicly?

Jesus anticipated repentance as necessary to receive the
inbreaking kingdom, or commonwealth, of God. The commonwealth of justice and peace and love was here at hand,
but a conversion experience, an "about-face," was needed
to embrace it. People could not go about their lives in the
same way if they were to be citizens of God's commonwealth.

We are repenting of our own homophobia to embrace the
good news of our citizenship. Now we are called to proclaim
that good news to help others repent of their homophobia.

At the same time, we listen for others who call *us* to repentance: a hurt lover, an offended friend, an unwanted
stranger, a disfranchised group. Welcoming God's commonwealth is the task of a lifetime.

Help me to repent to receive and then proclaim your reign,
Sovereign God.

Esau said, "I am about to die; of what use is a birthright to me?"

                                                              Genesis 25:32

Jacob cheated his brother Esau out of his birthright. Esau was hungry, and Jacob offered him bread and lentil stew in exchange for his hereditary claim as the firstborn.

From time to time I would be invited to a halfway house for boys arrested for prostitution to address their questions about God. Having survived on the street as castaways and runaways, they lived for the moment. It was difficult for them to "settle down" and attend school for the seemingly distant reward of a diploma or future employment. One young man blew all the money he'd been saving to rent a limousine to take him and his friends to a gay teenage dance club.

In another halfway house our church began for female prostitutes, a lesbian who had begun a job said she couldn't bear to open up her first paycheck. "I used to make that much money in one night," she told me. She finally cashed it, saying, "There are just some things that are more important."

Our birthright of human dignity is too important to exchange for whatever we hunger for in life. Our inheritance of God's commonwealth is too valuable to exchange for anything of lesser value. And our long-range vision should never be compromised by short-term achievements in church or society.

We claim our birthright as citizens of your commonwealth!

For you did not receive a spirit of slavery to fall back into fear, but you have received a spirit of adoption. When we cry, "Abba! Father!" it is that very Spirit bearing witness with our spirit that we are children of God, and if children, then heirs, heirs of God and joint heirs with Christ.

Romans 8:15–17

Like today, early Christians held strong positions about how to express themselves spiritually. In Romans, Paul reminds them they are no longer slaves who are told what to do. Rather, they are adopted children of God.

Many of us hold strong positions about how we are to express ourselves sexually as Christians. Some of us are contradictory, expecting from a lover or friends or leaders what we don't demand of ourselves. Others of us are hurtfully consistent, demanding of all others what has been good for us, or even what we *think* would be good for us.

We may review our behaviors in the light of our growing awareness that we *and those with whom we relate* are children of God. But we must not be enslaved by those who would make ultimate their own moral conclusions.

A woman faithfully cared for her lover who became a quadriplegic in an accident. Eventually she grieved that her Christian commitment consigned her to a nonsexual future. In counseling with a minister, she decided to allow herself a sexual relationship with a "limited partner." Now she finds herself a better caregiver to her primary partner.

If we lived under "the spirit of slavery," our "masters" could take responsibility for us. As it is, living as God's children, we take responsibility for ourselves.

Deliver us from slavery to both libertine and legalist impulses.

*"The land that we went through as spies is an exceedingly
good land. If [God] is pleased with us, [God] will bring us into
this land and give it to us, a land that flows with milk and
honey. Only, do not rebel against [God]; and do not fear the
people of the land, for . . . their protection is removed from
them.*

Numbers 14:7–9

Because the Israelites rejected this optimistic report from
Joshua and Caleb, they were condemned to wander the
wilderness until the older generations died. Those of us
who fail to believe and follow our faithfully optimistic leaders may suffer a corresponding fate.

In the early seventies, lesbian activist Sally Gearhart
wrote an article subtitled, "What the Church Needs Is a
Good Lay——On Its Side." She joined a chorus of feminists
claiming that the patriarchal hierarchy of the church now
had its "protection . . . removed from them" and optimisti-
cally calling for a collective, communal approach to deci-
sion-making. Biblically, God is discerned in community with
others. Surely God's commonwealth needs every citizen to
piece it together.

If all the powerless of the church got together, we'd be
the majority: women, people of color, people with disabilities, lesbians, gay men, bisexual and transgender persons. If
God is pleased with us, God will bring us into a land that
flows with milk and honey, unafraid.

We trust in you, Center of our common wealth.

"They disobeyed the kings' command and yielded up their bodies rather than serve and worship any god except their own God."

Daniel 3:28

King Nebuchadnezzar said this after witnessing Shadrach, Meshach, and Abednego survive being thrown into a fiery furnace at his command, because they had refused to worship his idol.

God's law is higher than human law. There are times when we lay our bodies on the line to protest injustice. We refuse to bow to the god of heterosexuality, no matter what "kings" demand.

A governor of California vetoed a gay rights bill passed by the state legislature. It had happened before at the hand of his predecessor. But this time, the governor had indicated support for our community in the campaign, and we felt betrayed.

We took to the streets across the state, demonstrating our anger. The governor was in Los Angeles that night attending a dinner. I joined thousands who marched from West Hollywood to the site of the dinner at the county's art museum. We chanted, "We're here! We're queer! We're fabu-lous! Get used to it!" It felt *damn* good.

The governor had vetoed the bill because he thought it would be bad for business. When another gay rights bill was passed the following year, he did not bow to the god of business the second time he had a chance to sign it into law.

Bless our angry resistance to injustice, God of righteousness.

"For where your treasure is, there will your heart be also."
Matthew 6:21

In this verse, Jesus succinctly illustrates the reason for the spiritual quest: discerning our treasure.

Someone recently said to me that there are no atheists, that we all worship some god. Many of the gods we worship are not worthy of our allegiance. In *The Intimate Connection,* theologian James Nelson defines spirituality as "whatever shapes our lives take toward the objects of our ultimate trust." Not all spiritualities are fulfilling.

I often discover what's important to me in dialogue with others. It's not surprising to me, then, that Christian spirituality begins with a dialogue with the Bible. Things in scripture that alarm me tell me as much about what I value as those things that please me.

Though we use our minds in reading scripture, we must let the Bible's words descend into our hearts to gain their full impact. There, our reaction to an irritating grain of scriptural sand may evolve a pearl, and our response to a pleasing biblical seed may bear fruit. The commonwealth of God is discovered by the heart, just as all great loves are discerned.

Spirit of God, descend into my heart.

"The treasure of heaven is like treasure hidden in a field, which someone found and hid; then in his joy he goes and sells all that he has and buys that field.

"Again, the kingdom of heaven is like a merchant in search of fine pearls; on finding one pearl of great value, he went and sold all that he had and bought it."

Matthew 13:44–45

In a dialogue I wrote for worship, a gay Kilroy is offered "A Guide to Investments" by his guardian angel. Kilroy invested a lot of his leisure time and discretionary funds in his appearance and entertainment. He spent more for Sunday brunch than he put in the offering. Kilroy's guardian angel warned him that if he didn't rearrange his priorities, heaven was going to seem like hell.

Though money is only part of our treasure, how we use it reveals what we believe to be vital. I learned over the years that getting a gay-positive line item in a church budget was crucial for church members and leaders to "own" the inclusiveness of God's commonwealth.

It's true for us as well. A couple who hosted me in Houston explained that, as they became more intentional in supporting their church, they decided to sell their large house and find a smaller, less expensive one. They found a less costly home, which in many ways was better than the one they sold! And now money they once spent on lavish parties helps provide communion for lesbian and gay Christians.

Guide us, Spirit, in our divestments and investments, to reflect the nature of your commonwealth.

[Jesus] also said, "With what can we compare the kingdom of God, or what parable will we use for it? It is like a mustard seed, which, when sown upon the ground, is the smallest of the seeds on earth; yet when it is sown it grows up and becomes the greatest of all shrubs, and puts forth large branches, so that the birds of the air can make nests in its shade."

Mark 4:30–32

West Park Presbyterian Church in New York City is not a "high-steepled" church, meaning a church with a big and influential congregation. Yet its rejection of a national church policy forbidding gay ordination became the mustard seed of a movement throughout its denomination. Other churches adopted "more light" resolutions, stating their support for the full rights of lesbians and gay men in the church and their search for illumination on our concerns.

Parallel movements began in other denominations. Eileen Lindner, associate general secretary of the National Council of Churches, has observed that if all churches that welcomed us within mainline denominations affiliated, they would comprise a denomination larger than the Metropolitan Community Church!

Lindner, who holds a doctorate in American church history, believes the future of the church may be cross-denominational affiliations based on constituencies and programs rather than a common history.

A mustard seed of resistance may provide branches in which we may nest in God's commonwealth.

Bless the branches of your mustard seed, Cosmic Gardener, as they stretch toward the light of your commonwealth.

And again [Jesus] said, "To what should I compare the king-dom of God? It is like yeast that a woman took and mixed in with three measures of flour until all of it was leavened."

Luke 13:20–21

I was invited to preach on lesbian and gay concerns at a pre-dominantly straight suburban church near St. Paul, Minnesota. That Sunday, shortly before the sermon, the congregation took in new members: six young heterosexual families with small children. I remarked afterward to one of the pastors that it seemed strange to speak about homosexuality in that context. I was told that two of the families were joining because they had left another church downtown when it fired a pastor for being lesbian. They wanted their children to grow up in a more hos-pitable environment.

We are like the yeast the woman of Jesus' saying placed in a loaf of bread. We are lightening up the church with our presence, helping it stretch beyond itself, as yeast leavens bread. We expand the commonwealth of God beyond our simple numbers, helping it become bread for the world, so there will be enough for all.

Bless the leavening of your Body, Christ Jesus, that we may feed God's commonwealth.

Once Jesus was asked by the Pharisees when the kingdom of God was coming, and he answered, "The kingdom of God is not coming with things that can be observed; nor will they say, 'Look, here it is!' or 'There it is!' For, in fact, the kingdom of God is among you."

Luke 17:20–21

Just as we look for manifestations of God's presence in everyday experience, we watch for glimpses of God's commonwealth in ordinary events.

A woman was asked by her congregation's governing council to word a resolution opposing the ordination of lesbians and gay men. They endorsed the resolution, as did a higher governing body, and she was sent as a delegate to the national convention. As she received materials on the subject, she studied them. When the issue came to a vote, she voted in favor of ordination. People back home felt betrayed. Her response was that she didn't know anything about the subject before!

The kingdom, or commonwealth, of God manifests itself in serendipitous and subtle ways. Jesus said that it is among us or, as it is alternatively translated, within us. Sometimes it's evident in the simple process of education and our willingness to learn.

Teach me, Spirit of Wisdom, to learn your commonwealth into being.

"Daughter, your faith has made you well; go in peace, and be healed of your disease."

Mark 5:34

Proclaiming the good news of God's commonwealth was associated with "curing every disease and every sickness among the people" (Matt. 4:23). And to seventy disciples he sent to proclaim the gospel throughout the villages, Jesus said, "cure the sick who are there, and say to them, 'The kingdom of God has come near to you' " (Luke 10:9).

A woman who had suffered a hemorrhage for twelve years touched Jesus in a crowd, and she was healed by her belief that simply touching the hem of his garment would make her well. Someone once interpreted what followed as a little impromptu street theater. Jesus asked, "Who touched my clothes?" The disciples were amazed at him, for there were lots of people touching him in the press of the crowd. But Jesus wanted to draw out this woman as an example of faith.

As a woman with a hemorrhage, she risked rendering a rabbi unclean by her touch, for she would have been considered ritually unclean. So she came forward, trembling. Jesus publicly confirmed her faith. Her faith delivered her from being ritually unclean and outcast.

None of us can render Jesus unclean by our touch. But Jesus can use our faith to heal both us and the society that casts us out.

Heal our diseases, Christ Jesus, by our faithful touch.

"'I choose to give to this last the same as I give to you. Am I not allowed to do what I choose with what belongs to me? Or are you envious because I am generous?' So the last will be first, and the first will be last."

Matthew 20:14–16

In the early seventies I attended an antiwar rally on my college campus. One peace activist began delivering a litany of his previous justice involvements, punctuating each with the refrain, "Where were you!?" Finally, a longtime friend of mine had had enough. When he named yet one more cause and shouted "Where were you!?" she shouted back, "I was in the fifth grade!"

During a national gathering of gay and lesbian folk in the Disciples of Christ, I joyfully witnessed the honoring of someone who had recently been ordained as an openly gay man. In accepting an award, he honored me and several others present by saying he was awed to receive this tribute in the presence of so many who also deserved praise. It occurred to me that our movement, like all progressive ones, is led by successive generations.

In the commonwealth of God, we all share equally no matter when we got into our movement. Jesus told a parable of an employer who hired people at different times during the day, but paid them equally at the end of it. When those who worked the longest began to complain, the employer reminded them of his freedom to treat them equally.

There is no seniority system in God's commonwealth.

Thank you, God, for the spiritual wealth you bestow on us equally.

My brothers and sisters, do you with your acts of favoritism really believe in our glorious Lord Jesus Christ?

James 2:1

A Mel Gibson look-alike appeared at church one Sunday, and several of the men stumbled all over themselves to go out of their way to say hello and be friendly. Other visitors went relatively unnoticed and ungreeted.

The epistle of James addressed favoritism in the church with regard to the rich and the poor. "Has not God chosen the poor in the world to be rich in faith and to be heirs of the kingdom that [God] has promised to those who love [God]?" the letter asks (2:5). Demonstrating partiality, you fail to "love your neighbor as yourself" (2:8).

At a national gathering of church women, all those attending a workshop on an inclusive church said they wanted their congregations to be open to everyone. Yet, when pressed, they came up with more than forty kinds of people they'd rather not have sit next to them in the pew.

A gay stranger sick from AIDS transformed a church in Iowa by asking them to pray for him each week. He sat next to parishioners who might not have chosen to sit next to him, so ravaged by illness. Once the postmaster for the area, now he served as a messenger of the inclusiveness of God's commonwealth.

Spirit, inspire us to welcome another as we would want to be welcomed.

And you shall hallow the fiftieth year and you shall proclaim liberty throughout the land to all its inhabitants. It shall be a jubilee for you: you shall return, every one of you, to your property and every one of you to your family. . . . The land shall not be sold in perpetuity, for the land is mine; with me you are but aliens and tenants.

Leviticus 25:10, 23

In the year of jubilee, all property leased for farming was to be returned to the family to whom it belonged. It could not be sold. It is unknown if this was truly the practice of the Israelites, but it is based on a humbling principle: The land is God's, and we are just tenants.

Many of our community are the caretakers of property. To recognize that what we have, whether land, houses, buildings, antiques, classic cars, or whatever, has been entrusted to us by God is humbling. A gay Christian in Hawaii told me that he views himself as a steward of his fine collection of antique furniture. He has not made his ownership ultimate; he cares for the items so they may be passed to future generations.

Though it sounds materialistic, how we treat matter matters. Matter has its own value, created by God. Native American religions recognize spirits in seemingly lifeless objects, a view that finds scientific expression in the theories of the atom, suggesting that all matter is constantly in motion, a kind of life.

Matter matters because it is God's, and it belongs to future tenants of this world.

May we be good stewards of all that is of the earth, as we sojourn on your land, Sovereign God.

Then [Jesus] called his disciples and said to them, "Truly I tell you, this poor widow has put in more than all those who are contributing to the treasury. For all of them have contributed out of their abundance; but she out of her poverty has put in everything she had, all she had to live on."

Mark 12:43–44

Anyone who has hitchhiked knows that it's most often the drivers in less expensive cars who offer a ride. Surveys reveal that the middle class give proportionally more to charities than the wealthy. Jesus did his own survey of those contributing to the temple treasury and found this widow, who put in her last penny, more generous than anyone.

It seems that those who are closest to the experience are the most likely to help: the driver one step removed from the hitchhiker; the middle class one step removed from the poor; the widow one step removed from absolute destitution were it not for her faith.

Women have been more responsive to our cause than men. Maybe it's because women are one step removed from our experience. Our culture disfranchises them for their sex just as it disfranchises us for our sexuality.

Embracing feminism is not just a lesbian thing. It's an appropriate spiritual connection for us all.

Thank you God, for women who know and alleviate our suffering!

*Then Jesus said [regarding self-righteous religious leaders], . . .
"They love to have the place of honor at banquets and the best
seats in the synagogues. . . . But woe to you . . . hypocrites! For
you lock people out of the kingdom of heaven. For you do not
go in yourselves, and when others are going in, you stop
them."*

Matthew 23:1, 6–7, 13–14

A remarkably representative blending of those infected with
HIV gathered for a retreat outside Detroit: black, white,
straight, gay, bisexual, women, men, asymptomatic and the
very ill. Alongside them stood family members, medical and social workers, and ministers. The effort many expended to attend would put to shame those of us who forego such spiritual
opportunities merely because they are inconvenient.

The Spirit moved among us, bringing down barriers of
race, gender, sexuality, and yes, even religion. One participant confessed he'd not been prepared for all the "God-
talk" of the retreat, but he had taken Communion for the
first time in twenty years!

What he didn't know was that the local governing body
of the sponsoring denomination had insisted on having one
of its own ministers bless Communion, despite the several
clergy present. Their man breezed in shortly before the service, celebrated Communion in an affected accent, and left
without having communed with us. It occurred to me that
those on the retreat had *already* received communion. It
was a communion that this minister neither provided nor
enjoyed.

Thank you, God, for your commonwealth devoid of pretense!

[Jesus said,] "But I am among you as one who serves."
Luke 22:27

Ronnie was the first person close to my age I knew to die.
Death was what happened to old people, not to people in the
third grade. Ronnie's heart was too large, literally. The night before his needed open-heart surgery, he demonstrated that his
largeness of heart was more than physical. Another child in his
ward, afraid of the oxygen tent in which he was to sleep,
needed reassurance. So Ronnie climbed into his bed to show
him there was nothing to fear.

Ronnie died the next day, after what was then a rare and
experimental surgery.

A friend has learned he is HIV-positive. Ron has a larger
than normal heart, figuratively. When his lover developed
AIDS years before, he could not abandon him and had continued to love him in intimate ways.

I heard a respected therapist offer the generalization that
women need things to be good before sex, whereas men
use sex to make things good. It is not surprising that gay
men would climb into bed to make things better, even
AIDS. And so with Ron.

Something that grieves me deeply in comparing Ronnie
and Ron is that the church would look only on the first as
an "innocent." Yet both Ron and Ronnie shared the same
life-threatening condition: largeness of heart.

Jesus did, too.

Bless me with the largeness of heart to serve others!

"These people who have been turning the world upside down have come here also."

Acts 17:6

While proclaiming the gospel in Thessalonica, Paul and Silas are accused of turning the world upside down. Religious leaders drag their host, Jason, to city authorities to complain that he is harboring them. It looks like the inhospitality of Sodom all over again.

How rarely are those who proclaim the gospel today accused of turning the world upside down! Most preachers do not question the structuring of our society, often for fear of sounding "political." Yet Christian faith requires us to view social and political systems in a new way.

Pope John Paul II has spoken of God exercising a "preferential option for the poor." Christianity has from the first taken root most firmly in the hearts of the powerless. India's "untouchables" embraced Christianity because they had few rights in the caste system. African-American slaves welcomed Christian faith to endure the humiliation of being treated as mere property. Central American *campesinos* and *campesinas* ("peasants") espoused liberation Christianity that called for a reordering of their nations' governments.

We, too, have been accused of wanting to turn the world upside down. But it's not us. It's God's commonwealth.

Create revolutions of the Spirit that transform our world!

Is not this the fast that I choose:
to loose the bonds of injustice,
to undo the thongs of the yoke,
to let the oppressed go free,
and to break every yoke?

Isaiah 58:6

The prophet Isaiah rightly proclaimed that any spiritual discipline, such as fasting, that does not manifest itself in liberation and justice is not of God.

Many very religious people will be very disappointed in God's final evaluation of their lives to discover that pious sentiment alone is an insufficient expression of thanksgiving. "To share your bread with the hungry, and bring the homeless poor into your house" (58:7) is better in God's eyes than simply saying grace over one's own meal.

We who know what it's like to be denied the bread of communion and the hospitality of God's house have a sense for what it means to be hungry and homeless. If we expect our hunger to be met and to be welcomed into God's commonwealth, we must expect no less of ourselves in regard to the hungry and homeless of our world. And how can we expect liberation for ourselves if we do not work for the liberation of all?

A motto on the beams of the chapel of my childhood Christian school said it well: Attempt great things for God; expect great things from God.

When I answer another's cry for help, Yahweh, then you will say, "Here I am" (58:9).

But be doers of the word, and not merely hearers who deceive themselves. . . . So faith by itself, if it has no works, is dead.

James 1:22, 2:17

Many of us were reared on the concept that belief was what mattered. If we accepted, or believed, Jesus Christ, that saved us. But faith is more than intellectual assent. It is also action.

Coming of age as lesbians and gay men, we realized that love was what mattered. Love was what helped most of us accept our sexuality as a gift from God. But love is more than an emotional assent. It is also action.

Love without demonstration has no credibility. So it is with faith. Faith without works has no life for James, just as love without works has no life for us.

For James, if we do not do what we say we believe, we forget our identity. During the 1955 Montgomery, Alabama, bus boycott by African-Americans, an elderly grandmother, asked if she was tired of walking rather than riding the bus, said, "It used to be my soul was tired and my feets rested; now my feet's tired, but my soul is rested." Acting on her beliefs gave peace to her soul, as it will to ours.

Help me act on your Word so that it may be well with my soul.

They shall beat their swords into plowshares,
and their spears into pruning hooks;
nation shall not lift up sword against nation,
neither shall they learn war any more.

Micah 4:3

Just as Yahweh lay a bow on its side after the flood to signal divine disarmament, so God's commonwealth proves disarming. Floods of animosities will subside, and resources used for weapons of destruction will be used for instruments of justice. Nations will need to convert their economies to accommodate a peaceful *oikumene,* the New Testament Greek word for world.

Peacemakers have argued that preparing for peace may avert war. Instead of studying how to wage war, we do better studying how to make peace with justice. At the least, it offers us a different vision from which to work.

I wonder if lesbian and gay Christians are prepared for the peace that will follow our struggle for acceptance. Will we easily be able to lay down our defensiveness in an open and affirming congregation? Will our bitterness prevent us from enjoying the fruits of peace in a culture that guarantees our civil rights? Will the peace we achieve keep us from engaging in making peace and justice for others?

Come, let us go up to the mountain of God, that God may teach us God's ways, and that we may walk in God's paths (4:2).

"Blessed are the peacemakers, for they will be called children of God."

Matthew 5:9

Jesus blessed peacemakers as children of God. To be a child of God meant one contained the essence of God. Peacemakers contain the essence of God. God is a peacemaker.

We wouldn't know that God is a peacemaker if we read the Bible uncritically, or studied church history without spiritual discernment. From the chosen people's battles to conquer the Promised Land to the "holy" wars of the Christian crusaders, God could be understood as a warmaker rather than a peacemaker. But humanity has frequently ordained its own violence as God's will.

That's why Christians do better to rely on the Word of God——Jesus Christ——in interpreting the words of God——the Bible. Jesus Christ is the key to understanding both scripture and God. Jesus' "sword" was his proclamation of God's commonwealth. Jesus' "strategy" was his healing touch. Jesus' "secret weapon" was the cross. That God resurrected him supports his choice of persuasion over coercion.

The commonwealth of God is not something taken by force. It is like a butterfly emerging from a cocoon: we cannot safely hasten the process, but we can create the peaceful environment in which it may unfold its wings and fly.

Bless us as peacemakers, that we may be your children, God.

How beautiful upon the mountains
are the feet of the messenger who announces peace,
who brings good news,
who announces salvation,
who says to Zion, "Your God reigns."

Isaiah 52:7

Think of the first person who helped you understand it was okay to be gay or lesbian. Then think of the first person who helped you understand it was okay to be a gay or lesbian Christian. Perhaps the person was you. Perhaps it was another. Perhaps it was a person whose story you heard or whose words you read. It may even have been a biblical figure or writer. Whoever it was, how beautiful they seemed, how blessed the peace with your sexuality they enabled, how good their news that your sexuality and your spirituality could embrace! Like your first experience of God's salvation, you may have felt born anew and wanted to "sing for joy" (52:8).

We, in turn, bring good news to a world that suffers from the hell of the false division of spirit from body. All injustice grows from this denial of the sacred worth of every body, regardless of disability, gender, sexual orientation, color, age, and appearance. As the Lord's Prayer says in one translation, "Thy kingdom come in earth as it is in heaven." In earth. In our earthen bodies. In our mother earth. Heaven is simply the harmonious soul: an indivisible integrity of spirit and body in which human and divine will coincide.

Thy kingdom come in earth as it is in heaven. Amen.

For whenever I speak, I must cry out. . . .
If I say, "I will not mention [Yahweh],
or speak any more in [God's] name,"
then within me there is something like a burning fire
shut up in my bones;
I am weary with holding it in, and I cannot.

Jeremiah 20:8–9

I receive letters from closeted church folk who say they admire my courage for being out. Though I sometimes wish I could re- tire as a gay activist, I know with Jeremiah that "there is some- thing like a burning fire shut up in my bones" and that I would be yet more "weary with holding it in." The closet is ultimately more demanding than speaking our truth.

The truth is that my sexuality has profoundly shaped my spirituality. I better rely on prayer. I better affirm the grace of bodily experience. I better depend on God's uncondi- tional love. I better understand the evil of injustice. I better know sexuality as God's gift.

My sexuality has helped me theologize anew and interpret scripture afresh. It has gotten me through times of doubt that I was loved by God or anyone. The integrity of sexuality and spirituality gave rise to a passionate ministry for reconcilia- tion. Even the church's delayed affirmation and the specter of AIDS teaches me an eternal perspective that transcends the here and now, and an expansive perspective that transcends any particular form of spirituality.

Within me there is something like a burning fire! Help me to speak my truth!

The wolf shall live with the lamb,
the leopard shall lie down with the kid,
the calf and the lion and the fatling together,
and a little child shall lead them.

Isaiah 11:6

Reflecting with a group of ministers on how their congregations could become welcoming of gay people, one minister mentioned his confirmation class of eighth graders. "I believe one of the boys is gay," he said. "He may be the one to lead our congregation to a better understanding," he added, looking as if he shared the boy's burden.

In the rural region that the minister represented, it is true that an insider, a member of a farm family, will do more for changing attitudes than an "expert" or a gay person from the outside. This is also true of urban and suburban families. The more everyone understands that being lesbian or gay is a "family thing," the less threatening it becomes.

Though this may be a terrible burden to place on a child, children also are called to serve God's commonwealth, leading us to overcome our acquired prejudice and hatred. For our part, we must watch lest we narrow their wide-eyed wonder at the diversity of God's world.

Bless the little children, God, as citizens of your common-
wealth.

NATIVITY

"My soul magnifies the Sovereign,
and my spirit rejoices in God my Savior,
who has regarded the low estate of God's handmaiden.
For behold, all generations will call me blessed;
for the one who is mighty has done great things for me. . . .
[God] has scattered the proud in the imagination of their
hearts . . .
and exalted those of low degree."

Luke 1:47–49, 51–52 (Inclusive Language Lectionary)

Mary sang this psalm because she believed she would give birth to a whole new world. The nativity, or birth, of Jesus would be the nativity of a new movement of God's Spirit. As that Spirit swept into primordial chaos and created a world, so it would sweep into primal human hearts and create a commonwealth.

Just as creation was an "inside job," an evolutionary movement toward self-consciousness, so redemption was an inside job, a revolutionary movement toward God-consciousness. Unlike most revolutions, this one would be nonviolent, embodied in a vulnerable baby born to a poor, unwed mother in a stable.

Mary may have intuited that this nativity would give birth to many more nativities of the Spirit——among them, our own nativity as lesbian and gay Christians. She knew future generations would call her blessed. And so do we.

Our soul magnifies the Sovereign, and our spirit rejoices in God our Savior!

Do not remember the former things,
or consider the things of old.
I am about to do a new thing;
now it springs forth, do you not perceive it?

Isaiah 43:18–19

A minister who had once been gay-positive became gay-negative after his sister came out as a lesbian. Perhaps for him it was okay for his friends to be gay, but he wouldn't want his sister to marry one! During a presentation, I saw him nod approvingly at everything I said, from scriptural interpretation to the blending of sexuality and spirituality. Puzzled by these nods of approval following his earlier statement of disapproval, I sought him out afterward to ask why he opposed gay acceptance. "You can't keep changing the rules," he said. "If you change the boundaries one week, you've got to change them next week."

Like any human institution, the church's primary governing force is inertia. "We've never done it that way before!" are its seven deadly words. To change the church's course requires a mammoth expenditure of energy over time. Individuals fear change, and many look to the church as an anchor in the metamorphic storms sweeping the world.

But God's Spirit beckons us from the future, away from the past. Even now, it is doing "a new thing."

Prepare our hearts for your future, embryonic Spirit.

"See, I am sending my messenger ahead of you,
who will prepare your way;
the voice of one crying out in the wilderness:
'Prepare the way of the Lord.'"

Mark 1:2–3

Gospel writer Mark here quotes the prophet Isaiah in reference to John the Baptist, whose preaching prepared the people for Jesus.

The Bible is filled with messengers, preparing us for God's presence. For Christians, all the messengers point ultimately to Jesus. And modestly, Jesus himself claimed that he came to point people to God. In turn, we, the church, past, present, and future, also prepare the way for God.

Early Christians called themselves the people of the Way (Acts 9:2). Though saved, they were people in process. The world was also in process, preparing for the fulfillment of time, also known as the day of judgment or the end of the age.

We are also people of the Way. Though saved, we are people in process. And we are preparing the way for a new understanding of God's Word made flesh. We are voices in the wilderness, but our baptism of the Spirit will bless the church as it approaches God.

May we prepare the church to make room for your Spirit, God.

O that you would tear open the heavens and come down!

Isaiah 64:1

As a child, a gay friend demanded proof of God's existence. Seeing a spot on the wall, he prayed that if God existed, it would disappear under his thumb. It did. Then he looked at his thumb and found a squashed bug! He wondered what to make of the episode.

As an adult, I saw a spot on my ankle that looked like a KS lesion. This was before I had taken an HIV test, and I feared the worst. I was in the shower, and I prayed to God that it would wash away. I placed my thumb on it, and it disappeared. I thanked God.

Others have KS spots that do not disappear. For them I share Isaiah's sense of urgency directed at God: "O that you would tear open the heavens and come down!" Other gays and lesbians have pled for God's presence with similar urgency.

Jesus' people were voicing comparable cries at the time of his nativity. Oppressed by the Romans, they sought deliverance. Questioning the favor of God, they languished. "How long, O Lord?" they wailed in desperation.

Simone Weil wrote in her *Spiritual Autobiography,* "Waiting in expectation is the foundation of the spiritual life." If she is right, we are deeply spiritual people as we wait expectantly for God to cure people's hatred and reveal a cure for AIDS.

O that you would tear open the heavens and come down!

"Greetings, favored one! [God] is with you. . . . Do not be afraid, Mary, for you have found favor with God."

"Blessed are you among women, and blessed is the fruit of your womb."

Luke 1:28, 30, 42

Recovery author and workshop leader John Bradshaw uses an exercise in which a small group takes turn proffering affirmations upon one seated in the middle, statements we should have heard when we were born, like, "Welcome to the universe!" or, "I'm so glad you're a girl/boy!"

The Bible is filled with blessings that we, too, should have heard from the moment of our nativity. Using scriptural quotes, I have led lesbian and gay Christians to hear these affirmations through a comparable exercise. Giving and receiving them produces tears, joy, content, and peace.

A delighted surprise occurs when some of the blessings were originally directed at others. The two verses for today are examples. Both were spoken to Mary, the first by the angel Gabriel and the second by her kinswoman Elizabeth. If your name is substituted for Mary's, and if "womb" is used for women and "loins" for men, the affirmations may be personalized. Using these is not necessarily to affirm our procreative capacities, but to celebrate our sexuality.

God is with me! Blessed is the fruit of my womb/loins!

"All this is but the beginning of the birth pangs."
Matthew 24:8

We know that the whole creation has been groaning in labor pains until now; and not only the creation, but we ourselves, who have the first fruits of the Spirit, groan inwardly while we wait for adoption, the redemption of our bodies.
Romans 8:22–23

Jesus, in the Gospel of Matthew, and Paul, in the epistle of Romans, compare the culmination of history to a woman in childbirth. The metaphor is apt, because nativities cause pain and anguish but result in the joy of delivery.

For Jesus, the time was imminent and to be marked by geophysical and political disruption and the persecution of the faithful. For Paul, the nativity was in process, and would deliver the earth and our bodies "from its bondage to decay" to "freedom" and "glory" (8:21).

Think when you first fell in love: how awe-full and how awful it was! Something wonderful had happened, and yet you expected something yet more wonderful to happen. That's true also of faith. Believing in God is wonderful, yet a person of faith believes this is only the beginning.

These awe-full and awful feelings are what are described as "birth pangs" by Jesus and "labor pains" by Paul. They remind us that there is more to come. Wait and see.

Bless us in the anguish of labor and the joy of delivery!

For you yourselves know very well that the day of the [Sovereign] will come like a thief in the night. When they say, "There is peace and security," then sudden destruction will come upon them, as labor pains come upon a pregnant woman, and there will be no escape!

1 Thessalonians 5:2–3

When I was growing up, my family used as a devotional a book called *Raptured!*, a horrible depiction of the end times based on the book of Revelation. Not knowing why, I found myself very anxious and nervous during this period.

It is a sad commentary on American Christianity that another book of that ilk, Hal Lindsay's *The Late Great Planet Earth*, is a bestseller. Most biblical scholars recognize that the writer of Revelation, like most prophets, was not predicting the future, but interpreting his present.

There is a foreboding quality to some biblical passages anticipating the day of Yahweh, such as this one from Paul, who here echoes Jesus. But God does not want to frighten us into faith, despite the scare tactics that have been used against us by some Christians. God wants to love us into faith, so we may share the assurance Paul offers in the verses that follow, "For God has destined us not for wrath but for obtaining salvation through our Lord Jesus Christ."

You have made us "children of light and children of the day" (5:5), so we need not be anxious about thieves in the night.

"It is like a man going on a journey, when he leaves home and puts his slaves in charge, each with his work, and commands the doorkeeper to be on the watch. Therefore, keep awake—for you do not know when the master of the house will come."

Mark 13:35

On an elevator with other prospective Princeton seminary students, I heard one say, "Just think, if Jesus came right now, we'd all just shoot out the top of this elevator!" That was one of the reasons I went to Yale.

The nativity of Jesus reminds us that God's entrance into our world is seldom so dramatic. Despite the fantastic stories surrounding his birth, the fact is, few people cared about or even noticed his coming into the world. Mary and Joseph couldn't even find a room at the inn.

Jesus compared God's entrance to a master of a house about to return from a journey. But this is a metaphor for a Master who has never really left the world. As Abraham, Sarah, and Lot entertained angels unawares, as the travelers to Emmaus invited Jesus to dinner unknowingly, so faith helps us see that God returns every day to God's house—— our community, our church, our home. God returns in the stranger seeking help from a lesbian and gay community center. God returns in lesbians and gay men coming home to the church. God returns in our lover home from a stressful day at work.

Are we ready?

Help us keep awake, ready to receive you, Master of our home.

Rejoice in the Lord always; again I will say, Rejoice. Let your gentleness be known to everyone. The Lord is near. Do not worry about anything, but in everything by prayer and supplication with thanksgiving let your requests be made known to God. And the peace of God, which surpasses all understanding, will guard your hearts and your minds in Christ Jesus.

Philippians 4:4–7

We are a gentle people. We are a people who party hearty——socially and spiritually. This scripture reminds us not to sweat the details. It reminds us to offer up everything to God in prayer——both requests and thanksgivings. It reminds us of the peace that passes our understanding which surrounds us when we do so.

Why? Because God is near. We have nothing to fear. We have everything to celebrate.

At the national gatherings of my church, the booth for lesbian and gay concerns is always the most busy and festive. I believe there is a theological reason for that. We are exciting because we see God's day coming.

Surround us with your peace, as we rejoice in your nearness, God of our prayers!

"But the hour is coming, and is now here, when the true wor-shipers will worship [God] in spirit and truth."

John 4:23

"Until we recover theology as the delighted, passionate, imaginative, refreshing, terrifying, intelligent exploration of the inexhaustible God, we have no right to claim the interest or attention of the secular world."

Most of us would probably agree with Elizabeth Templeton's evaluation, quoted in Joan Puls' *Hearts Set on a Pilgrimage.* Joseph Campbell thought the mistake of the church in the twentieth century was to reduce the Christian gospel to morality. I think some of us make the related mistake of reducing it to justice.

I better understand what has been a mystery: why self-respecting gay men and lesbians who have options sometimes choose to worship with congregations that don't openly welcome them rather than with those that do. Those that welcome us often focus on justice to the detriment of prayer, sacraments, and the mystical and aesthetic expressions of faith.

To worship "in spirit and truth," I believe, is to worship inspired and embodied, giving thanks and bringing justice.

Delight us with your Spirit of praise and service, O God!

My little children, for whom I am again in the pain of child-birth until Christ is formed in you . . .

Galatians 4:19

An injury to my back reminded me how a problem in one part of the body affects the whole, causing a generalized malaise. I thought of a man who has always been quick to complain of aches and pains, who nonetheless has outlived the wife who cared for him, and who now depends on a daughter who either fits into the category of codependent or compassionate, depending on who makes the call. The daughter has been severely ill herself, but her father goes on about his own phantom afflictions.

My mind jumped from his body and mine to the Body of Christ, the church. Though it has inflicted real pain upon its lesbian, gay, and bisexual members, it protects those members who are spiritual hypochondriacs: those who claim they will be hurt if we find acceptance in the church. This looks more like codependence than compassion to me.

The pain causing the church's malaise has been misdiagnosed as homosexuality, when in reality, it is the pain of childbirth: the Body of Christ being formed once more within the church's womb, a body that includes lesbian, gay, and bisexual members.

Be born once more, O Christ, within us!

And [Jesus] sighed deeply in his spirit and said, "Why does this generation ask for a sign? Truly I tell you, no sign will be given to this generation."

Mark 8:12

The sign Jesus left us was a cross.

A gay seminarian told of feeling alone and rejected at his first summer camp. An older boy, a camp counselor, comforted him. The younger boy felt warmed and cared for in a way he had never felt before. On the last day, the older boy gave the younger a cross he had fashioned with two twigs and string. To this day, that cross is the seminarian's most valued possession.

His telling me that story prompted me to open the box of a similar icon upon my return home. It is a small silver cross given me by a gay minister with whom I had spoken. He had been given it by a teenager at a summer camp. Though there had been no open expression of their feelings, the cross had served as a conduit for the first love the minister had experienced from another man.

The sign of the cross communicates a willingness to give birth to love. God's willingness. And hopefully, ours.

I make the sign of the cross on my body, in preparation for life and for love.

*Then Jesus said to them, "Prophets are not without honor, ex-
cept in their hometown, and among their own kin, and in
their own house."*

Mark 6:4

Visiting a minister of a Metropolitan Community Church in a
small city, I agonized with him over his experience as a
prophet without honor. Because of hostility toward religion,
other gay and lesbian leaders often did not include his church
in community events. And, though he sat on the mayor's
human rights committee, the community passed over him
when acknowledging its leaders. His congregation was behind
on his salary and questioned his integrity for taking a second
job!

Years later, I commiserated with him again when he was
among the earliest diagnosed with AIDS, and his church at
first seemed hesitant to help. Now, as a longtime survivor,
he has found respect for an AIDS ministry.

Jesus, "amazed at their unbelief" (6:6), could do little
ministry among people of his hometown because they
"took offense at him" (6:3). Many of us identify with this, either in our community or in our church.

Prophets are often the unacknowledged midwives of the
nativities of the Spirit.

Bless your prophets, even when we do not.

*"I still have many things to say to you, but you cannot bear
them now. When the Spirit of truth comes, [she] will guide you
into all the truth."*

                                                    John 16:12–13

I caught a glimpse of God's future when I attended the celebra-
tion of a covenant between two women. Sally is a therapist,
and Cyndy is a minister, ordained openly as a lesbian within the
United Church of Christ.

The simple ceremony was led by a clergywoman from
Sally's Presbyterian church, but most who came were from
the UCC they both attended. Those who gathered on their
tree-shaded lawn were most remarkable in being unremark-
able. Friends of all ages, colors, abilities, and sexualities
comingled, imbibing a communion of more than refresh-
ments. The UCC minister introduced himself to me as a reformed opponent to gay ordination.

As Pachelbel's Canon was played by an ensemble, cham-
pagne was poured for "the blessings," extemporaneous
words between Cyndy and Sally, and our spontaneous
words of affirmation. A small Latina girl offered the final
toast.

Jesus had his own blessings for this couple, but he could
not have said them in his time. Now the Spirit led us to affirm the truth some disciples still cannot bear to hear.

Bless us in the birthing of covenant relationships, O Spirit.

"The wind blows where it chooses, and you hear the sound of it, but you do not know where it comes from or where it goes. So it is with everyone who is born of the Spirit."

                                                                    John 3:8

The Spirit is no respecter of denominations. Who would've imagined she would move a Baptist church in Raleigh, North Carolina, to vote overwhelming to welcome lesbian and gay members and to affirm lesbian and gay unions?

And yet, on March 15, 1992, Kevin and Steven were united before 250 guests at the Pullen Memorial Baptist Church, amid vigorous protests and threats of retribution from national and regional Baptist leaders. The Southern Baptist Convention executive committee had announced it would entertain motions to exclude churches that affirm gays and lesbians, an unorthodox departure for a congregational-based church that historically claims "no creed but Christ."

Meanwhile, also in Raleigh, Binkley Memorial Baptist Church licensed a gay minister!

Kevin described the decision and the ceremony as a "moving religious experience——we were really 'church' for each other." I should say!

Thank you, Spirit, for your outbursts of hope!

I will pour out my spirit on all flesh;
your sons and your daughters shall prophesy,
your old men shall dream dreams,
and your young men shall see visions.

Joel 2:28

Steve Pieters, an MCC pastor, was one of my first friends to be diagnosed with AIDS. Not long after, I had a dream about him. We were standing on the edge of a pool of water the size and shape of a grave. The water was not the color of the surrounding soil. Rather, it was bright blue, like the sky, and bright green, like a newly sprouted lawn.

In the dream, Steve took my hand and led me into the pool, reminiscent of being led into the baptismal pool in which I was baptized as a youth. Steps appeared beneath my feet, unseen from the surface. As I stepped into the cool, refreshing waters, I found myself crossing a threshold, entering an upright doorway. The blue that I saw was indeed the sky. And the green that I had seen was a lush valley descending from towering mountains, reminiscent of Shangri-La in James Hilton's classic novel, *Lost Horizon*.

The beauty gave me peace and joy as I had never felt. I felt comforted that death was a threshold, not an end.

Bless us with dreams and visions of hope and life to come.

"Here comes this dreamer. Come now, let us kill him and throw him into one of the pits; then we shall say that a wild animal has devoured him, and we shall see what will become of his dreams."

Genesis 37:19-20

Joseph was a self-affirming, unrepentant dreamer. Jealous of the grace that God bestowed on him, his brothers plotted to kill him, but Reuben suggested throwing him into a dry well. Then they sold Joseph to passing slave traders en route to Egypt.

We are self-affirming, unrepentant dreamers as self-affirming lesbians and gay men who dream of full rights. Our siblings in the church, jealous of the grace with which God has blessed us, might want to do away with those of us who rattle the church. But Reubens offer the church a more civilized alternative. Allan Boesak of South Africa has named this "The Reuben Option." It is to put dreamers into dry wells——closets——where they languish invisibly.

Little did Joseph's brothers know what role they had unwittingly played in God's providence. For in Egypt, Joseph's dreams would come true, and he ultimately saved their family from a famine.

Our dreams will also come true, and we will save our family of faith from a famine of dreams.

Send more dreamers, that our churches may be filled with dreams!

Then [Gamaliel] said, "Let them alone; because if this plan or this undertaking is of human origin, it will fail; but if it is of God, you will not be able to overthrow them—in that case you may even be found fighting against God!"

Acts 5:35, 38–39

Peter and the apostles enraged the religious authorities of their day, partly by affirming that the Holy Spirit had been given to themselves. The religious leaders wanted to kill them, but Gamaliel, a liberal spiritual teacher, offered the caution that, if their movement was not from God, it would die out of its own accord. But if the movement was a true nativity of the Spirit, nothing could stop it.

One might wonder why today's religious authorities who resist the nativity of the lesbian and gay movement do not heed Gamaliel's counsel. Even if they do not trust *us,* do they not trust *God?* Perhaps they sense this *is* a movement of the Holy Spirit, and that's what makes them apprehensive.

At a Pentecost service celebrating the ministry of lesbians and gay men, we sang Jim Manley's song "Spirit." It served as both a prayer of petition and an affirmation of faith: "Spirit, spirit of gentleness, blow through the wilderness, calling and free."

Spirit, blow through the wilderness of church courts and councils, for freedom is coming.

"Truly I tell you, people will be forgiven for their sins and whatever blasphemies they utter; but whoever blasphemes against the Holy Spirit can never have forgiveness, but is guilty of an eternal sin"—for they had said, "He has an unclean spirit."

Mark 3:28-30

Jesus said this when his opponents accused him of casting out demons through the power of Satan. And we could say it when our opponents reject our full participation in the church. They blaspheme against the Holy Spirit within us by naming it sinful, unclean, or evil.

A conservative uncle in Texas whom I describe in *Uncommon Calling* demonstrated his strong personal support after learning that I was gay by asking me to do his funeral when the time came. I wished him a long life by saying, "May I be ordained by the time you need my services!" When I sent him the book, he told me he read it nonstop, cover to cover.

When he died, my younger cousin honored me by asking that I fulfill his father's wish. But one day later, his older sister, a fundamentalist and biblical literalist, called to disinvite me. With all her Christian "sweetness" she said she did not want me to think she was rejecting me! She naively thought she had rendered no blow. In truth, she had rejected God's spirit within me.

We must keep faith with the Spirit, even when others reject it.

May Christians praise your Spirit within us, Holy God.

Jesus said to her, "Woman, why are you weeping? Whom are
you looking for? . . . Do not hold on to me."

John 20:15, 17

When I was in seminary, an African-American student gave a
sermon at Christmastime about Easter. "If there had been no
crucifixion and resurrection, there would be no Christmas!" he
declared. And it's true. The birth of Jesus was miraculous because of his rebirth.

Our birth and our life have become miraculous because
we have followed Jesus out of the tomb. We have been resurrected to life by our discipleship, our spiritual discipline
by which our sexuality and our spirituality have emerged in-
tact and integral. We experience at once a resurrection of
body and soul.

Jesus asked Mary whom she sought on that first Easter
morning of resurrection. Then he called her by name, and
she recognized him. But he warned her not to hold on to
him.

Many tried or try to hold on to us, to keep us just the way
we were. Parents, spouses, children, churches, careers, governments——all have wanted or want us the way we were,
or at least how they perceived us.

But they should not weep. Nor should they hold on.

Free me from expectations that keep me entombed.

"See, the home of God is among mortals. . . .
[God] will wipe every tear from their eyes.
Death will be no more;
mourning and crying and pain will be no more."

Revelation 21:3–4

The tingling sensation the audience has in the final scene of *Longtime Companion* is akin to the mystical vision of John in Revelation. Walking along the beach on Fire Island, the protagonists "see" all the friends they have lost to AIDS gathering for a party. Smiles flash, hair is playfully tugged, hugs are long.

Early Christians needed a similar vision in the midst of the persecutions and martyrdoms that they endured. John heard a voice from the throne of heaven saying that God now "tabernacled" with us, and would "wipe every tear from our eyes," bringing an end to death and grief and crying and pain.

Jesus' other name, Emmanuel, means God-with-us, and he comes to bring an end to death and suffering and sin. The whole of the Bible is about God-with-us, God's decision to move in with us, be our lover, and care for us. Nothing can separate us from God's love, not even death.

We pray for a cure for AIDS, just as you have given us a cure for death, God-with-us.

You have been born anew, not of perishable but of imperish-
able seed, through the living and enduring word of God. For
    "All flesh is like grass
        and all its glory like the flower of grass.
    The grass withers,
        and the flower falls,
        but the word of [God] endures forever."
That word is the good news that was announced to you.

                                              1 Peter 1:23–25

Peter quoted Isaiah's reminder that God's Word abides forever. Long after we're gone, the Bible that contains that
Word will also endure. How we interpret the Bible today,
how we live out its gospel, will help determine its meaning
for those who follow: lesbians, gay men, and the future
church. If we do not want it used to spiritually abuse our
posterity, then we must act now. If we want it to spiritually
empower unborn generations of lesbians and gay men, we
must "out" the good news of the Bible today so that they
will read it tomorrow. The Spirit at work in us helps the
Word come out of the words of scripture.

God's Word is an imperishable seed at work in us and
through us. As Ruben Alves has said, "Let us plant dates
even though those who plant them will never eat them. We
must live by the love of what we will never see."

As we are born anew by your imperishable seed, O God, bless
those who follow with your Word of love.

Love never ends. But as for prophecies, they will come to an end; as for tongues, they will cease; as for knowledge, it will come to an end. . . . And now faith, hope, and love abide, these three; and the greatest of these is love.

1 Corinthians 13:8, 13

A chaplain from Detroit began sobbing as conference songleaders taught us a new song about a young gay man named Kurt. On the night of his death, after a difficult visit with his family, he told a minister, "Love heals." The story, passed along by word of mouth, inspired a hymnwriter to compose a song with that refrain: "Love heals." The chaplain cried because *he was the minister to whom Kurt had confided his final thoughts!* He did not know that Kurt's story now lived in a song.

Long after the Bible is gone, God's Word of love will serve as a healing balm, overcoming pain, division, suffering, and death. God's love will transcend all words with which we try to capture and express it.

Anyone who has been in the arms of a lover or by the bedside of a loved one who is dying knows that words can never embody the heights and depths of love, love's rejoicing and love's suffering. That's why God's Word became flesh, because God's love is too full to remain abstract and must be incarnated in flesh and blood to touch us.

As Kurt prophesied, "Love heals."

We have faith and hope in your love, God.

Now faith is the assurance of things hoped for, the conviction of things not seen.

Hebrews 11:1

A national gathering of United Methodists refused to hear from an openly gay person during a four-hour debate in which they decided to affirm an earlier position that we were persons of "sacred worth" but that "the practice of homosexuality is incompatible with Christian teaching." If Mary and Joseph had shown up there, Jesus would have been born in a parking garage!

Fifteen representatives of Methodist justice groups protested, walking onto the conference floor between the delegates and their presiding bishop and holding a banner which read, "The stones will cry out!"——a reference to Jesus saying that even if his followers were silenced, the very stones of Jerusalem, perhaps of the temple itself, would cry out. Periodically throughout the debate, the banner would be lifted and a rumbling noise could be heard from hundreds of supporters stomping their feet in the visitor gallery.

A few weeks before my father died, he offered me a blessing after we experienced a similar defeat in my own denomination. He said, "The next time you go tilting at a windmill, I hope it falls down." Though he knew he would not live to see it, he was certain that we would win.

And so are we.

Keep us from any lack of faith, Blessed Assurance!

*But the angel said to them, "Do not be afraid; for see—I am
bringing you good news of great joy for all the people: to you is
born this day in the city of David a Savior, who is the Messiah,
the Lord."*

Luke 2:10–11

Angels made this announcement of Christ's nativity not to a religious gathering or council, but to a bunch of literal outsiders,
shepherds tending their flocks. Jesus himself was an outsider,
born in a stable to a poor, unwed Jewish teenage girl. He was
destined not to be a priest, but a carpenter.

But from the outside looking in, he discerned what had
gone wrong in the spiritual quest of his people. Spirituality
had become overly codified, rigid, restrictive. It was the pet
of the wealthy, the powerful, the educated, and the self-
righteous. God had been domesticated.

During the annual gathering of lesbian, gay, and bisexual
Christians at the Kirkridge retreat center in Pennsylvania, a
young lesbian pleaded for us not to simply seek acceptance
in the church, but to use our being "out" of the mainstream
to transform both the church and society.

Our nativity as outsiders may give birth to Christ once
more.

*Make your Word flesh in us, that we may call the church to
repentance.*

"What no eye has seen, nor ear heard,
nor the human heart conceived,
what God has prepared for those who love [God]."

1 Corinthians 2:9

Evangelist Billy Graham eventually became embarrassed by his early, naive depiction of heaven, according to a 1993 *Time* magazine cover story. "We are going to sit around the fireplace and have parties," he had once told audiences, "and the angels will wait on us, and we'll drive down the golden streets in a yellow Cadillac convertible."

As a child, I feared heaven would be boring because there would be no television. As an adult, I overused Jesus' image of the messianic banquet until a gay church member frankly told me that he didn't think sitting around eating all the time sounded like anything he would want to do!

In this verse from his letter to Corinth, Paul alludes to Isaiah to declare that Christians have been given a new revelation. But it also suggests that we still don't know all that God has planned for us. There are nativities of the Spirit yet to be.

We look forward to what you have prepared for us, Loving God.

Then Paul stood in front of the Areopagus and said, "Atheni-
ans, I see how extremely religious you are in every way. For as
I . . . looked carefully at the objects of your worship, I found
among them an altar with the inscription, 'To an unknown
god.' What . . . you worship as unknown, this I proclaim to
you. The God who made the world and everything in it . . .
does not live in shrines made by human hands."

Acts 17:22–24

During the time I was working on these meditations, I
stood on the Areopagus, the hill west of the Acropolis,
where Paul preached to the citizens of Athens. From there I
could see the ruins of temples once dedicated to other di-
vinities, as well as longstanding churches honoring the God
Paul proclaimed.

Our "gods" come and go, but God remains forever. The
images, metaphors, and buildings in which we try to capture God also come and go. The Athenians, erecting an altar
to an unknown god, were on the right track. There is a part
of God that will always be unknowable and mysterious.

Many Christians think they know God and, with the
Athenians, are "extremely religious." But they only know
God in part. If they learn our experience of God, they will
know more. For it is the collective, communal experience
of God that gives us the fullest picture.

Thank you for your mystery, and that we may learn more of
you through one another.

No one has ever seen God; if we love one another, God lives in us, and [God's] love is perfected in us. . . . God is love, and those who abide in love abide in God, and God abides in them.

1 John 4:12, 16

In the PBS series and the book based on the series *The Power of Myth,* Joseph Campbell explained the liabilities of mythologies to interviewer Bill Moyers. "You have the three great Western religions, Judaism, Christianity, and Islam——and because the three of them have three different names for the same biblical god, they can't get on together. They are stuck with their metaphor and don't realize its reference."

This insight informs not only our view of struggles among religions, but within religion. As the church, we need to open ourselves to receive the God behind our particular view of God and the broader community of faith beyond ours.

The church must similarly open itself to the reference behind the metaphor of heterosexual marriage in the Garden of Eden, which is the covenantal companionship and the mutuality of lovers regardless of gender.

Ultimately, as 1 John declared, it is all about love, for God is love.

May we know you more by loving others more, God of love.

Then I saw a new heaven and a new earth.

Revelation 21:1

A well-known Christian educator from the South, who was not gay, used an unintended double-entendre in a letter to a gay friend. The writer awe-fully mentioned "the glory holes of God" through which blessings had come.

I thought back to the "glory holes of God" that had sustained me through the years. The tree in our front yard that I climbed as a child. The foothills I hiked surrounding my school. The cliffs and beaches of the shore. And now, the grove of trees outside our windows, from which I watch cardinals, squirrels, falling leaves, and occasionally, lightning storms or snow flurries.

These are the openings through which I have caught a glimpse of God's glory and splendor that placed my fears in perspective and led me to new nativities of the Spirit. These are the windows through which I have understood the vision of a new heaven and a new earth. These are the *true* glory holes.

Thank you for opening me to a new heaven and a new earth!

"Look, I have set before you an open door, which no one is able to shut. . . . Let anyone who has an ear listen to what the Spirit is saying to the churches."

Revelation 3:8, 13

The open door of our closet cannot be shut.

One like Christ (1:13) told the visionary John to say this to the church in Philadelphia of Asia Minor, the city of brotherly and sisterly love. "I know that you have but little power, and yet you have kept my word and have not denied my name" (3:8), Christ adds. "I am coming soon; hold fast to what you have" (3:11).

When Jews were forced to wear yellow stars by the Nazis, Etty Hillesum wrote of a man on a bicycle who gloried in his Jewish identity: "He was wearing a huge golden star, wearing it triumphantly on his chest. He was a procession and a demonstration all by himself as he cycled along so happily. And all that yellow——I suddenly had a poetic vision of the sun rising above him, so radiant and smiling did he look" (*An Interrupted Life* [New York: Simon & Schuster, 1985], p. 134).

Today, we proudly wear the pink triangle——what the Nazis forced homosexuals to wear. And we wear it with the cross, another intended symbol of shame transformed by God to a symbol of pride. We have little power, and yet we have kept God's word and have not denied God's Word. Our "patient endurance" (3:10) will be rewarded with a place in the temple of God, and we will bear God's name and Christ's name (3:12).

We are lesbian, gay, and bisexual Christians! Thanks be to God! The church will have to get used to it!

"Master, now you are dismissing your servant in peace,
according to your word;
for my eyes have seen your salvation,
which you have prepared in the presence of all peoples."

Luke 2:29–31

When the baby Jesus was first brought to the temple, two elderly prophets, Anna and Simeon, recognized him as the salvation of the world, and praised God. The Holy Spirit had revealed to Simeon that he would not die before seeing the Messiah, and he took the baby in his arms and thanked God with the words of today's text. Now he could die in peace.

One evening I attended an AIDS requiem, performed by lesbian and gay choirs in a cathedral-like church. The AIDS Quilt had been displayed along its walls and halls all weekend, and within my sight from where I sat, I could see panels memorializing two close friends. As I viewed the people who were gathered in the pews, I recognized them as a living, human quilt: varied colors, sexualities, genders, ages, faiths, abilities, and health statuses, woven together to wrap and warm this cold stone church with our multicolored, multitextured human experience.

My eyes saw God's salvation in this living quilt, surrounded by "so great a cloud of witnesses" on the woven quilt. And I thought how salvific for the Body of Christ, the church around the world, if it could be wrapped and warmed by this quilt of compassion!

My eyes have seen your salvation, O God of glory! Thanks be to God!

Scripture Index

7:20–23, June 23; **7:34**, Aug. 20; **7:38**, Feb. 14; **8:43–48**, Feb. 3; **10:5–6**, Jan. 31; **10:9**, Nov. 16; **10:29, 37**, May 8; **10:36–37**, Mar. 12; **10:41**, Oct. 9; **11:9**, July 24; **12:7**, Feb. 7; **12:11–12**, Sept. 4; **12:48**, May 7; **13:16**, Aug. 16; **13:20–21**, Nov. 14; **13:34**, Oct. 10; **16:31**, Oct. 18; **17:2**, May 6, May 7; **17:18**, May 19; **17:20–21**, Nov. 15; **18:1, 4–5**, Apr. 27; **18:13, 14**, Feb. 13; **19:40**, June 28; **22:48**, Mar. 27; **22:27**, Nov. 22; **22:48**, Mar. 27; **24:5**, Oct. 30; **24:30–32**, Oct. 22

John 1:1, 14, Jan. 5; **2:10**, Mar. 25; **2:29–31**, Dec. 31; **3:8**, Dec. 15, May 12; **3:16**, Mar. 2; **4:14, 39**, Sept. 11; **4:17–18**, Sept. 12; **4:23**, Dec. 10; **6:35, 49**, July 17; **8:12**, July 3; **8:31**, June 9; **9**, Feb. 3; **9:34, 39**, Aug. 15; **10:10**, Sept. 24; **10:11, 16**, July 29; **10:14–16**, May 5; **10:16**, Apr. 25; **11**, Mar. 29; **11:25–26**, Oct. 20; **12:3**, Mar. 26; **12:24**, Mar. 30; **12:42–43**, Feb. 24, Feb. 25; **13:8, 9**, Sept. 25; **13:23**, Mar. 26; **14:1–3**, Oct. 21; **14:6**, July 21; **14:18–19**, July 25; **15:4**, Oct. 8; **16:12–13**, Dec. 14; **17:22–23**, Oct. 4; **20:15, 17**, Dec. 20; **20:29**, Feb. 29

Acts 2:6, May 12; **2:43–44**, May 21; **4:32**, May 20; **5:35, 38–39**, Dec. 18; **7:55**, Jan. 28; **8:36**, May 13; **10:34–35, 47**, May 14; **16:28**, June 30; **17:6**, Nov. 23; **17:22–24**, Dec. 27; **20:35**, May 22

Romans 1:26–27, Aug. 22; **2:29**, Apr. 11; **3:22–25**, Apr. 14; **4:9**, Apr. 19; **5:1–2**, Apr. 21; **5:2–3**, Feb. 22; **8:14**, July 20; **8:15–17**, Nov. 8; **8:18**, Feb. 23; **8:21, 22–23**, Dec. 6; **8:26**, Feb. 20; **8:31, 37–39**, Mar. 4; **12:20–21**, Jan. 31

1 Corinthians 1:26, Sept. 1; **2:9**, Dec. 26; **3:16**, July 4; **6:19**, July 5; **7:29–31**, June 21; **10:30**, Aug. 27; **11:24, 25**, Oct. 24; **12:4**, Sept. 22; **12:12–13, 26**, May 1; **13:3**, Mar 11; **13:8, 13**, Dec. 23; **15:40–43**, May 31; **15:49**, Jan. 7; **15:54–55**, Oct. 23

2 Corinthians 3:18, Jan. 25; **4:8**, Feb. 21; **5:1**, July 31; **5:17**, Apr. 22; **5:18**, Apr. 23; **6:2**, Aug. 31; **9:6–7**, May 22; **12:9**, Sept 8

Galatians 1:15–17, Sept. 23; **3:19**, Apr. 19; **3:28**, Oct. 3; **4:19**, Dec. 11; **5:1**, July 8; **5:13**, July 9; **5:22**, Aug. 30

Ephesians 1:16, Jan. 12; **1:17**, Sept. 16; **2:4**, Apr. 20; **2:5**, Mar. 30; **2:8**, Apr. 18; **2:10**, Jan. 8; **2:12–13, 19**, Nov. 1; **2:14**, Oct. 6; **2:14, 15–16**, Aug. 28; **4:1–3**, Sept. 29; **4:4–6**, Oct. 2; **6:12**, June 17; **6:13–17**, June 20